The Pictorial
Encyclopedia of
Fashion

The Pictorial Encyclopedia of
Fashion

by Ludmila Kybalová
Olga Herbenová
Milena Lamarová

Translated by
Claudia Rosoux

Hamlyn · London/New York/Sydney/Toronto

Designed and produced by Artia for
The Hamlyn Publishing Group Ltd.
London · New York · Sydney · Toronto
Hamlyn House, Feltham,
Middlesex, England

Published 1968 in the U.S.A. by
Crown Publishers, Inc., New York.
Third impression 1972

Library of Congress Catalog
Number 68–14771

Printed in Czechoslovakia

ISBN 0 600 03068 7

Contents

The modern student of the history of costume, as well as the designer of historical films and plays, is indeed fortunate in his epoch. Never before in the history of mankind have there been so many sources of information, so all-embracing a documentation of the subject, so little excuse for being 'out of period'. We are apt to forget how comparatively recent this development is.

In the Ancient World lack of communications made it impossible to travel easily from one place to another; and a man might spend his lifetime in his own village, confident that the rest of the world consisted entirely of villages like his, inhabited by people dressed exactly like himself. Nor, as clothes changed so slowly, was he conscious of any development in time. His forbears had dressed in the same clothes as he wore himself, and he saw no reason why his descendants should not do the same.

Wars and conquests brought knowledge of other peoples. The wall paintings in Egyptian temples, for example, show quite clearly that their creators were aware that the clothes they themselves wore were not the same as those worn by negro or Semite captives. The Ancient Greeks knew that the 'barbarians' on their borders wore trousers, which they did not do themselves. But if they ranged fairly widely in space they do not seem to have had much sense of the changes wrought by time. They do not seem to have been aware, even, that the clothes of the Cretan civilization they had destroyed were very different from those of Classical Greece.

Indeed the Ancient World showed very little interest in such matters, although something which we can legitimately call 'changing fashions' was certainly to be found in imperial Rome. And when the world reverted to barbarism in the Dark Ages any such interest would have been inconceivable. The Crusades however, by introducing Western man to a civilization so different from his own, forced him to realize that 'paynims' and Saracens dressed differently, and were indeed much more advanced in luxury and sophistication than he was himself. Certainly the result was to change his own style of dress and made possible the development of 'fashion'.

Fashion, in our sense, can be seen emerging in the last half of the 14th century. Beginning in the luxurious Courts of France and Burgundy at that time, it soon spread in the West, so that it is possible in remote England to note the differences in the headdresses of ladies between (say) 1380 and 1400. The great discovery was that women, instead of being wrapped up like parcels, as they had been for nearly a thousand years, could, by such devices as tight-lacing and décolletage do much for the enhancement of their bodily charms. These discoveries still, today, form the basis of fashion.

The woman of 1400 could not be unaware that the clothes she wore were different from those of previous generations. The time-sequence, so to speak, had been discovered, but there was little consciousness of the space-variation, except of course, for the contacts with the Near East. In the piazzi of Venice the traders of Western Europe met the Levantine merchants who were nearly all wearing caftans and turbans. The Turks were already in control of Constantinople and the greater part of the Balkans. It was impossible to ignore them, and so the idea was firmly lodged in the European mind that the clothes of 'far away' were Turkish clothes.

Of historical knowledge there was as yet very little, but with the Renaissance and the discovery of classical remains, another notion came to be accepted, that if the clothes of 'far away' were Turkish the clothes of 'long ago' were Roman. This was about as far as the contemporaries of Shakespeare had got, as can be seen in the only surviving drawing of costume in a Shakespearean play. The playgoers who went to the Globe to see *Titus Andronicus* took for granted the strange mixture of Roman, oriental and contemporary costume presented to their eyes. Indeed in the theatre this attitude persisted until almost the end of the 18th century.

However, certain efforts had already been made to increase knowledge. One of the earliest attempts to produce a *Pictorial Encyclopedia* of costume was Ferdinando Bertelli's *Omnium fere gentium nostrae aetatis habitus* published (significantly enough) at Venice in 1563. He followed this up with a work entitled *Diversarum nationum habitus* published at Padua in two parts in 1591 and 1594. Much of the 'foreign' costume is imaginary but the book is highly authoritative for the North Italian dresses of its own period which can assumed to be authentic. It is amusing to find the device of the movable flap (to be exploited in the 19th century by the designers of fashion plates and the manufacturers of Valentines) which enables us to study both the skirt of the Venetian courtesan and the pantaloons beneath it, (see Illustration 239).

German publishers were already in the field (indeed the illustrations of Italian books of the period are largely drawn from German sources, notably the wood engravings of Jost Amman) with a volume published in 1577 at Nuremberg, by Hans Weigel: *Habitus praecipuorum populorum . . . singulari arte depicti.* From France in 1567 came a *Recueil de la diversité des habits, qui sont de présent en usage*, published in Paris. Much of the material, unfortunately, is purely fanciful, including a '*Femme sauvage*' and a '*Ciclope*'.

Probably the most famous of the early books on costume was Cesare Vecellio's *Degli Habiti antichi et moderni di diverse parte del mondo*, published at Venice in 1590. It found its way all over Europe and was almost certainly known to Shakespeare. It is not altogether an original work as editors of the period had no more inhibitions about plagiarism than Shakespeare himself. One of the illustrations is that of a '*Nobile Inglese*'. The second part of the work is devoted to the costumes of Asia and Africa, depicted with very varying degrees of authenticity.

Meanwhile new schools of portraiture had arisen and as the paintings produced were frequently engraved, those interested could at least learn something of the clothes worn by important personages in all the countries of Europe. The present work inevitably draws largely upon such sources; and as it is now possible to reproduce in colour from the paintings themselves we are able to learn of the colours of the costumes as well as their forms. Here is to be found a mass of documentation which, almost paradoxically, was not available to the painters' contemporaries, for the ordinary man and woman could have seen very few of their products, hidden away as they were in the palaces of kings and nobles. The days of great public exhibitions of painting were, of course, still far in the future.

The various engraving processes, however, began to play an increasing part, especially in the 17th century when the popularity of men like Abraham Bosse and Wenzel Hollar implies considerable public interest in contemporary costume. The advantage to us is that such artists sometimes show us the dress of the common people. From paintings alone one might come to the conclusion that everybody wore fine clothes and wore them all the time. Hollar is particularly valuable in this respect, for his work, published in London in 1640 and entitled *Ornatus Muliebris Anglicanus, or The Several Habits of English Women from the Nobilitie to the Country Woman, as they are in these Times*, contains twenty-six plates mostly representing the daily wear of the English middle classes.

Three years later Hollar brought out his *Theatrum Muliebrum*, depicting the different styles of feminine costume in all the principal European countries. He also published a series of exquisite etchings representing such costume accessories as muffs, fans, hats, watches and *châtelaines*. And, towards the close of the

17th century there was a burst of activity in France, with the work of Jean Dieu de Saint-Jean and the Bonnart family. The engravings of all these artists provide an invaluable record of French contemporary costume.

It is unfortunate that the troubles of the closing years of the reign of Louis XIV brought this admirable tradition to an end; for there was very little more in the way of costume engraving in France until the magnificent series known as *Le Monument du Costume*, which appeared in the 1770s. The gap is partly bridged, so far as England is concerned, by the engravings of William Hogarth, after his own paintings, which were published in the 1740s.

Then, as we approach the end of the 18th century, something entirely new appears. This innovation was the fashion plate. All the engravings we have been discussing were, or purported to be representative of costumes actually worn. The aspiring *bourgeoise* might gain a hint or two from the depiction of what 'the Lady of Quality' wore, but the intention was not to prophesy the coming mode. The fashion plate was intended to do precisely this and, of course, played an important part in the democratization of fashion.

It goes without saying, therefore (although it is not always realized) that students of the history of costume should use fashion plates with a certain degree of caution. Every dress that we see in a fashion plate did not *necessarily* become a dress that was actually worn; but, with this proviso, it is obvious that fashion plates not only provide one of the main sources of costume documentation for the whole of the 19th century but give us also a *dated* series which serves as a kind of check-list for the dating of contemporary paintings.

Among the first true fashion plates are those included in *La Galerie des Modes*, a series of beautifully engraved and hand-coloured plates issued in Paris between 1778 and 1787. These provide an ample documentation of Parisian modes in the decade before the French Revolution, showing not only the costumes themselves, both for men and women, but valuable details of accessories and underwear. This publication was paralled in England by Heideloffs' *Gallery of Fashion* issued in monthly parts between 1794 and 1803. It was followed by a whole succession of fashion magazines.

Meanwhile there was an ever increasing interest in historical costume, stimulated by the Romantic Movement. Illustrators and theatrical designers were no longer content with a vague approximation to the clothes of long ago and far away, and there was a growing demand for accurate and exhaustive information. This demand was met by histories of costume, notably by Fairholt, Planché and

Racinet, and these ambitious works are not entirely superseded even now. But, of course, they suffer from the difficulty of producing really accurate and convincing versions of the material available. Neither line-engraving, wood-engraving nor lithography could really give an adequate reproduction of a painting and the colour had to be added by hand or by the laborious process of chromo-lithography.

In the present century the use of photography and improved techniques of colour reproduction have abolished this handicap. The modern student no longer needs to view the pictures of the past through a distorting medium which involved re-drawing on the part of a later artist.

During recent years there has been an enormous increase in the costume histories available and some of these have attempted to cover the whole field from primitive to modern times. The present publication, *The Pictorial Encyclopedia of Fashion*, takes us back to the fourth millennium B.C. and continues the story to the present day. Its value and originality lie in the method of presentation which has been adopted. The first part of the work is a straightforward history; the second is a detailed study of separate categories: hair and beards, headdresses and hats, ruffs, collars and cravats, underclothes, accessories and jewellery, men's costume, liturgical vestments, shoes and stockings, overcoats and children's dress. Each of these sections is arranged chronologically for ease of reference and each of the numerous plates is provided with a caption and a commentary. The plates themselves are well chosen and include a number of mid-European examples not often to be found in books published in France and England. English readers should be glad to have in their hands a work at once so authoritative and comprehensive: not just another 'history of costume' but a *Pictorial Encyclopedia* of the greatest value.

Introduction to the History of Fashion

Introduction

Fashion in·its widest sense comprises all outward manifestations of civilized behaviour which receive general acceptance for a limited period of time. These include moral standards, table manners, car designs as well as styles of dress. It is the latter, however, that spring to mind at the mention of the word fashion – that constant change in outward form, which is inaccessible to rational explanation.

Man's apparently foolish craving for novelty and change has always been a favourite theme with satirists and caricaturists, but this must not blind one to the fact that fashions in dress – the theme of this book – play a very important part in civilized human society, to say nothing of their importance in the economy of that society. Every fashion change hides within itself the promise of the ultimate ideal of beauty, and the consumers, male and female, are only too willing to believe in the possibility of fulfilment and feel obliged again and again to bow to the dictates of a new fashion.

The human body is the basis of all fashion. Each epoch develops its own aesthetic conception of the ideal human shape. This is demonstrated most clearly by the variations in the ideal of feminine beauty. One need only compare Ruben's buxom beauties with the tall, slim and elegant line preferred today.

Clothes can accentuate as well as tone down certain parts of the body, so as to make the silhouette approach as nearly as possible the prevalent ideal. They can correct faults and create an illusion. Characteristic examples are the medieval predilection for a slightly protuberant belly in the female form, as can be seen in many contemporary works of art, and the preference in Rococo times for an exaggeratedly tiny waist.

The apparent bodily proportions, too, can be strongly influenced by the composition of the attire. The most frequently encountered tendency in the history of costume is a striving for an increase in stature. The optical illusion of an increase in height or girth – by means of a crinoline for instance – served to enhance

dignity and social importance. Occasionally the length of the dress or the amount of material used pointed to the social position of the wearer.

Not till the 20th century, when the figure was at last allowed to develop its natural line, was it no longer necessary to submit the body to the torture of a tightly laced corset, a practice reminiscent of the Chinese and Japanese fashion of stunting the growth of a small girl's feet and of similar customs among primitive tribes.

The European standard of decorum has remained fairly constant. The exposure of women's legs earlier this century was a revolutionary innovation, and in general today's clothes leave ever increasing portions of the body bare. Ideas of modesty vary according to habit and tradition in different parts of the world (for instance, custom requires Moslem women in less advanced countries to veil their faces). The criterion of modesty is usually the extent of the 'décolleté'.

An early example of décolleté can be seen in the Snake Goddess of Crete (Ill. 50). Monuments of Greek origin, too, display a wide variety of necklines. The low-cut dress reappeared in the Middle Ages, when it was employed by Burgundian fashion not only for the bosom but also for the back. In the sensuous times of the Renaissance, too, when the figure was encased in a corset which lifted the bosom high, dresses were cut very low – except in Spain where, characteristically, strict dictates of Spanish fashion prohibited the wearing of low necklines, which were not worn again until the Baroque period and which were cut lower still at the time of the Rococo.

It is impossible to overlook the erotic element in the history of fashion, where it is represented in a variety of ways – from low-cut dresses and transparent materials (which are again in fashion today as they were at the time of Napoleon) – to the deliberate stressing of the male genitalia in the masculine attire of the Middle Ages. Sexuality has a significant in-

2 *Petit Courrier des Dames*, 1839.
The wasp waist, achieved by tight
corseting, was not achieved
without discomfort for the ladies
of the period.

3 *Journal Amusant*, Paris, 1868.
A caricature of the tall wigs and
long trains of the period of
Napoleon III, which completely
distorted the natural proportions.

4 *Modes Parisiennes*, 1868. The
bustle and the waist-concealing
polonaise spoiled the natural line
of the feminine back.

5 Alfred Grévin. 'The Tournure'.
The caricature shows the
characteristic deformation of the
figure by the *trompeuse* (a false
bust) and the *tournure* (or bustle).

6 *Kladderadatsch*, Berlin 1881.
'The uplifted bust'.

2

3

4

5

6

fluence on fashion; it is one of the factors which subconsciously affect the way in which clothes are used and judged.

The history of fashion is probably nearly as old as the history of costume itself. From the moment, when man discovered the function of clothes as a protection against the vagaries of nature, it cannot have been long before he began to consider their aesthetic aspect. Clothes proved to be the object which could perhaps most easily serve as a vehicle for his artistic sense and, to this day, they have remained the means whereby he can outwardly express certain ideas about himself and the world in general.

To clothe the naked body with a garment may be regarded as symbolizing chastity and modesty. But such an interpretation seems almost too narrow and limited. After all, even the amulet was once a form of clothing: it served as a barrier or bridge between the exposed vulnerable human body and the good or evil spirits of the surrounding world. Examples of the symbolic significance of certain kinds of dress may be found in the rigorous rules which governed the clothes worn by Egyptian pharaohs, Roman senators, Spanish monarchs or the ranks of medieval nobility.

In one way or another the clothes we wear are affected by tradition even today, and historical events have played no small part in influencing fashion now as in the past. Under the guillotine of the French Revolution not only heads, but wigs rolled – literally as well as figuratively. Not to wear a wig henceforth became as obligatory as is the wearing of jeans among certain groups of young people of today. Clothes have meaning; they reveal secret attitudes.

Although clothes are among the most individual creations of civilization, fashion, which follows clothes like a shadow, stimulates the imitative instinct. Psychologists regard imitation as a form of biological self-defence, the natural reflex of the herd-animal. The comparison with human society is an obvious one.

A fashion is meant to be copied by everyone, but, paradoxically, the fashionably dressed individual expects to stand out in a crowd. Man adapts himself to his surroundings, he adopts the current fashion – and at the same time he seeks to distinguish himself by means of this very fashion; he copies others, yet in so doing he attempts to find the style which suits him best and helps him to realize his image of himself. Fashion is thus a fashion of opposites.

People in general tend to look above themselves and to model themselves on prominent personalities. The history of fashion has many examples to offer for influential leaders of fashion, from Isabel of Bavaria (1371–1435), Queen of France, to the popular television stars of today. Moreover man loves disguises. Cinderella's pumpkin is a universal theme.

Where is the birthplace of fashion? Not by any means anywhere. One might say 'in Paris of course'. But it is not a matter of course. Throughout the centuries many countries and towns have claimed to be leaders of taste. Fashion arrived on the banks of the Seine by a circuitous route, and Italy, Spain and later also England were stations on its journey through Europe.

The power that fashion commands over neigh-

7

bours and countries further away, over entire continents even, is often a question also of political power; fashion and politics frequently go hand in hand. Italy's contribution took place at the time of the Renaissance and the flowering of the City States, at the head of which stood Florence and Venice; they were the centres of Italy's profitable trade with the orient. Already in the 13th century magnificent silk fabrics were produced in parts of Northern Italy; in Milan there was a flourishing velvet industry. It will be seen that centres of fashion always exist side by side with a lively textile industry. This is exemplified today by the part played by Lyons, famous for the manufacture of silk, as well as, more recently, the production of artificial fibres, in France's predominance in the world of fashion.

The Duchy of Burgundy was, for a century preceding the battle of Nancy in 1477, a leader of fashion in Europe. Ghent, Bruges and Ypres were the commercial pillars of this Duchy. The woollen industry of Flanders, which processed English wool, stood then at its peak, and the Cloth Hall at Ypres was mag-

7 *Modebilder zur Theaterzeitung*, 1834. In the 1830s the silhouette became more voluminous and pompous. Wide coats and skirts were typical.

8 Leonetto Cappiello. Marthe Brandes. Drawing. Although wide skirts had disappeared by the end of the 19th century, bust and waist were still tightly laced.

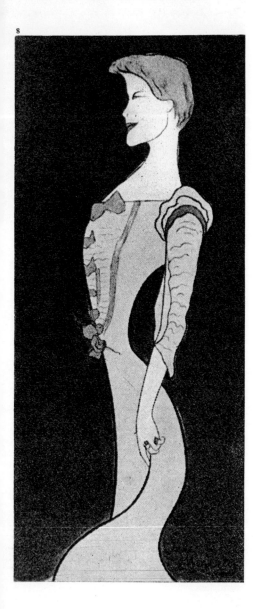

nificently adorned. Schiller described Burgundy later as 'the most voluptuous and splendid court in Europe, Italy not excepted'. But with its battles Burgundy also lost its supremacy in the world of fashion, and a century noted for its excesses in style and the exaggerated luxury of its costume came to an end.

Spain then took its place and dictated the fashion during the markedly masculine era of the Counter Reformation. Black was now the dominant colour, to which homage was paid by the rulers of an Empire in which the sun never set. Beside the stiff costume of the proud reserved nobleman the crinoline signified dignity and decorum. But the conservative circles in Spain – who were basically anti-fashion, as conservatives always are – held fashion, impatiently striving for change, in too much restraint. After 1600, when the political hegemony of Spain had been broken, the balance of power shifted to France, and Paris, with its zest for living, stepped into the lead of fashion. Casanova wrote: 'Paris is perhaps the only city in the world which changes its appearance completely in the course of five or six years.'

It is true that London, like Madrid and Paris the seat of an influential court in a united country, has been a real rival of the French capital since the 18th century. It is a paradox in the history of fashion that Paris of all places, according to a 1768 report sent from there by a German writer, suffered a bad attack of 'anglomania'. The proximity of the two countries was already encouraging a lively exchange of ideas, which cannot conveniently be reduced to the phrase: 'What Paris means to the fashionable woman London means to the well-dressed man.'

The connection is closer than this – an intermingling of two essentially different but complementary types: imagination and fantasy in Paris and a feeling for the practical and sporting in London. The 'English suit', the 'tailor-made', tailored coats and rainwear are Britain's domain in the world of fashion. London's claim to be the leader in the correct wear for men, which originated in Savile Row, the home of fashionable men's tailoring, has remained uncontested – in spite of interesting

9

10

11

9 Hans Holbein, the Younger. 'Unknown Woman'. Kupferstichkabinett, Basle. The décolleté of antiquity came back into fashion in the late Gothic period, since when it has been in favour, with a few short interruptions, until the present day. The Renaissance lady wears a square-cut neckline, laced bodice, long sleeves and her head is covered with a beret.

10 Johann Kupecky. The family of the Artist. Museum of Fine Arts, Budapest. At the time of the Baroque the neckline was sometimes cut so low as to expose the entire breast.

11 Portrait of Sophia Western. Engraving after the painting by John Hoppner. The broad-brimmed hat is tied under the chin with ribbons. The dress is cut low and edged with frills, and the scarf, which has been added, adorns rather than conceals the breast.

12 *Allgemeine Modenzeitung*, 1836. All the various necklines of the 1830s have broad beribboned lace collars, which cover the shoulders.

attempts in Paris, in spite of the imaginative creations of Italian designers, in spite of the colourful and easy-to-wear leisure clothes that came from America after the war and created a new market, in spite of Carnaby Street.

Two of the best known creators of fashion of this century, Mme Schiaparelli and Nina Ricci were Italians (an argument for the unbroken creative tradition of Italy, which has recently acquired renewed prestige in the shoe as well as in the dress industry) but, of course, they were Italians in Paris.

Two of the most successful fashion designers in the 19th century, Worth and Redfern, were Englishmen, but Englishmen in Paris. The journal *Modenwelt*, among others, wrote in 1865: 'Whether one likes it or not, Paris is without question the uncontested sovereign seat of high fashion, whence its queen sends out her commands across the globe. . . .'

12

The French rulers, from Louis XIV to Napoleon III, and not excepting the great Napoleon himself, have always paid gracious attention to fashion. If one also considers the geographical position of this capital of a mighty state, the long tradition of a highly developed textile industry and the skill of the Paris tailors and seamstresses, it is not surprising that this exuberant city became the supreme fashion centre, whose eccentric ideas, with some modifications, were taken up everywhere in the world by the dress trade.

The Houses of the most famous French designers used to be situated within an area limited by the Rue de Rivoli in the South, the Chaussée d'Antin in the North, the Rue Royale in the West and the Rue Taitbout in the East. Here, or in the immediate vicinity, they reigned: Worth, Paquin, Paul Poiret, Redfern, Lanvin, Lucien Lelong, Coco Chanel, Jean Patou, Christian Dior – this was the domain of the Haute Couture, the name given to the small illustrious circle of the most prominent Paris fashion designers, and to the society which they formed. Today the couture houses are concentrated in the area of the Rond Point, near the Champs Elysées.

The founder of the Haute Couture is that young Englishman, who came to Paris at the age of 20, knowing no French and with 117 francs in his pocket: Charles Frederick Worth. Fifteen years later, in 1860, his young wife brought about the decisive meeting with the elegant and influential Duchess Metternich, whose intercession with the Empress Eugénie made Worth the uncrowned king of Paris fashion. In due course he counted no less than nine queens among his clients. For the solemn opening of the Suez Canal he is said to have supplied the Empress alone with no less than 150 model dresses. Worth's name is connected with the crinoline, and when it had had its day Worth created the bustle, allegedly because he liked the folds in the back of a woman's dress, which she would hitch up when turning in the street.

At one of his fashion shows models, the so-called mannequins (from the Flemish Maeneken, a diminutive of man), are said to have made their first appearance. In the early years after the foundation of his fashion house Worth's wife frequently and successfully

13, 14 The influence of fashion – here English fashion – according to a caricature in *Simplicissimus*, 1902–1903: 'This is what Herr and Frau Schmidt looked like when they left for London – and this is what they looked like when they returned a week later as Mr and Mrs Smith.'

15 Charles Frederick Worth, the English founder of Paris Haute Couture. Circa 1858, at the time when his Salon was in the Rue de la Paix.

16 Charles Vernier. *Le Charivari*, 1856. Among the strangest creations of fashion are the hooped skirts. Mocked at and attacked they dominated the fashion scene for the last time, during the reign of Napoleon III and the Empress Eugénie. At that time the couturier Worth, whose name remains linked with the crinoline, was at the height of his fame.

15

16

17 Sarah Bernhardt, by Georges Clairin.
Musée du Petit Palais, Paris. Great and
famous actresses, whether of stage or screen,
have always been active supporters of fashion.
Sarah Bernhardt was certainly one of the
most influential.

I Hans Baldung Grien. The Martyrdom of St. Dorothea. Národni Galerie, Prague.

IIa Bohemian Master after 1370. Votive-picture of Jan Očko of Vlašim (Bohemia). Národni Galerie, Prague.

IIb Antonio Vivarini and Giovanni de Alamagna. Saint from the altar-piece of the Church of San Francesco in Padua (detail). Národni Galerie, Prague.

III Studio of Michael Pacher. Birth of the Virgin. Castle Gallery, Rychnov n.Kn. (Bohemia).

IV From a German illuminated manuscript of the 15th century. Pages carrying helmets during court celebrations.

played the part of a mannequin. Predecessors of these models – whose profession today is as strenuous as it is well paid – were the Roman coloured terracotta figurines, 8 to 25 cm. (3 to 10 in.) high, which the Romans sent to the provinces in place of fashion plates. Later on the French used similar though larger figures, in order to demonstrate the latest Paris fashions in Vienna, Madrid, St Petersburg and Berlin.

At the end of the 19th century Worth and Doucet were the leading couture houses in Paris. Charles Frederick Worth died in 1894, but his sons had early entered the business. Among their clients, who were scattered all over the world, was the famous Italian actress Eleanora Duse, who, for thirty years, had all her stage costumes made by the House of Worth. Jacques Doucet was a highly cultured man, a collector and connoisseur of the arts. Many of his inspirations derived from the treasury of the 18th century, which was his passion. Sarah Bernhardt, another actress whose dresses were no less admired than her acting genius, was Doucet's client. Réjane, the well-known and popular Paris actress, was also one of his most faithful customers.

Everyone around the Rue de la Paix and the Place Vendôme, who was of any importance in the world of fashion was present in Paris during the brilliant World Exhibition of 1900. Much to the disgust of the men the fashion section of the exhibition was presided over by a woman, Mme Paquin. She was the first woman of Haute Couture and she received the ribbon of the Légion d'Honneur. Her creations and her art of launching them (on one occasion a dozen attractive models displayed her designs at the great races at Longchamp) were as famous as her clients, which included La Belle Otéro. Mme Paquin also visited Berlin and became court dressmaker to the Empress of Germany.

Paul Poiret (1879–1944) was one of the most influential creators of fashion of all time. The pose of conquering hero, which he assumed so convincingly during the years of his greatest successes, was part of this dynamic couturier's style of life. His strong explosive colours, which stimulated his draughtsman Lepape, were inspired by visual art. Poiret reigned in

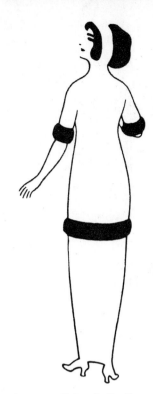

18 *Ulk*, Berlin, 1910. Poiret in Berlin: 'Poiret's posterior' ('Popoiret') or 'Some can – some shouldn't.'

19

20

the period just before the First World War; in 1927, however, his House had to be closed. This extravagant, autocratic personality, in all of whose activity there was a theatrical streak (he worked a great deal with the theatre), whose fabulous parties were notable events among the élite, would not recognize that time had overtaken him. New personalities appeared: Mme Vionnet, Mme Schiaparelli. Coco Chanel, whose name has today already become a legend, introduced a new ideal of simplicity into the world of the Haute Couture. She argued that true elegance could only be achieved by allowing full freedom of movement, and that a fashion which does not find favour with the masses is no fashion. She was the first representative of the Paris fashion houses who worked for the ready-to-wear market. Towards the end of the twenties her workshop employed more than 2,000 workers. Typical of her creations is the famous 'Chanel suit', which has always been both youthful and practical.

Christian Dior (1905–1957) was the most outstanding couturier of the period following the Second World War. He realized that, after the drab uniformity of war, women longed to be feminine again and that it was up to him as a fashion designer 'to adorn and beautify wo-

21

19, 20, 21, 22, 23 A cross-section
of Paris fashion in the twenties, as
depicted in influential fashion
magazines of the period, such as
Vogue or the *Gazette du Bon Ton*.
The models illustrated are from the
Couture houses of Jean Patou (19),
Rodier (20), Worth (21), Lanvin (23)
and by the artist Man Ray (22).

men'. He created the 'New Look' with its revolutionary lengthening of the skirt, which, in his own words, was a reaction against poverty. In his book *Je suis Couturier* he said: 'We had behind us a time of war, of uniforms, of women in the services with broad shoulders like a boxer's. I sketched flower-like women, gently curved shoulders, rounded breasts and reed slim waists and skirts that spread out like flower petals.' Dior's overwhelming success illustrates the importance of the fashion creator's instinct for the time and the spirit of the age.

At the inception of each new fashion stands the imaginative couturier. He derives the stimuli for his collections from all kinds of sources. In one season Mme Schiaparelli owed the inspiration for her creations to the magic of the American circus of Barnum and Bailey. Paintings and exotic ballets, great exhibitions and the tide of events, films, travel, successful novels, all are the raw material for the fashion designer. He can escape from the present to the tender romance of past periods – or seize time boldly by the forelock. In 1965 Emilio Pucci, the leading couturier of Florence said, 'For the first time in history man can move freely in the universe. The Haute Couture cannot overlook this fact.' The 'Astronaut-look', the 'Space-look', entered conversation. Space creations immediately appeared in the leading international fashion magazines. A jeweller from Geneva exhibited in London under the title 'Météorites et Bijoux'. 'I dream,' he said, 'of jewellery that will reflect nature, space, the secrets of the ocean depths, and the space-age, which has begun.' Fashion is a mirror of the age, in retrospect at least, and the fashion designer is the medium through whom its spirit finds expression.

Every fashion, nevertheless, requires sponsors. Not until it has been recognized and accepted in certain élite circles, does it become high fashion. Its curve then rises with its increasing popularity and the circle of those whom it pleases grows steadily bigger. When everyone has copied it and it has reached its peak or, in other words, when the fashion threatens to become a uniform and therefore ceases to be fashionable, the cycle either ends abruptly or

24 *Simplicissimus*, 1914–1915. The fashion designer is accustomed to make use of any inspiration his epoch may have to offer. Thus the latest creations of Paris Haute Couture elegantly and characteristically reflect the exotic presence of the various foreign auxiliary troups.

25 There has always been a mutual interchange of ideas between film and fashion. Here the artist and fashion creator Christian Bérard helps the actress Edwige Feuillère try on an historical costume.

it declines gradually. And this is the greatest of fashion's many paradoxes: its objective – acceptance by the masses – carries with it its downfall.

In French to be in fashion is to be *en vogue*. *Voguer* means to float or glide, which graphically suggests the ups and downs of fashion; it is in a constant state of flux. Fashion cycles vary enormously with different types of garment. Less expensive ones, summer dresses or hats, for instance, very quickly become out of date, they change from season to season. A few novelties, if a large section of the consumers regard them as useful, eventually become standard wear. This dependence on the seasons – spring-summer and autumn-winter are the main phases – is characteristic of the process of fashion.

In order to become generally known, a fashion needs to be publicized with illustrations which can serve as a guide. Before the designs are formally shown, there is a period of great secrecy during which every precaution is taken to prevent spies from catching a glimpse of the drawings. But the couture house must, as soon as the fashion show is under way, do everything in its power to publicize its new collection. By tradition French fashion has at its disposal the instrument of a first rate and world-wide publicity. French fashion magazines have always been of a high standard. The first illustrated fashion journal, the *Cabinet des Modes* appeared in Paris in 1785 (followed a year later in Weimar by Bertuch's *Journal des Luxus und der Moden*). An exclusive paper like the *Gazette du Bon Ton* which appeared before and after the First World War, is still today regarded by many as an ideal. Writers of renown, among them Cocteau, Giraudoux, Colette, and artists like Raoul Dufy and Christian Bérard have contributed to this standard. Today the last word on fashion is spoken by *Vogue* and *Harper's Bazaar*. These magazines have helped fashion photography, in the last twenty years, to attain to its present very high artistic level – albeit to the detriment of fashion drawing.

A fashion is not meant to be confined to shows and photographs. Before the 'man and woman in the street' can come to terms with it via television, illustrated papers and fashion journals, a new fashion which at first almost always raises a smile, must be launched in public by a small self-possessed élite. They will be seen on the boulevards of the capitals, at gala premieres, at race meetings, in fashionable resorts and restaurants. In the English-speaking world the small number of people who have the means, the time and the taste to indulge in setting the fashion in this way are said to be 'with-it'. They are the ones who stand in the spotlight of publicity, who belong, whose opinions matter. It is important to add that today anyone is 'with-it' who has grasped the essence of a new fashion and who carries it off with aplomb. Not all who are 'with-it', however, look chic and elegant, since neither their nature nor their figure permit it. Conversely there are many elegant people who are by no means in the forefront of fashion. True fashion leaders can only be those who manage to be both 'with-it' and elegant – and there are not many.

The range of influence of such an élite – formerly it consisted largely of the aristocracy, popular actresses and spoiled society women – was for a long time limited to political and cultural centres. In the provinces there was always a strong resistance to it, born of habit, custom and tradition. Only very gradually was the fashion of the metropolis taken up and brought into accord with the demands made upon clothes by work and everyday life. But this has changed now – although the provinces still lag behind, they are quicker to follow fashion than they used to be.

The beginning of the machine age in the 19th century brought about a reassessment of values, which did not leave clothes and their social function untouched. It concerned all the classification of clothes as chattel. Medieval costume represented capital. It qualified as movable goods, calculable in figures, and owing to the lavish use of ornament and jewellery it sometimes acquired the character of a transferable investment. It is not, after all, very long since personal garments were part of the dowry and were passed down from generation to generation. But the growth of the clothing industry changed everything. In 1770 in Paris the first important clothes factory was founded. The repeal and simplification of the Guild laws, during the French Revolution, brought about conditions which led to mass-production on a larger scale. Already in the first years of the revolution several large manufacturers of clothes and underwear had sprung up. In 1824 the business 'La Belle Jardinière' was founded in Paris for the production of ready-made clothes. This soon overtook other enterprises of a similar nature and, to this day, is among the leading firms of its kind.

With the boom in the textile, clothing and chemical industries in the course of the 19th century, fashion became more democratic. Through the mass-marketing of ready-made clothes prices could be lowered. The *dernier cri*, the latest fashion, no longer interested a small circle only, but became the preoccupation of millions. The economical significance of the ready-to-wear trade was gradually brought home to the Haute Couture, for the First World War had altered the structure of its clientele. There were fewer courts and a smaller number of the aristocracy left. The creation of collections for a considerably larger circle replaced the personal relationship between couturier and client.

Today private customers still account for about 60% of the total turnover at some Paris fashion houses; their main profits derive, however, from their collections being purchased by large stores and wholesalers - as well as from sidelines, such as the production of perfumes, powder, shoes, stockings and corsets - which are sold in the couturier's boutique. The international ready-to-wear trade is an even larger purchaser; the times have gone for good when (it was in 1936) Jean Patou and Lucien Lelong could be called enemies of the Haute Couture, because they had expressed the opinion that the wishes of the clothing industry would have to be considered.

Quality, in the sense of the durability of the product, understandably is an enemy of fashion change. But the concept of quality has altered - no one today would seriously think of passing on articles of clothing from one generation to another. Quality no longer means durability - future changes in fashion have already unconsciously been taken into account (a kind of built-in obsolescence). Today much greater stress is laid on how the garment will wear; its elasticity, crease resistance, water and dirt-repelling quality; whether it is 'non-iron' and will keep its shape. These are the demands the purchaser makes of the material and on which he bases his modern concept of quality. The ever increasing variety of new fibres and fabrics coming on to the market, coupled with skilled propaganda, ensures the continuing interest of the consumer. The latest additions are paper clothes which, being very cheap, will give the wardrobe even greater variety and versatility.

It is still true to say that good clothes lend a cachet to their wearer, a distinction which today is achieved by very subtle means. The more uniform the outward appearance - measured by international standards - the more numerous are the variations in material and colour. It is not so much the cut, but rather the texture and colour of the material which accentuate the character of the garment. Clothes produced wholesale are accessible to everyone. Individual taste is shown in the choice and in the combination of the separate parts of dress. Those who desire to wear distinctive dress must resort to made-to-measure clothes and exclusive materials. Deliberate understatement - such as using mink for lining raincoats - is a sign of exclusiveness. Sometimes it would seem at first glance that fashionable clothes are concerned too much with trivia and pay too little heed to the functional. There are, however, numerous examples in history which show that utilitarian garments can and do become articles of fashion. The garment concerned becomes symbolic of the wearer's philosophy of life. Jeans, for example, which to begin with, were cheap working clothes, became for a time almost compulsory wear among a certain group of young people. The significance of jeans, though unstated, was so strong that it managed almost to obliterate the otherwise inescapable impression of uniformity. Girls, who were seen on all occasions wearing jeans and a shaggy sweater, demonstrated their dependence on their generation and obedience to their group, rather than their aesthetic judgment or their personal taste.

26

27

Interesting evidence of the connection between clothes and social class is the designation of office workers, etc. as 'white-collar workers'. The gulf that separates people who work with their brain from manual workers is thus neatly expressed by means of a characteristic garment.

Fashion, in general, endeavours to give a youthful and fresh appearance to the wearer: it aims to rejuvenate. Anthropologists have demonstrated that tattooing and decorating the face with clay ornaments among primitive tribes was intended not only to adorn, but also to hide wrinkles. The very essence of fashion is change and it is thus closer in spirit to the dynamic tempo of living of the young.

But the wearing of high fashion clothes used to be the prerogative of the wealthy. Turning the pages of the fashion journals of the past century one finds throughout models for 'ladies', that is to say for women whose husbands were in a secure position and able to meet the cost of these model dresses. The 20th century, however, brought mass employment of women, as well as a relatively high income for young people in general. Both factors influenced fashion to an extent never known before.

The fashion designers rose to the occasion. Because the professionally active women declined to wear superfluous and purposeless embellishments, women's fashions of the twenties possessed many marked characteristics of men's clothing. The drastic shortening of the skirt to the knee, the discarding of corsets and the short hair styles introduced a new concept of simplicity and broadmindedness in dress.

The large number of new and young consumers, thirsting for change and able and willing to spend money, give an important impetus to the fashion creator. Fashion is no longer directed towards people of mature years but rather towards youth and its mode of living.

Moreover, every activity and every hobby seeks a corresponding echo in dress. Once the problem of a garment's fundamental purpose had been solved, fashion took a hand; graphic examples are women's suits and bathing costumes. The suit which, to begin with, was modelled on the man's suit, because of its usefulness and versatility, in due course became a classic garment. The skirt length varied as did the width of the lapels or the size of the buttons but the basic idea remained the same.

It took several decades before the basic shape of the bathing suit became stabilized. The original embarrassment caused by its design, not altogether due to the necessity of exposing a large part of the body, the clumsy attempts to borrow ideas from other articles of clothing particularly underwear, only make us smile today. But once the right formula had been found, the design for the upper part at any rate was soon employed for dresses, especially evening dresses.

Mass-production made it possible to have different clothes for a great variety of purposes. The original division into everyday or working clothes and holiday or Sunday clothes became a long string of specialized garments: indoor clothes, outdoor clothes, party clothes, evening clothes, leisure clothes, travel clothes, etc. One type influenced another. At one time it seemed a far cry from long sports trousers to evening clothes but today there are trousers especially intended for evening wear.

There is said to be an old Indian law which threatens the severest penalty – death by hanging – to those wearing the clothes of the opposite sex. This tradition testifies, within the framework of the history of costume, to the sexual significance of clothes. Clothes demonstrate the polarity of the sexes, which is shown in many ways, but they also express a challenge and a wish to please. This is no longer true of masculine dress. The cavalier of the Renaissance employed a great quantity of lace; the chiselled armour of the medieval knight was a veritable work of art. Church and municipal laws censured the excessive use of ornament, the extravagance of masculine attire. Modern man no longer fights with the sword under the colourful pennant of his king; the lute of the troubadour is silent and pastoral plays today are forgotten. The attributes of man's social importance are less obvious, his rank is hidden beneath a sober suit which, at first glance, seems indistinguishable from other suits. But who would dare

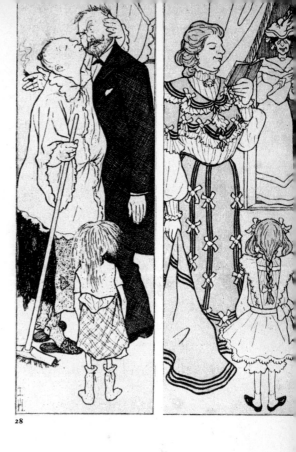

28

26, 27 In the history of fashion women's clothes from time to time resembled men's to such an extent that they became an object of caricature. Today, too, women's clothes often borrow elements from the clothes of the opposite sex, such as hats, ties, jackets, trousers. *Above*: 'Which is the man and which the woman?' English caricature, 1787, Collection Grante-Carteret. *Below*: 'Why does that old ass keep staring at us? Has he never seen a woman?' *Lustige Blätter*, Berlin, 1927.

28 The family in private and when visitors are expected. From the series *Bilder aus dem Familienleben* (Pictures from family life), Th.Th.Heine, *Simplicissimus*, 1905, Munich.

Through the ages no attempt which would bring the male body into accord with the contemporary ideal of beauty has been omitted. Pointed shoes, padded doublets, trunk hose, bells, ruffs, ribbons, codpieces, dags, corsets and wigs, were worn by all and not only by a few daring spirits. There were indeed a few for whom fashion was a very serious matter: in the 17th century it was Monsieur Alamode, and in the 19th there were the dandies of London and Paris.

29 Wenzel Hollar, 'The Jealous Lad'.
'Good Lord, there's Fred
    with a plume in his hat,
I'll get one just as bright,
And if he won't leave my
    Gretl alone,
We'll have to have a fight.'

30 Willem Buytewech. Standing Cavalier. Museum Boymans von Beuningen, Rotterdam. The fashionably dressed cavalier is wearing a broad hat, doublet, knee-length breeches with ribbons and roses on stockings and shoes. His suit is covered with a large number of buttons and a large cape is wrapped around his body.

31 Franz Hals. The Laughing Cavalier.
Wallace Collection, London. Moustache,
slashed sleeves, broad lace collar with
ribbons and a broad sash – all these typify
the cavalier.

32 Already by the end of the 18th century
the dandy led the fashion. This photograph
from the middle of the 19th century shows
him in outdoor clothes, where the top hat
(here in grey) was indispensable.

assert that man has lost his desire to please
women?

True, he does so no longer by means of
Brussels lace. In the machine age male
interests have shifted rather beyond fashion –
above all towards the car. Its shape, colour and
accessories, which are all elements of fashion,
have come, in fact, to symbolize the role
played by the armour or the embroidered tunic
of past centuries.

There are many people who can never pro-
nounce the word fashion without a tone of
disparagement. Regarded superficially, it has
indeed an air of frivolity and foolishness. But
in fact every alteration in the cut of a dress is
an unequivocal means of expressing the deep
human longing for change. In reality fashion
mirrors the entire philosophy of life of society.
Every single human being pays homage to it,
whether voluntarily and with enthusiasm or
passively and thoughtlessly; fashion keeps
them all in thrall. It forms part of the web of
everyday existence; it is the very colour of the
tapestry of life.

Four Thousand Years
in The History of Fashion

33 Isis receives Rameses III and his son.
Painting in a tomb of the XXth Dynasty,
Valley of the Queens, Thebes. Ceremonial
robes of the Pharaohs of the New Kingdom:
The Pharaoh (*centre*) wears a collar which is
wider at the corners, a tunic and the royal
loincloth.

Ancient Egypt 3000 B.C.–200 B.C.

The artists of ancient Egypt have left us a very detailed picture of their culture, but although they obviously took great care to be faithful to their subject in every respect, their paintings and reliefs lack a sense of perspective, and clothing is almost invariably shown from the front. The garments appear rigid and are depicted without the verve and flow which would make the figures come to life.

Although the Egyptians wore little clothing on their splendid bodies, they knew how to make perfect textiles. As raw materials they mostly used cotton and flax. At the time of the First Dynasty (2900–2706 B.C.) the only garment worn in the region of the lower Nile was a small loincloth of cotton, which was sometimes attached to a girdle – and this fashion continued among Egyptian peasants, soldiers and slaves until the time of Caesar. Even kings and members of the rulers' families, priests, judges, and high officials usually wore loincloths, but these were lavishly adorned and made of costly materials.

Another garment worn by the Egyptians was a sleeveless tunic which could be combined in various ways with the loincloth and its girdle. Later a robe of rich materials, which had evolved from an original fur wrap, became part of the clothing of noble Egyptians. Priests included a leopard skin amongst their robes. Kings and priests were generally depicted wearing sandals, the rest of Egypt's inhabitants went barefoot. The pioneer Egyptologist Adolf Erman pointed out that to no other convention of dress did the Egyptians remain faithful for such a long period of time. 'At a time when there was a whole hierarchy of garment and wig and when, moreover, there was earnest striving towards greater cleanliness, young and old, men and women, even when dressed in the most elegant clothes, still almost always went barefoot. In the Old and Middle Kingdoms, women do not seem to have worn sandals at all and the men of the aristocracy only wore them occasionally, out-of-doors perhaps, in cases of necessity, but usually gave them to their sandal-bearers to carry.'

Egyptian women did not consider it necessary to cover their breasts: slaves and the wives of the fellahin did so only exceptionally. The tunics and loincloths of the women were generally longer than those of the men. The tunic reached to the ankles and the loincloth to the knees. The tunic clung tightly to the body, had necklines of varying depths and straps which were arranged either above or below the breasts.

Soon after the establishment of the New Kingdom (1580–1074 B.C.) when Egypt was at the height of her powers, a light skirt or robe known as kalasiris was introduced for the members of both sexes of the higher ranks. The kalasiris appears either as a skirt, which covered the lower part of the body from the hips down and was supported on shoulder-straps, or as a robe, which came up to the neck. It was either sleeveless, or provided with short and tight or longer and rather loose sleeves. Presumably it could either be cut from pieces of cloth which were sewn together at the sides or woven into an elastic one-piece garment. In this form it would resemble a tube of even width, which perfectly adapted itself to the shape of the wearer. The kalasiris may be regarded as 'the true national costume of the female population of ancient Egypt'.

In the course of thousands of years of history, clothes underwent only minor changes. The inhabitants of Egypt adhered to tradition and evidently did not feel any great desire for innovations. This would explain not only the relative uniformity, but also the conservative character of Egyptian attire. Styles of hair and beards changed the most.

With the exception of garlands or coloured bands with trailing ends, which the women wore with festive clothing, head coverings were reserved for the rulers. The King of Upper Egypt wore a white crown and the King of Lower Egypt a red one. When in about 2800 B.C. the country was united under King Menes, the first recorded king, this fact was made manifest by the rulers wearing a double crown in the colours of both parts of Egypt.

The wig, which was known to the ancient Egyptians, was originally intended as protection from the sun. On festive occasions the Pharaohs would wear a false beard which was stuck on. The nobles in all periods, moreover, had a variety of sticks, all with particular names and each with a special meaning.

The Egyptians had their bodies massaged with aromatic oils and treated their hair with ointments. Ointments were one of the necessities of life; it is difficult today to appreciate the importance of their role. Hungry, unpaid workers lamented in the same breath the fact that they had nothing to eat and that they had no ointments! The women lengthened their eyes and brows with black and used green eye-shadow. They painted their fingernails with yellow-red henna. The tombstones of noble Egyptians tell of strange occupations: we read of guardians of ointment vessels and of keepers of cosmetics. Men as well as women wore jewellery, the women also artificial flowers. Particularly popular were necklaces and bracelets which were worn both below and above the elbow, as well as anklets. In the second millenium the production of jewellery in Egypt reached a very high standard: the kings' jewels are masterpieces of gold and precious stones.

Ornaments and jewellery were considered indispensable among many of the people of antiquity, and this is why they were put in the tombs with the dead. They have been found in thousands of Egyptian, Babylonian, Assyrian, Sumerian, Persian, Phoenician and Etruscan tombs, not to mention Greek and Roman burial sites. Ornaments and jewellery, therefore, are a valuable testimony of the lives of ancient peoples.

34 The Lady Hanoutou. Wooden figure, XIXth Dynasty, Egyptian Museum, Cairo. The elegant lady wears a large wig and is dressed in a kalasiris of fine cotton.

35 King Mycerinus between two goddesses. IVth Dynasty, Egyptian Museum, Cairo. The goddesses wear wigs, the typical headdress of the Old and Middle Kingdoms, and tight-fitting kalasiris. The King's head is covered with the mitre of Upper Egypt and he wears a loincloth.

36 Nefret, wife of Prince Rahotep. Detail of a double statue from Medum, IVth Dynasty, Egyptian Museum, Cairo. The queen's wig is characteristic of the Old Kingdom and she is dressed in an undergarment with shoulder-straps and a smooth tight-fitting kalasiris of a white material.

37 The daughters of Djehuty-hetep. Painted clay, XIIth Dynasty. Their hair style, adorned with lotus blossom, is typical of the Old Kingdom. They wear tunics with shoulder-straps which leave the breasts bare.

38 The Goddess Isis accompanies Queen Nerfertari into the next world. Painting in the tomb of Queen Nerfertari, XIXth Dynasty, Thebes. Nefertari (*left*) in a white kalasiris with gold collar, the symbols of royal power on her head; the Goddess (*right*) in a tight-fitting patterned garment, with a veil over her shoulders.

36

37

39 Queen Nefertari at prayer. Painting in Queen Nefertari's tomb, XIXth Dynasty, Thebes. On the queen's head is the symbol of royal power, the so-called Vulture Cap, and she is dressed in a white, pleated kalasiris.

40 Funeral procession. Painting in the tomb of Ramose, XVIIIth Dynasty, Thebes. The subjects are clad in short white loincloths, the typical wear for countries with a hot climate.

41 Semitic women. Painting from the tomb of Khnumhotep, XIIth Dynasty, Beni Hassan. Short kalasiris simply cut, of blue, green and red patterned and probably printed fabric.

42 Servants from the House of Sebekhotep. Painting in Sebekhotep's tomb, XVIIth Dynasty, Thebes. Short wigs, tunics with sleeves made of fine white cotton fabric, longer loincloths.

39

40

41

42

In 671 B.C. Esarhaddon, King of Assyria, and a member of the illustrious Dynasty of Akkad, founded by Sargon, invaded and conquered Egypt, which remained an Assyrian province until 663. The conquerors came from Mesopotamia, the land on the upper Tigris.

Assyrian and Babylonian costume had reached an advanced state of development – above all in its elaborateness and in its richness of materials; the cut of the clothing was comparatively simple. In western Asiatic countries cotton, which since time immemorial had partly been imported from India and partly been produced in the country, had long been skilfully woven into fabrics of great beauty and variety. From it the national costume of both the Assyrians and Babylonians was made. This had some resemblance to the kalasiris of ancient Egypt.

This tunic-like cotton garment with sleeves ending above the elbow, reached to mid-calf. Its length, however, varied according to its purpose and with the different epochs. Soldiers and peasants wore a shorter tunic, which ended above the knee and was of simpler cut. Members of the ruling class had kalasiris which reached to the ankles.

In addition there was a rectangular piece of coloured cotton cloth, which was sometimes very long and was wound round the body in a spiral, at other times it was used as a kind of sash. Originally it may have been made of fur and later of some costly woollen material. The fringed sash or shawl, which was worn over the shoulder, with the ends slung round the waist, was probably a distinguishing mark of all higher state and court officials. The costliness of the attire indicated the rank of the wearer. The court of the Assyrian rulers was dominated by ceremony and protocol, and the lavishness of their costume expressed their need for outward show.

In Mesopotamia great attention was paid to hair-style and beard. The ruler above all had his hair dressed in very complicated styles. Only the lower ranks, soldiers and workers, wore their beard in its natural state and shorter. The higher ranks allowed their beard to grow to its full length. On the upper lip and cheeks it was carefully curled and under the chin it was regularly trimmed and along its entire length it was alternately braided and waved. The amount of trouble involved in this operation would lead one to suppose that artificial braids and wigs were not unknown. Cosmetics at any rate in early times had already reached a state of near-perfection.

Headcoverings were almost non-existent. The few to be found were precursors of the turban or fez.

43 Phoenician expressing greetings. Relief from the northern entrance of the North West Palace, 9th century B.C., Nimrud, British Museum. The noble Phoenician wears a conical tiara and rich jewellery: ear-rings, necklace and bracelets on both arms.

44 Relief from the Black Obelisk of King Shalmaneser, 9th century B.C., Nimrud, British Museum. The men wear long cloaks with fringed hems and their heads are covered with soft caps of conical shape, with the points turned down.

45 King Assurnasirpal. Relief in the throne room of the North West Palace, 9th century B.C., Nimrud, British Museum. Ceremonial court dress consists of the royal tiara with infulae, i.e. ribbons falling to the shoulders, a long tunic covered with a fringed mantle, and sandals, the soles of which are held to the feet by means of two straps.

46 Two Phoenicians. Relief from the northern entrance of the North West Palace, 9th century B.C., Nimrud, British Museum. Both men have broadly cut beards. One wears a conical cap, the other has curly hair, held together with a ribbon. Both wear long cloaks with broad fringed hems, ear-rings, necklaces and bracelets.

47 A winged god anointing King Assurnasirpal's cup-bearer. Relief in the throne room of the North West Palace, 9th century B.C., Nimrud, British Museum.

45

46

48 Priestess, the so-called Snake Goddess. Faïence figure from Knossos, 17th century B.C., Historical Museum of Crete, Heraklion. The goddess wears a turban with the symbol of the lion, a short bodice which leaves the breasts bare with 'wasp waist', flounced skirt and short decorative apron – the typical dress of Minoan culture.

Crete and Mycenae

The fate of the Greeks hung by a thread, the thread of Adriadne. Adriadne was the daughter of the all-powerful King Minos of Crete. It was with her help, and that of her thread that Theseus, son of the King of Athens, managed to free his home town from having to pay the tribute of seven youths and seven maidens, which each year had to be sent to King Minos' terrible bull, the Minotaur, in the Labyrinth. So tells the legend.

Owing to its advantageous position between Egypt, Asia Minor and the continent of Europe, Crete was in the 2nd century B.C. a powerful state which today is regarded as the cradle of occidental civilization. Its culture spread to Mycenae, the mythological seat of King Agamemnon in the north-eastern Peloponnese, which in turn created its own culture and eventually proved itself to be the stronger. However close the ties that bind Greece and Crete, Minoan costume was completely different from Hellenic. Both noble and commonmen dressed quite simply. A leather girdle supported the not very long loincloth, which sometimes had the form of short trousers. On some Cretan paintings broad, sack-like trousers may be seen, which reached to the knees.

The most richly adorned part of Minoan dress was the belt. In colder weather the Cretans wore a kind of cape sometimes made of leather. A similar cape, but coloured and decorative, was worn on festive occasions. Warriors were protected by leather armour.

The hair of the Cretans hung down to their shoulders and was combed smooth. Their heads were often covered by strange caps or small flat turbans. On their feet they wore light sandals, which were laced round the ankle; in winter boots were worn, which partly covered the calves.

Crete had a culture which loved splendour. It was an epoch of the highest development, with an amazingly refined feeling for form. Scholars believe that they have discovered in the surviving remains indications that the Cretans no longer enjoyed natural pleasures, but only artificial delights. The men with their slim waists that we see in pictures of the bull games, often appear decadent rather than manly.

It is clear that at that time society was dominated by the female. The snake priestess in her modish costume, with breasts uncovered, who is known to us through a small porcelain figure, has become the symbol of the entire Minoan civilization. 'La Parisienne' is the name which scholars gave to the heavily made-up girl in a fresco at Knossos; she seems as modern as a town girl of today. For this reason women's costume of this period is of greater interest to us than men's (which is simple by comparison).

The skirt always fitted closely over the hips and was bell-shaped, becoming broader at the hem. It appears to have been stiffened. Usually it was smooth and almost always came to the ankles, but embroidered and horizontally striped skirts were not unknown, even flounces were already to be found among the Cretans. But at no time does the Cretan skirt, which by our standards has a rather erotic effect, deviate from the basic bell-shape: it is broad at the hem and narrows strongly towards the hips.

Originally womens' clothes had no top – the breasts were simply left bare. Later a bodice was worn, which was laced tightly at waist and hips. It had short sleeves and sometimes a stand-away collar. The tight lacing lifted and usually stressed the barely concealed bust. During gymnastics young women wore only loin girdles and coloured ribbons with which they adorned their arms. On journeys or in bad weather Cretan women wore warm cloaks. Sometimes they covered their heads with small turbans and sometimes with broader hats. They generally wore only sandals, but on certain occasions boots.

Cretan women loved jewels and ornaments. They not only liked to wear rings, necklaces and ear-rings but also diadems, slides, golden pendants and pins with which they adorned hair and clothes. The Cretans were masters at fashioning precious metals, and they decorated gold and precious stones with beautiful engravings. The stones most used were steatite, agate, porphyry, amethyst and jasper.

50 Woman with ivory vessel. Reconstruction of a painting from Tiryns, circa 1400 B.C., National Museum, Athens. Some of her hair is left loose and the rest is tied in a kind of chignon. A short-sleeved bodice, which leaves the breasts exposed, forms a 'wasp waist'. The gored skirt is of a patterned material.

51 Dance scene. Gold ring from Mycenae, 17th to 14th century B.C. The dancers' breasts are bare and their long skirts are decorated with irregular flounces.

52 Bracelet from Mycenae. 16th century B.C. The bracelet, the typical ornament of the women of Crete, is decorated in the centre with a realistic-looking flower.

53 Prince with plumed crown. Stucco relief from Knossos (restored). Probably 16th century B.C. Historical Museum of Crete, Heraklion. Festive hair-style with hair left loose and turban with long feathers. The loincloth emphasizes the slim waist.

50

49 Praying woman (said to be from Troy) State Museum, Department of Antiquities, Berlin. The woman's hair-style consists of a complicated arrangement of braids. She wears a short bodice, which forms a 'wasp waist' and a skirt with flounces at the hem.

51

52

53

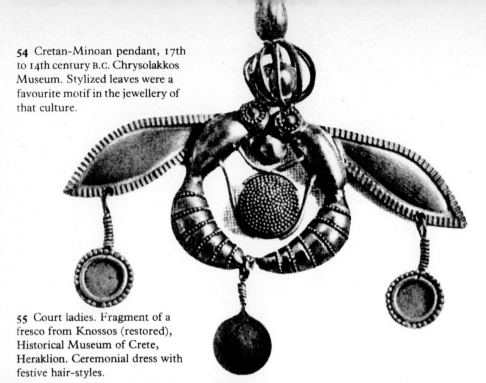

54 Cretan-Minoan pendant, 17th to 14th century B.C. Chrysolakkos Museum. Stylized leaves were a favourite motif in the jewellery of that culture.

55 Court ladies. Fragment of a fresco from Knossos (restored), Historical Museum of Crete, Heraklion. Ceremonial dress with festive hair-styles.

56 Dancer known as 'La Parisienne'. Fresco
fragment from Knossos, 1500–1450 B.C.,
Historical Museum of Crete, Heraklion. A
young Cretan woman with festive hair-style,
consisting of loose, flowing hair, and wearing
a bodice with very low neckline.

57 Euthydicos Kore, shortly before 480 B.C.
Acropolis Museum, Athens.

Greece in Antiquity

The clothes of the ancient Greeks indirectly promoted not only care of the body, correct posture and a healthy way of living; they positively induced thoughts on beauty and harmony. The effect produced by Greek dress was aesthetic rather than erotic. Nudity was regarded as completely natural.

There was no marked difference between the clothes worn by the sexes. Men and women could share the same garment if they wished to economize.

What mattered most was the manner in which each person wore his clothes. In this respect the Greeks might be said to have employed the means of the sculptor: it is remarkable what works of art they were able to conjure up from the two rectangular pieces of cloth which formed the basis of their dress. The graceful folds achieved by skilful draping were its chief ornament and provided the possibility of making fashion changes.

The oldest costume of the Greeks in pre-Homeric times, and especially of the Dorians, was the rectangular woollen cloth, which was draped round the body without being girded and fastened at the shoulder with pins. The garment was basically the same for both sexes and was called chlaina for men and peplos for women. Since the peplos was left open down one side, its wearers were graphically described as 'women who show their hips'. Over it they wore a short cloak also made from a rectangular piece of material.

This Doric dress constituted a new and unique principle in clothing: it did not need cutting out and had no seams. Comparatively early, however, the chiton, from the Semitic word keton, meaning cotton, was introduced by the Ionians from their Semitic neighbours in the East. It was similar in shape to a tunic, cut out and sewn, and after a short period of development it was also draped; girding it at the waist created the effect of a blouse, the so-called kolpos. This overfold on occasions served as a pocket.

During the hot months the Greeks wore no other garment; poorer people did not, in fact, own anything but the chiton (underwear was as yet unknown). In the cold season the wealthier people wore instead of the short cloak the larger rectangular himation, which again was not markedly different for men and women. A woman could wear the himation over her head, giving it the effect of a hooded cloak. It was considered good manners for a woman to hide her hands inside the himation. Tradition has it that the notorious Xanthippe refused to wear her husband Socrates' himation at a procession, whereupon the philosopher remarked disapprovingly 'You do not go out to see but to be seen.'

The chlamys, worn by youths and soldiers, was a knee-length and lighter version of the himation, also made of wool. It is said that spinning and weaving were the constant activities of unmarried Greek women. Sandals were the only footwear for men as for women, but even when Athens was at the height of her prosperity naked feet were not a sign of poverty. In their homes Greeks always went barefoot.

On journeys the men wore a flat hat with brim and chin-strap, called petasus, or a small spherical leather cap, or again sometimes a conical felt hat called pilos, or the conical Phrygian bonnet with its tip hanging forward. For a long time women wore no head-coverings, because custom forbade them to move freely in public places. They lavished all the greater care on their hair-styles. Their hair, elaborately curled and carefully pinned up, was for them indeed one of the most important objects of fashion.

The favourable warm climate above all necessitated protection from the sun. For this purpose the straw hat was found most suitable. It was generally flat and rather broad and decorated at most with a cone in the centre.

On the use of colours in Greek clothing more information may be gained from literature than from the pictorial arts. Only a small proportion of coloured relics have been preserved, too small in quantity to provide a real clue.

According to ancient sources Greek dwellings, temples and statues were coloured and it is probable that the natural colours of wool and flax were not the only ones to be found in clothes. The Ionian Greeks in particular probably wore coloured clothes under the influence of their eastern neighbours.

The entire setting of Greece, the sun and the sky above a blue Mediterranean, the landscape and the inhabitants with their sunburnt complexions, their expressive eyes and lips and their luxuriant growth of hair, cry out for colours rich and strong to do them justice.

Homer described the coloured chlaina of the men, decorated with motifs of flowers, figures and even stars, which were woven into the material. Democritus from Ephesus in the 6th century B.C., too, admired the colourful clothing to be seen in the Ionian towns. Favourite colours were white, yellow, purple and lilac. Certain colours had a particular meaning. Thus saffron yellow was regarded as solemn; fiery red distinguished the Commanders of Sparta; garishly coloured stripes were the signs of the hetaerae. The most popular patterns were stripes, lozenges and circles.

Greek women loved jewellery and trinkets and would adorn themselves with bracelets, necklaces, ear-rings, rings on their fingers and on their toes, as well as diadems and ornamental pins and clasps of every kind.

Particularly in later centuries the Greeks lived lives of such luxury that they even came to reproach each other for their excesses. But even in earlier times Demosthenes was reproached for the costliness and ostentatiousness of his clothes.

58 Caryatid from the Erechtheum, Acropolis, Athens, 420 B.C. The female figure wears the typical Greek peplos, sleeveless, richly draped and gathered at the waist by means of a belt and reaching to the ground.

59 Rider and horse from the procession of the Panathenaea. Detail from the west frieze of the Parthenon on the Acropolis, Athens. The youth is wearing a knee-length chiton and over it a chlamys, which is fastened at the neck and falls in folds down his back; its end is slung over his arm.

50. ATHÉNA « MÉLANCOLIQUE ».
MUSÉE DE L'ACROPOLE

60

61

60 The mourning Athena. Dedicatory relief, 460 B.C., Acropolis Museum, Athens. In token of her rank the goddess wears a helmet. She is dressed in a girded peplos which falls in regular folds to her ankles.

61 Athena. Detail of a metope from the temple of Zeus at Olympia. 460 B.C.

62 Nike, goddess of Victory, donning her sandal. Fragment from a balustrade in the temple of Nike on the Acropolis, Athens. Late 5th century B.C.

63 Demeter. Roman copy after a Greek original, middle of 5th century, Vatican Museum, Italy. The goddess wears a girded peplos, which is fastened at the shoulders with clasps and hangs down to the ground in heavy folds.

64

64 Peleus fighting Thetis. Peithinos-bowl, 5th century B.C., State Museum, Department of Antiquities, Berlin. The garments are somewhat stylized, falling into almost too regular and rich ornamental folds. Peleus is wearing a short chiton, Thetis a full himation.

65 Woman pouring wine for old man. Bowl, 5th century B.C., Corneto Museum. Both figures are dressed in richly draped chitons. In addition the old man wears a himation and the woman a chlamys.

65

66 Standing Muse. Relief from the Muse pedestal at Mantinea. Late 4th century B.C., National Museum, Athens. Over the long chiton a wide, draped himation has been thrown.

67 Woman with fan. Terracotta statuette from Tanagra. Late 4th century B.C., State Museums, Berlin. The woman is dressed in a long chiton and wrapped in a softly draped himation. On her head is a hat, the so-called pilos. In her hand is a heart-shaped fan.

68 Apollo from the West pediment of the temple of Zeus at Olympia, 460 B.C. The god is depicted with the typical hair-style of the period, in which the hair is held together with a narrow ribbon and arranged in regular curls.

69 Orpheus among the Thracians. Attic crater from Gela, 5th century B.C., State Museum, Department of Antiquities, Berlin. The armed Thracians wear helmets and chlamys. Orpheus's hair is long and adorned with a wreath. He is draped in a himation.

68

69

70 Large helmet of tinned bronze. 7th century B.C., Villa Giulia, Rome. Such helmets, high and pointed in shape, were characteristic of the Etruscan warriors of that epoch.

The Etruscans

To this day no one knows exactly where the Etruscans came from. Research has made little progress and our knowledge of them today is hardly greater than in ancient times when it was thought either that the Etruscans were an ancient indigenous people or, more probably, that they were immigrants from Asia Minor. The enigma which obscures their origins as well as their script and language will probably never be completely solved. Nevertheless the tomb paintings – above all in the necropolises of the larger towns – give us a vivid impression of their lives. In the 6th century the domain of this mighty confederation of cities extended from the valley of the Po to beyond Rome. Here the Etruscans were in direct contact with the settlers of the Greek colonies in southern Italy, whose art and culture exerted a lasting influence on them.

Arts and crafts played an important role in the Etruscan towns which were situated chiefly in the Tuscany of today. The Etruscans were also famous seafarers. Members of the aristocracy employed their time in tournaments, sport and hunting. The influence of the Etruscans on the peoples of Italy was considerable. Their clothing, known to us from frescoes and painted vases, played an important part as a link between Greek costume on the one hand and the formation of Roman dress styles, of which it was the immediate predecessor, on the other.

The men wore knee length chitons, similar to those worn in Greece, with or without sleeves; workmen wore the exomis which gave greater freedom of movement. Older men lengthened their chitons and the wealthier added ornamental hems as decoration. Over the chiton a cloak was worn, similar to the himation and called a tebenna.

This tebenna was a kind of wrap in the shape of a rectangle or a semi-circle; the Etruscans usually wore the latter type. It was put on by laying one end forward over the left shoulder; the bulk of the material was pulled across the back and the other end passed underneath the right arm and slung backwards across the left shoulder. A tebenna made of high-quality materials and lavishly decorated formed part of the ceremonial dress of the Etruscans. In addition, men would wear shorter cloaks after the manner of the Greek chlamys. They wore head coverings in the style of Phrygian bonnets or the Greek petasus.

Archaeological discoveries show the Etruscans to have been a life-loving, cheerful people. They regarded life after death as a continuation of life on earth and believed the dead to be just as ready for battle and full of zest as the living. Comfort and luxury were taken for granted by the Etruscans – at least by the upper classes. In contrast to other nations of the period, women took part in social affairs on an equal footing with men. At festivals Etruscan women may be seen attending dances and banquets and as spectators at athletic contests.

The women wore longer tunics, similar to the Greek chiton, and often decorated with ornamental hems; over this they wore tebennae, which on festive occasions were embroidered and also provided with decorated hems. The hair was braided in plaits or in complicated knots, which were gathered into a fillet or held in place by a band.

The décolletée was adorned with golden necklaces and the tunic held together with clasps – the fibulae (see Ill. 78). Golden bracelets and rings were obligatory ornaments. There was a certain air of the oriental about Etruscan costume.

It is not surprising that Etruscan women had a highly developed taste in jewellery. At the transition from the 7th to the 6th century, this people was one of the mightiest in the Mediterranean, both on sea and land, with trade connections in far distant countries. Excavations show that Etruscan craftsmanship had reached a very high level, especially in metal work, ceramics and ivory carvings. The techniques of hammering, embossing, casting and engraving appear to have been well known. Connoisseurs are agreed that Etruscan goldsmiths, in particular, achieved works of such beauty and perfection as have never again been equalled. Etruscan tools and vessels of bronze were in great demand all over the world.

71 Statue of a goddess. Early 6th century, Etruscan Museum, Chiusi. Typical hair-style of the Etruscan women, who wore their hair in plaits.

72 Minerva Parigi. Musée du Louvre, Paris. The goddess is pictured in soldier's clothes: on her head is a helmet and she is dressed in a tunic which is shorter than a woman's. Her raised hand probably held a spear.

73 Female figure from Perugia. Early 5th century B.C., State Museum, Department of Antiquities, Berlin. The woman's tight-fitting tunic reaches to the ankles. She also wears a short cloak and on her head is a conical cap. Her hair is plaited. Her garments are decorated with ornamental hems. Her feet are completely encased in characteristic pointed boots.

74 Worshipper in front of the statue of a goddess. Clay tablet, Musée du Louvre, Paris. The male figure is dressed in a short chiton with ornamental hem and a short cloak. Interesting are the high boots with upturned elongated points.

75 Orestes avenging his father. Relief, Carlsberg Glyptotek, Copenhagen. The women wear lightly gathered chitons and cloaks, the so-called tebennae. The garments show Assyrian influence, as does Orestes' beard and the women's head coverings.

76 Youth with drinking cup. Detail of Musicians' Group. Fresco from the tomb of the Leopards, 470 B.C., . National Museum, Tarquinia. The hem of the short cloak is in a contrasting colour. The hair is kept tidy with a fillet.

77 Bracelet from Vetulonia. 7th–6th century B.C., Museo Archeologico, Florence. The Etruscans became extraordinarily skilled in the production of their jewellery.

74

75

76

77

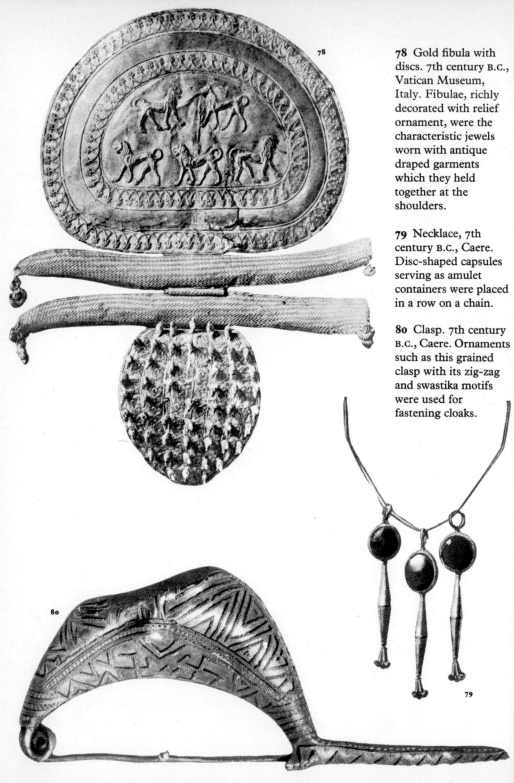

78 Gold fibula with discs. 7th century B.C., Vatican Museum, Italy. Fibulae, richly decorated with relief ornament, were the characteristic jewels worn with antique draped garments which they held together at the shoulders.

79 Necklace, 7th century B.C., Caere. Disc-shaped capsules serving as amulet containers were placed in a row on a chain.

80 Clasp. 7th century B.C., Caere. Ornaments such as this grained clasp with its zig-zag and swastika motifs were used for fastening cloaks.

81 Flute player. From the Musicians Group in the Tomb of thẹ Leopards, 470 B.C., National Museum, Tarquinia. A fillet keeps the hair in place. The cloak, ornamented with stripes, is reminiscent of the Greek chlamys; the sandals too, which consist of thin straps, resemble Greek sandals.

82 'Prima Porta' Augustus. Circa 20 B.C., Vatican Museum, Italy. The Emperor is represented as a general. His armour, the so-called lorica is richly decorated with relief ornament. The breastplate is fixed to the back with shoulder buckles. Underneath it he is wearing a leather doublet with short pleated shoulder bands and a tunic.

The principal features of Greek dress were taken over by Rome. Clothing underwent a gradual change from modest and simple styles in the early days of the Republic to ostentatious and luxurious splendour towards the end of the Empire. It was fashionable in Imperial Rome to wear layers of different types of garments and to change clothes frequently. Martial tells of a young dandy who changed his clothes seven times during a banquet in order to wear a different garment for each course.

The national costume of ancient Rome was the toga, which corresponded to the Greek himation. By the end of the 3rd century B.C. the development of the toga was more or less complete. At about this time men, and especially women, began to dress with such unrestrained pomp, that already in 215 B.C. the Senate was obliged to take measures, by means of the law of the Tribune Oppius, to curtail the luxuries of the women belonging to the most exalted Roman circles.

Underneath the toga a kind of loincloth was worn, which later became the sole garment worn by slaves doing heavy work, during gymnastics and when bathing in public. The toga was certainly very impressive and lent its wearer a solemn and dignified appearance. It also made him adopt an attitude of repose or move in a slow and relaxed manner; it stood in sharp contrast to the simple clothes of the plebeian.

All draped garments which were not sewn together at the seams provided the possibility of expressing individuality and personal taste, since the wearer, each time he dressed, could drape the material in a slightly different manner. This enabled him to create a somewhat different garment for himself on each occasion. Also the folds of the toga adapted themselves far better to the posture, the movements, in short, the temperament of the wearer, than does the European dress of today. Fashion changes could therefore be brought about easily and quickly and with a minimum of effort and expense.

The writer on costume, Carl Köhler, explained: 'In order to don a toga one had to fold it approximately in half lengthwise, forming it into thick folds, and casting it over the left shoulder, so that about one-third of the total length hung down in front. The remainder was then pulled across the back and passed under the right arm and then thrown back, again across the left shoulder. In consequence of its width the left arm was almost completely covered. Finally the part lying across the back was spread out till it covered the right shoulder, and the end hanging over the left shoulder was made shorter by pulling up the toga over the chest and allowing the overfold thus produced to hang forward.'

The Roman tunic corresponded to the Greek chiton, which was worn by both men and women. During the later period of the Empire, as many as three tunics were sometimes worn; the one nearest to the body generally was made of fine linen and used as underwear. The one uppermost became the immediate predecessor of the stola.

The stola was a richly ornamented garment, which sometimes ended in a bow and sometimes had sleeves. Usually it was worn girded, although this was not an irrefutable rule. It was worn above all by aristocratic matrons. The palla, considerably smaller and lighter than the toga, was often made of fine wool and mostly coloured, though not brightly. Soldiers wore a garment which was also frequently worn by the poor, the lacerna. This corresponded to the Greek chlamys; in rainy weather it was worn over the toga. From Gaul the legionaries brought back a hooded cloak, named sagum, which they rechristened cucullus. The soldiers of the Roman Legions did not protect their legs with trousers, but bandaged them like puttees, or else they wore stockings.

The hair styles of the Romans were always simpler than those of the Greeks, who often let their hair grow long and waved it artificially. Till the 3rd century B.C. a beard of medium length was customary; later the men were

clean-shaven. In the year 120 A.D. the Emperor Hadrian personally reintroduced the beard. It is significant that many men began to cut their beard as soon as it began to grow grey. The beard, therefore, was a sign of youth.

During the intervening four centuries the beard was regarded as an attribute to learned men and philosophers. Barbers' shops in Rome and elsewhere in the Empire were largely kept by Greeks. Talkativeness was characteristic of hairdressers then as now.

In the time of the Republic the hair of the Roman women was dressed comparatively simply. During the period of the Empire hair styles became more and more complicated, and the wives of rich patricians had no difficulty in employing several slaves merely to dress their hair. There was a grain of truth in Ovid's complaint that he was unable to enumerate the different hair styles on account of their infinite number.

When Roman women wished to dress their hair in accordance with the latest fashion, they employed implements similar to those used by the women of our day: combs, brushes, curling tongs, nets, hairpins, slides, mirrors, pomades, bleaches and dyes. Red hair, especially, was the vogue in Rome, and during the wars against the Teutons, golden-haired women were very popular. Roman women employed goat tallow and beech ash in order to achieve the red or blonde shades. The women of Rome also wore wigs made from the hair of captives and German slaves. In Rome the use of powder and rouge as beauty aids was fairly general and spread further with the growing love of luxury. There were many kinds of rouge for cheeks and lips and also black for brows and lashes. White make-up was intended to bring out the beauty of the complexion and a very faint blue was used to emphasize the veins.

Even in Republican Rome luxury had already reached such proportions that Cicero was forced to remonstrate with the aristocratic Roman women on the conspicuousness of their dress, and to reproach Catiline for shaving his legs and for wearing transparent garments. Many Roman writers and historians rightly remark on the excesses in dress practised by the women during the period of

84

83 Marcus Aurelius reprieving captured Teutons. Relief from the Arch of Constantine, 176 A.D., Palazzo Conservatori, Rome. The soldiers in the group are dressed in short tunics, lorica and lacerna, fastened at the shoulders. The prisoners (*bottom right*) are wearing girded tunics and cloaks.

84 Bust of Caracalla. Museo e Gallerie Nazionale di Capodimonte, Naples. Hair and beard are trimmed short in the typical Roman fashion. The cloak is asymmetrically fastened at the shoulder with a fibula of metal.

77

85 Peitho with Eros. Wall painting from the House of the Punishment of Cupid, Pompeii, circa 25 A.D., Museo e Gallerie Nazionale di Capodimonte, Naples. The goddess, with earrings and bracelet, is wearing an ankle length stola which is fastened at the shoulder with fibulae. Over this she wears a palla. Her hair is covered with a kerchief.

86 Scylla. Painting found at the Torre Marancio. Biblioteca Apostolica, Vaticana. The simple full-length stola and the palla, thrown over the left shoulder, are reminiscent of the goddess's clothing in Ill. 85.

87 Medea from Herculaneum. Circa 75 A.D. Museo e Gallerie Nazionale di Capodimonte, Naples. Medea is dressed in a stola, but her palla is slung round her hips.

SCYLLA

the Empire. At that time ladies of the higher strata of society competed with one another as to who wore the most fashionable clothes and this obliterated social differences in dress. The most prolific source for our knowledge of the colours, magnificence and luxury of Roman dress and jewellery are the finds made during excavations at Herculaneum and Pompeii. A large portion of the wonderful murals which came to light in the villas of the rich citizens may now be found in the Museum at Naples. But a number still bear witness on the spot to the splendour that reigned even in a Roman Province.

88 Toga statue of Augustus offering sacrifice, from the Via Labicana. Circa 10 A.D., Museo e Gallerie Nazionale di Capodimonte, Naples. The richly draped toga, worn by the Emperor, is the typical garment of the free Roman. The draping of the toga followed strict rules.

89 Statue, known as Livia, from Pompeii. Museo e Gallerie Nazionale di Capodimonte, Naples. The young Roman woman is dressed in a stola and wrapped in a palla, which also covers her head. Her hair is elaborately arranged in curls according to current fashion.

90 Painting of a mummy of a
young man. Middle of 2nd
century. Pushkin Museum,
Moscow. The youth's short hair is
covered with a laurel wreath
which, from ancient times, has
been a symbol of glory and victory.

91 *L'Arringatore.* Bronze statue
of an orator, circa 100 B.C.,
Museo Archeologico,
Florence. The orator is dressed in
tunic and toga. The sandals,
which have broad straps and are
laced high over the ankles, were
called calcei (sing. calceus).

90

91

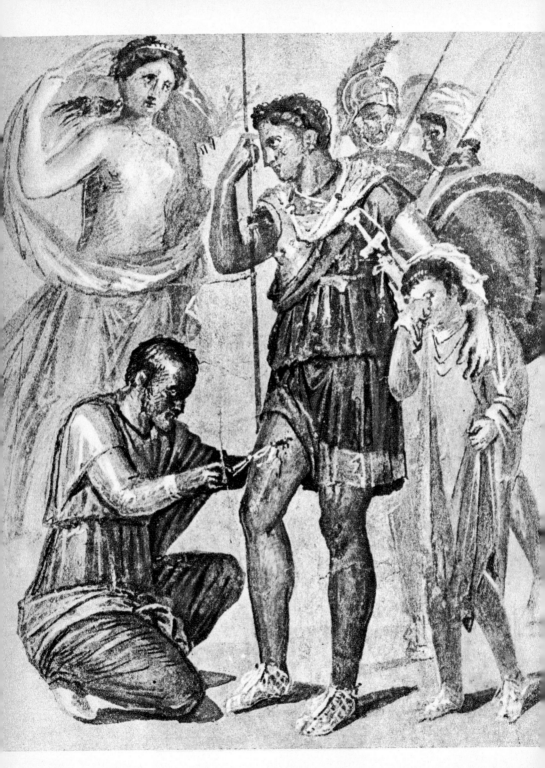

92 The wounded Aeneas. Wall
painting from Taso di Sirico in
Pompeii, National Museum, Naples.
Aeneas is dressed in a short tunic and
has thrown a cloak, the chlamys, over
his shoulders. On his feet are sandals.
The warriors standing behind him are
wearing the characteristic Roman
soldiers' helmets; the man tending
him is dressed in a tunic with sleeves.

93 The Sacrifice of Iphigenia. Wall
painting from Pompeii, circa 65 A.D.,
Museo e Gallerie Nazionale di
Capodimonte, Naples. Agamemnon
(left) has pulled his toga over his
head; on his feet are high sandals,
the calcei. The men who are
carrying Iphigenia are wearing short
cloaks, the chlamys. The priest
(right) is dressed in tunic and cloak.

94 Bracelet. Rome, 1st century A.D.
The snake was the symbol of fertility
and of a fruitful harvest. It was widely
used as a motif in jewellery, especially
rings.

95 Christ, the Good
Shepherd. 4th century,
Lateran Museum.
Christ is depicted in a
short girded tunic, with
sandals and 'puttees',
which are bound up to
the knee.

96 Tomb relief from
Palmyra. 2nd–3rd century
A.D., National Museum,
Damascus. The
tombstone depicts a noble
Roman couple. Both are
dressed in the wide cloak,
the palla, and the toga.
The woman is lavishly
adorned with jewels:
diadem, earrings,
necklaces, a fibula to
fasten her cloak,
bracelets on her wrists,
and rings.

ΙC̄ ΧC̄

ΡΩΜΑΝΟC
ΒΑCΙΛΕΥC
ΡΩΜΑΙΩΝ

ΕΥΔΟΚΙΑ
ΒΑCΙΛΙC
ΡΩΜΑΙΩΝ

97 Christ crowning the Emperor Romanos and his wife Eudoxia. Ivory relief from the cover of an Evangelistary from Bescançon, 10th or 11th century, National Library, Paris.

The Eastern Empire, with Byzantium (Constantinople) as its focal point and capital, came into being as a result of the re-orientation of the Roman Empire. Constantine the Great (306-337) was the creator of this 'Christian Roman Empire' which was Greek in language and culture. Byzantium reached the zenith of its greatness in the 9th and 10th centuries, but lasted until the 13th.

During this millenium Byzantium had taken over the mantle of Rome and carried on many of its ideals and ideas. Banking was highly developed and trade between East and West increased steadily. From the middle of the 6th century there existed in the East Roman Empire, and especially in Greece and Syria a silk industry which was independent of the imports from India and China.

The manufacture of silken fabrics and purple dye was a state monopoly in the Empire. Expensive silks could only be worn by high state officials and the costliest fabrics were reserved for members of the Imperial family. As the Empire gained in importance, so the pomp of official ceremonial increased. Apart from the Emperor and his retinue, paintings and sculptures depicted almost exclusively high state officials and princes of the church, whose dress was extraordinarily stiff and magnificent.

With rising power, greater wealth and an increasingly refined feeling for form, Byzantium began to influence European fashion. In the 10th century, when the German Crown went to the House of Saxony, Germany was, next to Russia, the most important buyer of Byzantine products. Otto II and the Grand Duke Vladimir married the daughters of Byzantine Emperors. In addition to jewellery, silken fabrics found their way into Germany via Venice and Amalfi. In this way fashionable costume in central Europe gradually acquired unmistakable oriental and Byzantine traits.

It is not surprising, in view of its origins, that the clothes worn in the Byzantine Empire had, to begin with, many features of Roman costume. Soon, however, Persian and Arabic influences made themselves felt, especially with regard to material and colour. The cut continued to develop broadly on lines based on classical Roman dress. Both sexes wore Roman tunic-like garments with sleeves and cloaks which corresponded either to the Roman sagum or to the lacerna. The Byzantine cloaks were somewhat longer than the Roman and the people had them made from costly materials. In this way a person's rank or office was more easily recognized than in the former Western Empire.

From the beginning of the 11th century court officials and other high ranking officers of the state began to wear a rather tight blouse without any kind of trimming, which could be fastened and was totally different in character from Roman dress. Byzantine costume gradually grew longer, sleeves became an indispensable part and lengthened to the wrist. The costume was made of heavy, richly decorated materials, shot through with gold. A large area of the dress was covered with pearls and precious stones; its edges were decorated with golden borders; all this further increased the impression of stiff formality. The gold embroidery and precious stones were intended to reflect the light in the same way as wall mosaics.

From the beginning of the 12th century women enveloped their bodies as completely as did the men, and their clothes were no less rich and stiff. Byzantine dress stood in sharp contrast to the airy clothes of Greece and Rome. Its most marked characteristic was the total concealment of the human body; the human shape was completely obscured, the clothes were stiff and fitted nowhere closely to the body; they were opaque and almost enveloped the entire body.

The pomp and splendour of Byzantine dress found its ultimate expression in the clothes worn by the Emperor. Over a gold embroidered stola of white silk he wore a purple cloak, which was fastened at the shoulder by a jewelled clasp. This cloak was richly decorated with gold embroidery. Pearl-encrusted

silk shoes and a pearl diadem and the golden sceptre completed the Imperial robes, which were by no means reserved for special occasions.

98 The Empress Theodora and her entourage. Mosaic from the Choir of San Vitale at Ravenna. First half of 6th century. The garments are of patterned silk with woven or embroidered coloured borders; the Empress' robe has figured motifs at the hem. She wears a superhumeral with a broad collar, the members of her entourage are dressed in long tunics with cloak and tablion, fastened with fibulae in the manner of the Greek chlamys; one wears a paenula (*right*).

99 Bishop Maximian of Ravenna and two Deacons with Gospel and censer. Mosaic from the Choir of San Vitale, Ravenna. First half of 6th century. The bishop (*left*) in pallium and stola, the two deacons (*right*) in tunica laticlavia (with two vertical stripes). All are wearing sandals with toe and heel enclosed.

100 The SS Peter and Cosmas. From the apse mosaic of SS Cosma e Damiano, circa 530, Rome. St Peter is dressed in a tunica laticlavia with a pallium thrown over his shoulder. St Cosmas wears a paenula over his tunic. St Peter's sandals have narrow straps. St Cosmas' shoes entirely enclose the foot.

98
99

Va Pieter Brueghel the Elder. Hay-making (detail). Národni Galerie, Prague.

Vb Hans Wertinger, called Schwab. King Alexander and his surgeon, Philip. Národni Galerie, Prague.

VI Bohemian Master. Jan Bezdružický of Kolovrat. Second half of 16th century. Castle Gallery, Rychnov n. Kn. (Bohemia).

VII Jan Provost. Coronation of the Virgin (detail). Hermitage, Leningrad.

VIIIa Bohemia painter. Alžběta of Rožmitál, wife of Jan Bezdružický of Kolovrat. Circa 1580. Nelahozeves Castle, (Bohemia).

VIIIb Juan Pantoja de la Cruz. Anna, Queen of Spain, daughter of King Maximilian II. Nelahozeves Castle, (Bohemia).

101 Court ladies of the Empress Theodora. Choir mosaic of San Vitale, Ravenna. First half of 6th century. The women are wearing garments of patterned silk, the figure on the left has the typical round Byzantine collar with pearls.

102 Reliefs from the Throne of Maximian. Middle of 6th century, Archbishop's Palace, Ravenna. The four saints are dressed in various types of cloak, reminiscent of Roman cloaks in style and in the way they are draped.

103 Madonna with saints. Ivory relief, 5th century, Coptic Museum. The Madonna is dressed in the contemporary costume of ladies of rank – a long tunic and a cloak; the saint on the left wears a dalmatica and the one on the right a paenula.

101

102

104 The Consul Stilicho. Left
panel of a diptych, circa 400,
Monza Cathedral. The man with
spear and shield wears a short
tunic and a sagum, which is
fastened at the shoulder with a
fibula.

105 Madonna. Ivory relief,
Musée du Louvre, Paris. The
Madonna is wearing a tunic
which falls in rich folds.
The cloak is pulled over her
head and forms a kind of veil.

106 Statue of Emperor Honorius at Barletta. Middle of 5th century. This is late Roman soldier's dress: short tunic, leather doublet with pleated shoulder pieces and ornamental borders, a simple lorica and the sagum, the end of which is laid over the left arm and hangs down to the knees. The knee-high boots are of leather.

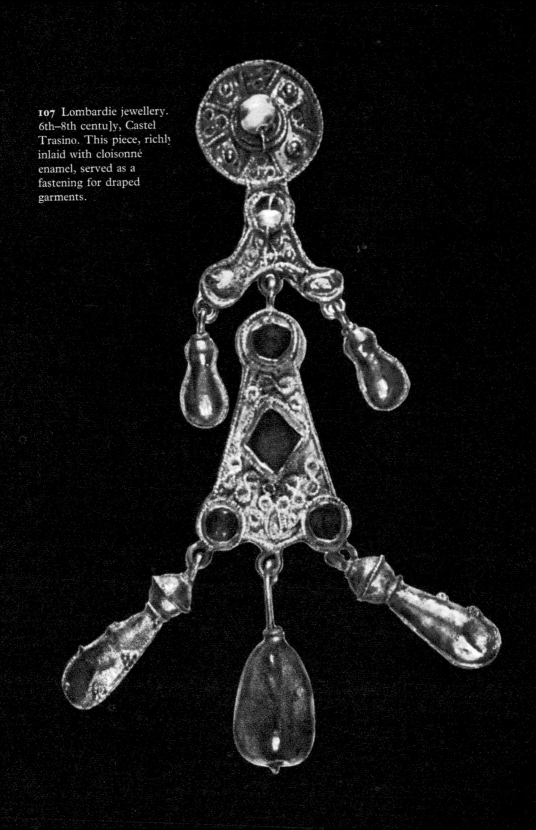

107 Lombardie jewellery.
6th–8th centu]y, Castel
Trasino. This piece, richly
inlaid with cloisonné
enamel, served as a
fastening for draped
garments.

The Period of the Migrations

The clothes worn by the Germanic tribes during the Migrations were not markedly different from those described by Tacitus, the great Roman historian, in the 17th chapter of his *Germania* (written 98 A.D.). These are his words in the translation by H. Mattingley (Penguin Classics): 'The universal dress is the short cloak fastened with a brooch or, failing that, a thorn. They [the Teutons] pass whole days by the hearth fire wearing no garment but this. The richest are not distinguished, like the Persians and Samaritans, by a long flowing robe, but by a tight one that shows the shape of every limb. They also wear the pelts of wild animals, the tribes near the Rhine without regard to appearance, the more distant people with some refinement of taste, for there is no other finery that they can buy. These latter people make careful choice of animal, then strip off the pelt and mottle it with patches of the spotted skins of the beasts that live in the outer ocean or the unknown sea. The dress of the women differs from that of the men in two respects only. The women often wear undergarments of linen, embroidered with purple and, as the upper part does not extend to the sleeves, forearms and upper arms are bare. Even the breast, where it comes nearest the shoulders, is exposed too.

'. . . The children grow up in every home, naked and dirty, to that strength of limb and size of body which excite our admiration.'

This well-known passage of Tacitus has been checked against the visual evidence provided by contemporary artists, and the following picture emerges: the man of means wore a garment of wool or linen, closely fashioned to the shape of the body. This garment must have had sleeves, for the lack of sleeves in women's dress is specifically mentioned. The man who was less well off wore a fur skin over his shoulders beneath his cloak, and when at home often removed both, leaving only his trousers; his wife, besides the amictus (a kind of cloak), wore only an undergarment of wool or linen, and in this she moved about the house.

This conception is supported by pictorial evidence, in particular on the columns of Trajan and Marcus Aurelius. On both, the typical Germanic warrior ready for battle is shown with the upper part of his body bare and either with or without cloak, while the German of trade and commerce invariably wears a more or less close fitting garment which varies in detail only; thus, in addition to a greater or lesser degree of tightness, it had a length which might barely cover the hips or else extend to the knees, sleeves long or short, and a wide neckline or a turned-up collar, but despite the differences in detail the basic shape remained the same and was unchanged for centuries.

This garment was worn by individual warriors of the Emperor's bodyguard on Trajan's Column and by the Marcomanni on the Column of Marcus Aurelius; it allows us to distinguish Sidonius Apollinaris from among the members of the royal train of the Visigoths and Burgundians as well as from among the Franks. This basic dress remained recognizable even after the changes in fashion that took place after the time of the Merovingians. Although the simple people of Gaul and Germania continued wearing their original costume for a long time, Roman elements appeared in the dress worn by the native aristocracy a short time after the first battle with the Roman conquerors.

Rome and Byzantium exercised a lasting influence on the Germanic tribes in yet another field. Their goldsmiths taught new techniques to the Teutons who were already highly skilled in the jewellers' crafts and who now developed a distinctive style of their own. The Lombardic jewellery, found in tombs, is perhaps for us the most impressive witness to the culture which existed at the time of the Migrations. Besides intricate ornamentation, often in the form of stylized heads of animals, with which buckles and clasps were frequently decorated, the new nations learned to do delicate filigree work.

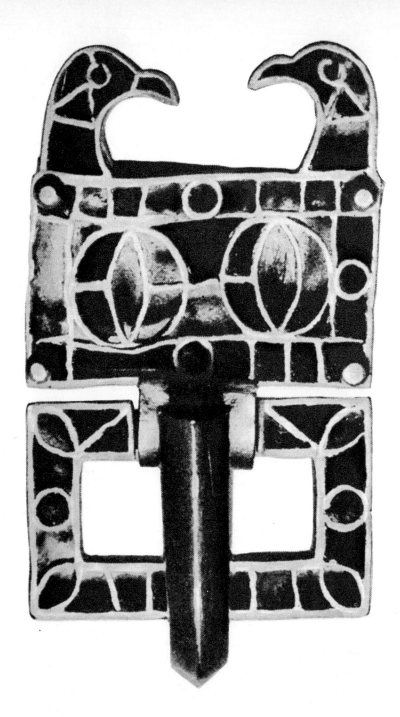

108 Belt buckle from the bed of the river Lambro. Museo Archaeologico, Milan. The gold buckle is in the form of two entwined birds. Dress clasps and belt buckles made of precious materials were used by both Germanic men and women.

109 Lombardic clasps of the 7th century, Desana.

110 Lombardic belt buckle of the 7th century, Desana, State Museum, Department of Antiquities, Berlin.

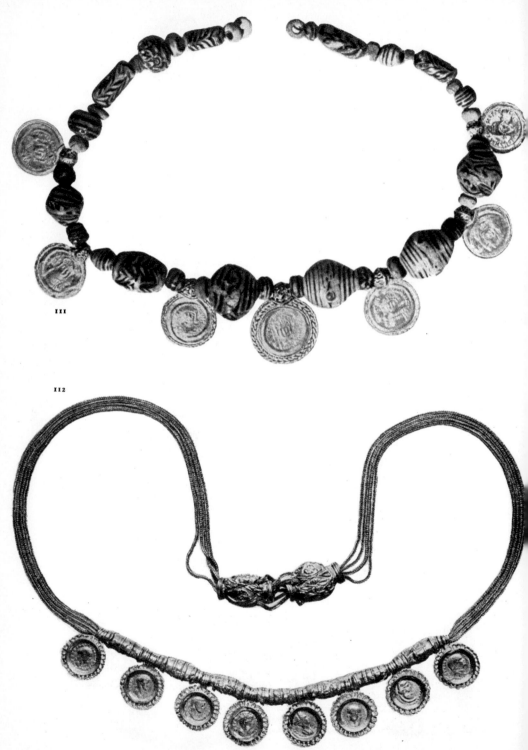

111

112

111 Lombardic jewellery – necklet. 7th century, Castel Trasino.

112 Lombardic jewellery – necklet. 7th century, Castel Trasino.

113 Dress brooch from the Gothic finds at Domagnano. Béhague Collection, Paris.

114 Lombardic clasp 6th–7th century. Nocera Umbra. Finds in antique tombs consisted mostly of necklets and clasps, but also included finger rings and diadems.

113

114

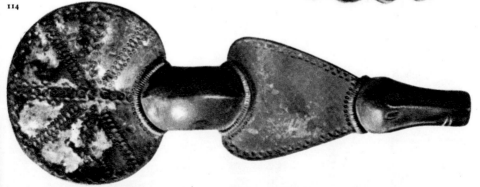

115 The Foolish Virgins.
Fresco from the church at Pedret.
First half of 12th century.
Museum of Catalan Art, Barcelona.

The Romanesque Period

Romanesque dress was much influenced by the ethnological and national characteristics of the various groups of peoples which formed at that time. Dress therefore differed greatly in the different countries and was regional in character. Economic and political intercourse was the exception rather than the rule. Contacts between the individual tribes and peoples were limited – often the only meeting point was the battlefield.

The costume of the period naturally continued to be influenced by Byzantine fashion, although this influence gradually diminished in the course of time. From the 11th century onwards only clerical dress showed any real distinct connection with Roman costume. Fashion among the ruling families, feudal lords and ecclesiastical dignitaries was more universal and came nearer to the Roman original than the clothes worn by ordinary people. Their clothes were simpler and adapted to their needs and environment.

The feudal system promoted social differentiations in dress. Already before the Carlovingian epoch a person's clothes would denote his position in feudal society. Many powerful lords, however, from the Emperor down to individual regional rulers wore clothes far less magnificent than those worn by the rulers of Byzantium. The reasons for this may have been economic as well as religious. It is interesting to read what Bishop Liudprand (c. 922–c. 972), when he was sent as Ambassador of Otto I to the court of Byzantium, had to say about the Byzantium court officials who relieved him of smuggled purple material. He calls them 'soft and effeminate men, who wear loose sleeves that hang down, women's bonnets and veils'.

In the Romanesque period the dress of the rulers differed from that of their subjects mainly in the material used and in decorative detail; the cut was not markedly different. In the 11th century rich people wore a relatively simple garment, but it was made of rich, coloured fabrics and decorated with em-broidery. The outer garments of both sexes were always more handsome and colourful than the undergarments.

Linen and wool were the materials most used, but the ruling classes also employed silk. The clothes of the rich were made from expensively produced materials, those of the common people from homespun linens or raw fleece. In the chronicles of Charlemagne we read that the peasants were ordered to wear dark and unobtrusive colours so that they might be distinguished from the gentlefolk at a glance. In fact, it was not only the colour which was prescribed for them, but also the quality of the material, and three centuries later they were limited even in the quantity that they might use: the width of the material had always to be the same, whether the garment was intended for a slim or a stout person. This primitive style, designed without much regard to the figure of the individual wearer, is still today retained in many national costumes.

The most important part of masculine attire was a sort of tunic, usually belted, which extended to the calves (the tunic of poorer people only came to the knee); in addition, long breeches and hose were worn. The footgear of ankle height was made of leather. In bad weather a kind of cloak made from heavy cloth was added, which was generally longer than the garment underneath.

In the 11th century men began to wear a short undergarment which covered the lower portion of the trunk. Sometimes it extended to the knee and consisted of that part and two 'tubes' of material, each of which was put on separately. The shirt, the precursor of which we can see in some contemporary pictures, was still a rarity.

It is interesting to note that women's dress during this epoch far more closely resembled the dress of late antiquity than did that of the men. This was especially the case among ladies of the nobility. The chief garment of the working woman was an ankle length tunic, loosely fitting and unbelted, with wide sleeves.

Byzantine influence was apparent in a small oblong scarf which covered the head.

In the 11th century women's dress consisted of an under and an upper garment. The undergarment reached the ground and usually had long, narrow sleeves; the upper garment was wider and shorter, with sleeves that, to begin with, ended at the elbow. Later the sleeves became elongated and widened towards the wrist in such a way that the tips reached to the knees.

At that time married women were sharply distinguished from the single by means of the headdress: married women always wore a scarf or veil. Single women had no head covering, the hair was worn simply, dressed either in a plain knot or braid, or else it fell loosely to the shoulders. Throughout the 12th and 13th centuries the scarf remained an important part of women's dress; it was put on with great care, often it gracefully encircled the chin.

In the early part of the Romanesque period women made their own garments, as well as those of their families. Indeed this work was not found degrading by the ladies of the upper classes. On large estates special buildings, or at least special rooms, were set aside in which servants did all the work under the supervision of their mistresses, from the weaving of the fabrics to the embroidering of the garments. Footwear, too, was made at home.

Towards the end of the 11th century handicrafts began to flourish in western Europe and at the same time the first tailors' guilds were formed.

116 Christ with the symbols of the Evangelists. Illustration from the Stavelot Bible, 1097, British Museum, London.
The long, richly draped tunic has a broad band of embroidery on the chest. Over it Christ wears a cloak.

117

117 The Evangelist Luke. Illustration from
the Lindisfarne Gospels, circa 710, British
Museum, London. The long-sleeved tunic
has ornamental borders at neck, wrist and
hem. The cloak thrown over one shoulder
is reminiscent of Roman costume.

118 St Peter. Relief from the binding of an
Evangelistary, 9th century, Library of the
Cathedral Chapter, Prague. This tunic too
has ornamental borders. The asymmetrical
draping of the wide cloak is reminiscent of
the Roman toga.

118

119 St Martin on horseback shares his cloak with the beggar. From the Altar at Montgrony, second half of 12th century, Vichy Museum. The picture shows the stylization and simplification of costume from a richly draped, wide tunic to a tight-fitting one with long sleeves. The belt here is merely an ornament, whereas with antique dress it would have served in producing the draped effect.

120 Vyšehrad Gospels, circa 1085, University Library, Prague. The Angel, Christ and the Saint are wearing the contemporary dress of the noble classes – the long outer tunic with richly decorated borders.

121 The Entry into Jerusalem. Illustration from Henry II's Book of Pericopes, 1007–1014, State Library, Munich.

122 St Joseph. Illustration from the Gospels, circa 1085, Library of the Cathedral Chapter, Prague.

123 Bohemian King. Illustration from the Vyšehrad Gospels, circa 1085, University Library, Prague.

119

120

121

122

123

X PORTA PENETRAT·QVERES

DE IESSE PCE DIT SPLENDID.

124

126

124 The worship of idols. Illustration from Haimon's Commentary to Ezekiel, early 11th century, National Library, Paris. The short tunic with long sleeves and belt was the only dress of the working people of the period.

125 Woman musician. Book illustration from the Tropaire de Saint-Martial at Limoges, 11th century, National Library, Paris. The long, narrow tunic widens towards the hem; the cloak has been pulled over the head so that it forms a kind of hood.

126, 127 Funeral procession. Wall-painting from the tomb of Sancho Saiz de Carillo at Mahaud. Late 13th century. Museum of Catalan Art, Barcelona. The typical Spanish dress worn by the men and women of the period differs from contemporary European dress in its colouring: the stripes of the richly patterned tunics are probably woven into the material; the cloaks are plain.

125

127

128 St Martin and the beggar. Wall Painting from Hix, middle of 12th century, Museum of Catalan Art, Barcelona. The 12th century artist has made realistic differences between the clothes of the rich man and the poor man. St Martin is dressed in a long tunic with ornamental borders, a cloak and leather shoes; the barefooted beggar is wearing a short tunic and short cloak.

129 Medallion on a Romanesque door panel. Circa 1200, Liège. (Origin uncertain, now set into a modern wall.) The man's dress consists of a tunic and the typical Romanesque semi-circular cloak, which is fastened at the shoulder with a fibula.

130 Charlemagne.
Bronze statuette,
9th century, Musée
du Louvre, Paris.
The Emperor's riding
habit consists of a
short tunic, a cloak
fastened at the
shoulder and laced
boots.

131 St Peter. Wall figure in the west porch of the Monastery Church of St Maria at Ripolli, second quarter of 12th century.

132 Fragment from the Tomb of the Abbot Odo. Middle of the 12th century, Musée Saint-Remi, Rheims.

133 Christ enthroned. From the tympanum of the church at Cervo, second quarter of 12th century.

134 Young girl.
Illustration from the
Velislav Bible, circa 1340,
University Library,
Prague. Exaggeratedly
fashionable dress as worn
in Bohemia during the
first half of the 14th
century: the young girl is
wearing a broad, stiffened
veil, which falls to her
shoulders, a long draped
dress and over it a
surcoat, which replaces
the elegant cloak.

Chivalry had its origin in south-western Europe, in Spain and southern France. It was not long before it spread to the whole of Europe. The 12th century undoubtedly saw a refinement of morals and the raising of woman to a social and cultural level she had never known before. The troubadours were pledged to the 'Service of Women' and the knight's code of honour bade him render homage to the female sex.

We are told that, during courtship, a set course of conduct had to be followed. 'The knight in love proceeds by four steps, each of which is characterized by the wearing of a certain colour. The *feignaire*, the secretly languishing knight, often becomes a knight errant in order that his deeds might give him the courage to confess his love. He wears green. On occasions he pays court, like Dante to another lady, so as not to betray himself as a *feignaire*. The *preiaire* has declared his love; humbly begging her favours, he has approached his lady. His colour is white, the colour of hopeful longing. The *entendaire* has been given a favourable hearing and his services accepted; as a vassal of love he wears red.

'There is yet another, a tender, delicate shade, which means that the lady has granted her favours. To what extent concerns no one; perhaps she has only told her knight that his feelings are returned; perhaps she has permitted him to watch her going to bed and to assist her – enough, she has made him happy by allowing him certain advances and by the warmth of her feelings for him. He has become her knight and wears yellow as a symbol of returned affection.

'This was the great system of courtly love (*l'amour courtois*) which is the basis of *courtoisie* towards all ladies, nay towards men and women everywhere. Because it was first practised at the courts of Spain and southern France it was called "courtly".'

The fundamental social changes which had elevated women to a new aesthetic ideal also brought about a new ideal of manhood. The strong masterful fellow, bursting with health and always ready for a fight, gave way to the refined, noble youth: Parzival, the chivalrous hero of Wolfram von Eschenbach's famous epic. The strong influence of the women of the period on manners and fashion, had the effect of making the men effeminate. They wore long and carefully curled hair which they sometimes even adorned with flowers; their faces were clean shaven.

The clothes worn by men and women were very similar; the only real difference lay in their length: a man's garment came to his knees whereas a woman's reached to the ground. As a result of the Crusades European fashion went through a period of uncertainty, of a groping after new forms, but eventually it emerged as a synthesis of national, Roman and Byzantine elements.

Since the end of the period of antiquity fashion had been intent upon concealing the bodily shape as much as possible, but in the course of the 12th and 13th centuries clothes were again designed to accentuate the human figure. In architecture, painting and sculpture, no less than in fashion, great stress was laid on slenderness and verticality. The costume of both sexes fitted closely to the body and was cut to form various hanging points in order to emphasize its vertical line. To this end certain appendages were added later, which dangled uselessly from the sleeves, the dags or dagges, which were deep indentations cut into the edges of a garment.

The aristocracy now no longer had their clothes made in their own workrooms, but by master tailors in the towns. In the course of the 13th century guilds became well established in western Europe. We know no details of the tailor's art of the period before the foundation of the guilds, because each tailor anxiously guarded the secrets of his craft. The guilds, however, had to have a written set of rules and regulations, and a number of instruction and pattern books have been preserved.

It was not until clothing was produced within the framework of the guild system that the differences between secular and clerical dress became marked, that special clothes were worn for social events, which differed from every-day garments, and that married women could be distinguished from the single by variations in their costume. Guild craftsmen not only produced clothes which were very well made for the period; they contributed towards the diversity and variety of medieval dress and to the development of fashion in general.

A man's complete suit of clothes, in addition to undergarment and tunic or robe, consisted of a cloak or mantle. The mantle was semicircular in shape and covered both shoulders; its lining was usually in a contrasting colour. This type of mantle was worn throughout the 12th and 13th centuries. One kind of cloak, which was the same length as the garment worn beneath it, had slits instead of sleeves through which its fur lining might be seen; this was called the suckeny.

In the 13th century this sleeveless, ungirded and frequently fur-lined suckeny also became popular with the women but their version was

longer. In the words of a writer on costume 'it was a pleasing garment in all its forms, particularly becoming to the ladies, and for this reason it gained an extraordinary popularity'. Eventually its use spread over the whole of Europe.

A belt was worn with the undergarment when it was used as a house dress, that is to say when

135 Atelier de Lérida. The life of St Clement. Fresco from Tahull, 13th century, Museum of Catalan Art, Barcelona. Festive and working clothes: (*left*) the long tunic with belt and cloak; (*right*) the short tunic with tight fitting hose; (*top right*) cloak with pointed hood.

136 Old Testament figures from the Porte Royale of Chartres Cathedral, circa 1145–1150. The court dress shows how much the tunic has already altered: the originally tight sleeves are now so wide at the wrist that they hang to the knees; the belt is worn at hip level.

137 The Annunciation.
Relief from the silver
canopy in the Cathedral of
Gerona, 1326. Mary (*left*)
is dressed in the typical
Gothic tight-fitting
garment with cloak. On
her head is the so-called
couvre-chef.

138 The Virgin Mary.
From the Passional of the
Abbess Kunigunde,
1314–1321, University
Library, Prague. Mary is
in the costume of the
married woman: a draped
cloak and a white veil.

139 Detail from the Annunciation of Mary. Book illustration, circa 1360, National Museum, Prague. This is the costume of the single girl: loose hair with coronet, tight-fitting garment and a light cloak, fastened on the breast with a brooch.

140 Bohemian Master. St Catherine. Circa 1400, Museum of Fine Arts, Budapest. The Gothic cloak of soft material falls in rich, cascade-like, flowing folds.

no outer garment covered it. Belts were thought to have magic powers; what is certain is that they conjured up a more attractive figure by emphasizing the slim waist which was prized by contemporary fashion. Wolfram von Eschenbach describes it in his verse:

You know how narrow
Ants always are in the middle,
But the maiden was slimmer still.

When married women went out of the house they covered their hair and neck with a scarf. Their hair was always most carefully arranged and worn in a great variety of styles.
Unmarried female serfs went bareheaded. Their long, mostly artificially waved hair was bound with hairbands or circlets made of a

141

142

143

Die Hebame. Baba.
obstetrix

Pharcs

141-145 Women, from the Velislav Bible. Circa 1340, University Library, Prague.

141 The fashionably draped cloak in longitudinal folds, shows the influence of France.

142 This was the fashionable headdress of the Gothic period: turban with veil, the hair either loose or held in a net.

143 The costume of married women consisted of an undergarment, a cloak fastened over the breast and a veil.

144 Young lady in festive dress: it has no belt and the sleeves have long streamers called 'tippets'. On her head is a ruffled veil which has a pleated or ruffled edge.

145 Working dress consisting of a tight undergarment with long sleeves and a cloak pulled over the head.

base metal. Noblewomen had bands made of gold or silver.

Late medieval costume was, on the whole, far more elegant and graceful than the costume of the early Middle Ages, but also more elaborate and expensive. At the time of the troubadours and minnesingers, dress needed the general bearing and gestures of the wearer to come fully into its own. The carriage, walk and movements of the people living in this epoch had a special character which was most tellingly expressed in dance.

The ideal woman had to have a slim figure, gently curved in the shape of an 'S'; the head slightly inclined forward, the breast seemingly drawn inward and belly and hips pushed outwards.

Gen: 3.

abel · adam · kayn

Gen. 4.

120

146 Pictures from the Velislav Bible. Circa 1340, University Library, Prague. Adam and Eve (*above*) are dressed in stylized pelts and their sons (*below*) are wearing contemporary working dress, short tunics with sleeves, which allow ample freedom of movement.

147 Illustration from the Liber Viaticus. After 1360, Národni Museum, Prague. This is what one must imagine Bohemian dress to have looked like in the 14th century: tight fitting hose and short tunics, girded round the hips.

148 Heinrich VII receiving a deputation of Jews after his coronation. From the Balduineum in the provincial archives of Koblenz. This traditional costume of the Jews with pointed hats had been decreed by the Lateran Council in 1215.

147

148

149

150

149 Ritter von Turm. 'Of a noble lady, as she stood in front of her mirror, preening herself, and how she saw the devil in the mirror showing his behind'. A young woman, fond of finery, in a laced bodice with long skirt and train.

150 Dancing country folk. Miniature from Charles of Angoulême's Book of Hours. Peasants' working dress in the 15th century was very varied. The women wear a veil, a tight undergarment with long sleeves and an apron or a short over-skirt; the men tight trousers, short belted cloaks with hoods or sleeveless jerkins.

151 Arrival of Queen Isabella of Bavaria in Paris on 20th June 1389. Miniature from the Froissart Chronicle, National Library, Paris. The ladies, dressed in the Burgundian fashion, wear the high hennin with frills and veil, a tight-fitting dress with belt at the waist and with low neckline. The men's costume already foreshadows the wide slit sleeves.

152 Illustration from Bohemian book. The dress of Prague bath attendants in the late 14th century is extremely simple: it consists of a tunic with shoulderstraps, girded at the waist and probably made of thin linen.

153 Dirk Bouts. Detail from the Burial of Christ. National Gallery, London. A white veil, which enveloped hair and forehead, and a long cloak, were the dress of married women and widows. The men too wore long cloaks: the man on the right has an interesting side-fastening.

154 Young girl, conscious of her appearance. From a manuscript of the 14th century, National Library, Paris. In this contemporary caricature the girl is depicted with 'tippets' on her sleeves. The curly hair is held in place by a crispine and a high comb. A small devil sits on each fantastic detail of her costume in order to emphasize its sinfulness.

155 Lower-Saxon Master. Late 14th century. Christ being taken prisoner. The short tunic with bells shows the influence of Burgundian fashion.

156 Fra Angelico. Annunciation. Civic Museum, Cortone. Mary wears a tight dress with long sleeves and a wide cloak which falls to the ground. Both garments are decorated with patterned borders. The angel's somewhat stylized garment is in a patterned, probably embroidered material.

155

156

157 Petrus Christus.
Portrait of a young lady.
State Museum, Department
of Antiquities, Berlin.

The French-Burgundian Fashion of the Late Gothic Period

The rich burghers increasingly copied the clothes of the nobility and the nobility on occasions borrowed the costume of the burghers. This is how it came about that in the 14th century the aristocracy laid aside the long tunic and donned the short urban coat. From the opening words of the French Court rules of the time it is clear that class limits in dress were no longer immovable: 'The King is aware that no people is as unstable and changeable . . . in dress as the French and that it is no longer possible to distinguish a person's rank and position by his clothes, be he prince, nobleman, free citizen or artisan, for it is permitted that each man may wear what he thinks fit.'

Accordingly not only did the nobleman vie with the burgher as to who was the most fashionably dressed but there was competition within these ranks. The merchant patricians in the towns had their own prescribed costume as did the artisans, servants and peasants. The clothes of the rulers and the high clergy naturally were privileged. Jews, prostitutes, hangmen, knackers and lepers had their special compulsory garb.

The vertical line of the previous epoch continued to remain fashionable. Everything was done to achieve a slender, pointed effect. Buttons acquired considerable importance, for without them it would have been quite impossible to put on or take off these figure-hugging garments. People began to have clothes made to measure, so as to achieve a perfect fit.

The Late Gothic fashion did not, however, come to its full flowering in France – where it began – for France was too much occupied and weakened by the endlessly dragging and fruitless Hundred Years' War against England. The rich colours, the beautiful fabrics, the noble lines but, alas, also the absurd excesses of the fashion of the time emanated from the Duchy of Burgundy, to which, in the 15th century, not only the northern part of present-day France belonged, but also Belgium and the Netherlands.

In her time Burgundy was one of the mightiest states with a very highly developed economy. The dominance of Burgundian fashion continued for the same length of time as the country's political eminence, that is to say, for the whole of the 15th century. Within the sumptuous, splendour-loving atmosphere of the Burgundian Court, the Age of Chivalry experienced its last expiring triumphs. Philippe de Commynes (1445-1509), eye-witness and chronicler of this turbulent epoch, recalls Burgundy's great days in his *Mémoires* which he began in 1489:

'In those days the subjects of the House of Burgundy lived in great wealth in consequence of the long period of peace which they had enjoyed, and because their lord was so good and kind that he levied but few taxes. It seems to me that his lands had a greater right to be called lands of promise than any others in the world. They abounded with riches and enjoyed the greatest happiness of peace, which they were only too soon to lose forever. All this began about 23 years ago. Profuse expenditure, costly garments in abundance for men and women, feasts and entertainments more sumptuous and opulent than at any other place of which I have ever heard tell. . . .'

The costliest fabrics, the most precious jewellery, golden bells and embellishments of all kinds were considered everyday things. The Burgundian Dukes themselves took the lead in this unprecedented expenditure. Of Charles the Bold, Philippe de Commynes has this to say: 'He was very splendid in his dress and everything else and, indeed, a little too much so. He paid great honours to all ambassadors and foreign guests and entertained them nobly. His ambitious desire for fame was insatiable. . . .' Even on his campaigns he surrounded himself with Burgundy's incomparable wealth: 'He lived in great pomp and magnificence in the camp to show his grandeur and riches to the Italian and German ambassadors who were sent to him: for all his valuable jewels, plate and rich furniture were with him. . . .'

While the Burgundian Court and the high aristocracy favoured darker hues and were not particularly fond of brightly coloured fabrics, the clothes of the rich burghers and their spouses were colourful and eccentric. Shortly after his accession to the throne in 1468, Charles the Bold surprised his courtiers by specifically ordering that black ceremonial dress be worn.

Fashion in the late Middle Ages had become so exaggerated that a series of sumptuary laws was passed in order to curb some of its excesses. The numerous prohibitions were designed not only to restrain extravagances in dress and in expenditure, but chiefly to maintain class differences in costume.

The most marked characteristic of Burgundian fashion was the pointed form of dress, footwear and hats. The women mostly wore narrow belts high under the breast, long trains and veils, which often touched the ground. The dresses, with deep necklines, were complemented by steeple hats. The cone-shaped hennin was extremely high, often as much as two feet.

Ostentation grew to such an extent that the Franciscan monks, in keeping with the asceticism of their order, refused absolution to women who wore long trains. The point of the shoe was often three times the length of the foot; sometimes it had to be reinforced and fixed with wire to the instep. The length of the shoe had to follow certain regulations. For instance, Dukes and Princes were permitted to wear shoes with points measuring two and a half times the length of the foot, the higher aristocracy twice the length, knights a length and a half, rich people one foot and the common people only half a foot.

The Habsburg knights had to pay dearly for their long iron-tipped shoes. At the battle of Sempach in 1386, in which Winkelried, the Swiss Knight, played such an heroic role, they were forced out of the saddle by the considerably smaller Swiss peasant army – after which the latter had no difficulty in decisively vanquishing the heavily shod and almost immobile enemy.

The characteristic garment of the men was a short, close-fitting and always belted doublet with high collar. The sleeves were sometimes slashed lengthwise, so that the white linen shirt was visible through the openings. The upper part of the sleeve, furthermore, was padded, giving it the shape of a flattened sphere. The front of the doublet was embroidered; shoulder, chest and back were often padded and the garment sometimes had a short skirt which was arranged in regular pleats.

Only the peasants still wore the long tunic of the early Middle Ages. Breeches and hose were now fused into a single garment, which covered the lower part of the male body from the hips downwards, in the manner of tights. A speciality of Burgundian fashion was the 'mi-parti'. Individual examples of it were in existence already in the 12th century, but it was most widespread during the epoch of Burgundian fashion. The garment was divided into two dissimilar portions by vertical, horizontal or diagonal stripes. This fashion developed as a result of the complicated medieval colour symbolism. Sometimes the two sides were cut differently; thus one sleeve might be wide and the other narrow. This garment was also worn by the women, but the fashion disappeared during the 16th century. Only the nobility were permitted to wear it; its use was forbidden to the common people.

The hems of the garment were often crenellated, 'dagged' or decorated with small ornaments. The materials most frequently employed were wool, cotton or linen. The ladies and gentlemen of the nobility had a predilection for costly damasks, shot with gold, and not infrequently trimmed with expensive furs. The rich also wore a great deal of jewellery and other embellishments.

A peculiarity of the age was the fondness for bells as decoration. They were even put on shoes. Men dangled them from their belts and women used them as trimmings for their necklines. This 'bell-craze' was most widespread in Germany, where it also met with the greatest number of prohibitions. In 1343, for instance, an edict was passed by the Town Council of Nuremburg to the effect that 'no man or woman might wear bells or silver tinsel of any kind on chain or belt'.

On their heads men wore a variant of the medieval collar-like hood, which came in many shapes and sizes. For decades these hoods or cowls were the predominating head covering. The hood had a point which sometimes stood straight up, but often hung down like a tail: in extreme cases an elongated point, or liripipe, reached as far as the knee. One version of the hennin, the hat of the ladies, looked like a truncated cone; it had great similarity to the Turkish fez.

An Austrian chronicler describes the period in the following terms: 'Each man dressed as he pleased. Some wore coats of two kinds of cloth; others had one sleeve considerably wider than the other – in some cases wider than the entire coat. Sometimes both sleeves were of such width and sometimes the left sleeve was decorated in various ways, with coloured ribbons and with silver tubes on silken cords. Some people wore a piece of cloth of a different colour on their chest, embellished with letters in silver and silk. Yet others had pictures on the left side of their chest. Some had dresses made so tight that they could not dress or undress without the help of others, or without undoing rows of small buttons which covered the sleeves right up to the shoulders and the entire chest and belly. Some people bound the hems of their dresses in a contrasting fabric, others cut numerous indentations into the hem instead. Everyone began to wear hoods attached to their clothes, which replaced the hitherto customary headgear of the men. Coats were made so short that they barely reached the hips.'

Two excesses of this extravagant fashion must be mentioned – the *braguette* and the *mahoîtres*. These were most pronounced in Burgundy. The latter were padded and bolstered shoulders which contrasted strongly with the otherwise close fitting male garment. *Braguettes* were cod-pieces. This fashion trait became so shameless that it was not considered indecent – and it can be verified – when

158 Roger van der Weyden. Donor and his wife, from the centre panel of the Altar of the Crucifixion, Kunsthistorisches Museum, Vienna. The woman wears a white veil, and both wear a fur-trimmed garment with slit sleeves.

the flag-bearer, during a procession, supported the flagpole on his protruding cod-piece. The Burgundian fashion found favour in Europe and for this reason spread rapidly. It had the greatest influence on neighbouring countries and their inhabitants adopted it almost without change. In countries farther away the fashion was modified according to taste. Modifications of Burgundian fashion may be seen to this day in pictorial works of the period. But it is the absurdities – pointed shoes, the mi-parti, folly bells and hats, which would have looked better on a dwarf – rather than the inherent elegance of the fashion, which were often depicted.

On examining contemporary portrayals of the people of Luxembourg we may observe that working women wore dresses of varying length, according to their calling. Since shorter garments were less decorative than longer ones, one may conclude that the longer the dress the higher the position of the wearer. Similarly, in men's clothing, the length of the costume sometimes indicated the level its wearer had reached in the hierarchy of officials. These variations in length did not, however, in any way affect the cut of the garment.

160

161

159 Roger van der Weyden. Holy Women. From the centre panel of the Altar of the Seven Sacraments, Musée Royal des Beaux-Arts, Antwerp. White veils were frequently worn by middle-class married women. The woman on the left is wearing a belted, pleated dress. The dress of the woman on the right has a tight fitting bodice, a very wide skirt with train, and removable sleeves.

160 'The Devil sits on the train.' From the 'Seelenwundergarten', Ulm, 1483. The contemporary caricature depicts a married woman in an exaggeratedly wide garment with long train, the sinfulness of which is shown by the presence of the devil.

161 Hans Memling. Portrait of Barbara Moreel. Musées Royaux, Brussels. This Dutch burgher's wife is wearing a cylindrical hennin with a transparent veil, which falls down her back. A heavy gold necklace graces her square décolleté.

162 Pętrus Christus. Portrait of a kneeling donor. National Gallery of Art, Washington. The Dutch burgher is dressed in a sombre garment of woollen cloth, trimmed with fur, with a sash thrown over his shoulder.

163 Hans Memling. St Ursula and her companions. From the Shrine of St Ursula in Musée de l'Hôpital Saint-Jean, Bruges. The Saint is portrayed in regal costume. The loose hair of the single girl is adorned with a jewelled diadem. Her undergarment is the so-called surcoat trimmed with ermine, and her festive cloak is held together by two clasps on a belt. Her companions, too, wear festive dresses with rounded necklines and borders of fabric or fur, as was fitting for members of the middle class.

162

163

164 Cornelius Engebrechtsz. St Constantine and St Helena. Alte Pinakothek, Munich. From about 1500 clothes made from heavy brocades, richly adorned, were part of court dress.

165 Petrus Christus. Portrait of a kneeling donor. National Gallery of Art, Washington. The Dutch burgher's wife wears a hennin, decorated with braid and embroidery, to which a transparent veil is attached, and a belted dress with a low, pointed neckline and broad train.

166 Albrecht Altdorfer. Praying Woman. Detail from the Altar of St Sebastian in St Florian. The lady of rank is wearing a veil of a fine, transparent fabric and a dress with a low, square-cut neckline, both front and back. The double sleeves reveal the sleeves of the undershirt. Neckline and sleeves are edged with ornamental borders. Her belt with folly bells was very fashionable in Germany in the 15th century.

164

165 166

167 Lucas Cranach the Elder. Betrothal of St Catharine (detail). Museum of Fine Arts, Budapest. St Catharine wears the costume of a young noblewoman: the lower hem of her brocade dress is trimmed with ermine. It has a low neckline, slit sleeves and broad belt. The saint on the right is similarly dressed. The motif of the pomegranate is embroidered into the hem of her dress.

167

168

168 Master E.S. Pair of lovers on a bench. School of Upper Rhine, 15th century.

169 Young men engaged in sport. Detail from an engraving of the 'Sun planets' by Finiguerra after a drawing completed in collaboration with Pollaiuolo. British Museum, London. The sports clothes consist of tight hose and a short jerkin, laced in front, with wide sleeves.

170 Jaime Huguet. Hangman's assistant from a retable at Sarria, Museum of Catalan Art, Barcelona. Male working dress consists of a short tunic, the front opening of which allows us to see the white shirt beneath, an apron, tight hose, slightly pointed shoes and a turban-like headdress.

171 Justus van Gent. Detail from the left wing of the Crucifixion of Christ. St Bavon, Ghent. The saint is depicted in the costume of an Italian noblewoman. She wears a turban high above a shaved forehead and a garment with wide embroidered sleeves, decorated with a net on the shoulders.

169

170

171

172

173

172 Roger van der Weyden. Birth of Christ. From the centre panel of the Bladelin Altar. State Museum, Department of Antiquities, Berlin. Mary and Joseph wear traditional dress. The donor is dressed in the contemporary clothes of the burgher, i.e. a short jerkin trimmed with fur, tight hose and pointed shoes.

173 Inglés Jorge. Marquis de Santillana. From a retable in the Buitrago, Madrid. Collection of the Duke of Infantado. The donor is wearing late Gothic dress: a turban, a cloth coat with a pouch called *aumonière* fixed to the belt. The page in the background is dressed in a short jerkin with slit sleeves which are wider at the shoulders.

174 Lucas Cranach the Elder. Princess. Museum Narodowe, Warsaw. The princess' dress is typical of Renaissance fashion in central Europe: it is of velvet and brocade with a laced bodice, which reveals the chemise. Round her neck are several gold chains.

175 Piero di Cosimo.
Portrait of Simonetta Vespucci.
Musée Condé, Chantilly.

The Renaissance

The great revival in Italy of fine art and particularly of painting, could not fail to exercise a decisive influence on the work of the most important textile manufacturers and master tailors. The contemporary view of perfection is defined in the words of the architect Leon Battista Alberti: 'Perfection is the harmonious accord of all parts to which nothing can be added and from which nothing can be taken away without disturbing the whole.'

The Italians of the Renaissance loved display. They built palaces, painted monumental pictures, and adored play-acting. They wore the best clothes they could afford and bought many and expensive garments. Although various extraneous influences were discernible in Italian fashion, it preserved nevertheless its individual character in its choice of style and colour combinations.

In the early days of the Renaissance, during the 15th century, when a slim figure and quick elastic movements were still the vogue, clothes required comparatively small amounts of material, but in the 16th century significant changes in taste became apparent; the outline broadened considerably and the garments now worn were made from new heavy materials which hung in loose folds and were dragged along the ground.

Venice, Florence, Milan, Genoa and Lucca, above all, had excellent textile industries which produced first-class brocades, velvets, satins and silks. Fashion was largely conditioned by these sumptuous textiles, which of necessity caused bodily movement to become slower and more formal, and garments made from them gave their wearers a dignified appearance.

The High Renaissance did not pay much attention to detail. Small embellishments, the pointed form – especially pointed shoes and hats – parti-colours and pleats were no longer fashionable in the 16th century. The slender youth and fragile maiden of the trecento and quattrocento had grown into the strong, resolute man with broad arms and shoulders and into the healthy, adult woman with full curves of the cinquecento, as we know them from the masterpieces of Leonardo da Vinci, Raphael, Michelangelo, Sansovino, Giorgione, Titian, Correggio and others.

The form of the body was either revealed or at any rate accentuated by the clothing. Catherine de Medici introduced to the French Court a fashion which resembled that of Crete. The low-cut dress was shaped to emphasize the bosom, which was either covered with a light transparent material, or left completely bare. Fashion changes took place frequently in the towns of Italy during the Renaissance. The Italians were by no means inaccessible to foreign influences in the 16th century. On the contrary, they gladly adopted French and Spanish ideas – often those that the people of France and Spain had previously borrowed from them.

The official costume of the men was always wider and longer than the clothes they wore in private life. They economized in neither the quality of the material, the richness of the folds, nor the width of the sleeves, which on rare occasions, might be as much as two feet in diameter. To begin with, the doublet was wide, then it narrowed somewhat and became higher, so that the shape of the shirt, too, had to be altered by raising the collar correspondingly. The sleeves remained huge and were its chief ornament.

The most characteristic item of male Renaissance costume was the *zimarra*. This was a gown of varying length with openings for the arms. Often it was faced or lined with fur and provided with false sleeves. Its cut and the embellishments on the shoulders showed up the figure and made it appear imposing.

The main dress of women was the simple *gamurra* with long sleeves and a bell-shaped skirt, over which was worn the elegant *cioppa*. This gown was often richly embroidered and brightly coloured, preferably in light shades. It was high-waisted with a train and decorative sleeves, which hung down loosely, without actually covering the arms. These were, of course, already covered by the long sleeves of the utilitarian *gamurra*. The outer garment of the men, too, sometimes had decorative sleeves.

Women's costume, in the 16th century, consisted of a long skirt, broad at the hem and narrowing towards the waist, and a short bodice, which generally had a large, rectangular neckline. To begin with skirt and bodice were sewn together to form one garment. Later this was no longer the case and as the fashion declined in popularity, the separate bodice and skirt became part of working dress.

The opulent sleeves which were as important an ornament in women's dress as in men's, were exchangeable and interchangeable and therefore were only loosely sewn in. Other accessories of Renaissance fashion were handkerchiefs, fans and large, perfumed and decorative gloves. The jewellery was in character with the costume, being large rather than dainty, and heavy gold chains especially enjoyed great popularity.

Headgear was considerably simpler in the Renaissance than under the régime of Burgundian fashion. In the early days of the Renaissance women wore a hat called *sella* (Italian for 'saddle'), which might be described as a somewhat toned-down variant of the two-horned hennin. Caps, resembling the future barrets, were also worn. In the 16th century the cap predominated with both men and women. That of the men was soft, round and of medium size, that of the women was wider and sometimes decorated.

For the most part, however, the head was left bare. Women admired a high forehead and for this reason they so arranged hair and eyebrows as to let the forehead appear higher. In other respects the hair was dressed in a variety of ways during the early Renaissance. Rich women braided pearls into their hair and crowned their heads with diadems encrusted with gems; young girls adorned their hair with garlands of flowers. Frequently the hair was put into delicate nets made from transparent veils.

During the High Renaissance the hair styles of both men and women became simpler. The hair was dressed so as to harmonize with the general air of restraint. The beards of the men added the final touch to their dignified appearance.

Italian women used a great many aids to beauty and continued to do so in spite of repeated prohibitions. They dyed and bleached their hair – blonde was very fashionable – and wore wigs; they painted their face, neck and breasts, not to mention eyes and lips. The face was adorned with beauty patches and the pupils enlarged with drops of belladonna. Both men and women made lavish use of perfumes; not only the body was scented but accessories, such as gloves, shoes and stockings.

176 Sandro Botticelli. Venus and Mars (detail). National Gallery, London. The hair of Venus is dressed in the style typical of Florentine girls with false hair pieces. Her softly flowing garment does not accurately correspond to the fashion of the day.

177 Masaccio. The Tribute Money. Fresco in the Brancacci Chapel of Santa Maria del Carmine, Florence. The hair and beards of Christ and the Apostles show the various styles fashionable in the Renaissance. The traditional garments consist of tunics and cloaks as worn in antiquity.

178 Paolo Uccello. Detail from the Miracle of the Desecrated Host. Gallerie Nazionale delle Marche, Urbino. Women's every-day dress was simple. The man is wearing a doublet and a Renaissance cap. The children's dresses are exact replicas of the clothes worn by the adults.

179 Domenico Ghirlandajo. The Birth of the Virgin. Fresco in the Choir of Santa Maria Novella, Florence. The women are dressed in Renaissance costume: the Saint in the middle wears the loose hair of a young girl and a richly patterned brocade dress. The women following her are dressed like married women or widows.

177

178

179

180 Piero della Francesca. The Queen of Sheba worshipping the wood of the Holy Cross. Detail from the choir fresco of 'The Story of the Cross' in the Choir of San Francesco, Arezzo. The Queen is shown here in a Renaissance headdress, with a crown over a fine, short veil.

181 Piero della Francesca. Battista Sforza, wife of Federigo da Montefeltro. Uffizi Gallery, Florence. The shaved forehead and the braided hair decorated with ribbons and jewels were typical of the Renaissance. The dress of velvet and brocade is adorned with several necklaces.

182 Fra Filippo Lippi. Detail from 'Madonna and Child' (or Madonna with a pomegranate). Palazzo Pitti, Florence. Another hair style of the Renaissance with pleated and embroidered veil.

180

181   182

183

184

185

183 Piero della Francesca. Detail of the Virgin, from The Annunciation. Detail from 'The Story of the Cross'. Fresco in the church of San Francesco, Arezzo. The smooth hair is covered with an open-work veil and adorned with a string of pearls. Under the embroidered cloak Mary is wearing a draped and belted dress.

184 Piero della Francesca. Women in the entourage of the Queen of Sheba, from the Fresco 'The Story of the Cross' in San Francesco, Arezzo. Renaissance hair styles with high shaved foreheads: on the left the hair is twisted round a circular base, on the right it is enveloped in a veil.

185 Alesso Baldovinetti. Portrait of a Lady. National Gallery, London. The dyed hair, which is combed high above the forehead is held in position with a piece of jewellery. The dress, of a soft material, has a deep décolletage, both front and back, and sleeves which are puffed at the top and embroidered with large flower motifs.

186

188 Solomon and the Queen of Sheba. Engraving by Roselli, after a drawing by Botticelli. British Museum, London.

189 Andrea Solari. Woman with guitar (fragment). Museo de Palazzo Venezia, Rome. The hair style with turban was popular in Italy especially at the beginning of the 16th century. The woman is wearing a low cut dress and sleeves slashed at the wrist.

190 Andrea del Sarto. The painter's wife Lucrezia. Prado, Madrid. The woman has twisted a striped scarf into a turban.

186 When the fashion of 'dagging' was at its height no garment was spared: even the cap showed this strange and bizarre embellishment.

187 Vittore Carpaccio. The Courtesans (detail). Museo Correr, Venice.
Both girls in this frequently reproduced painting are dressed according to their profession in fantastic and sumptuous garments with very low necklines and slashed sleeves, through which their underwear can be seen. The curly hair is combed onto the face and combined with false hair-pieces.

187

IX Alonso Sanchez Coello. Marie Maximiliana of Pernštejn. Nelahozeves Castle, (Bohemia).

X Jacob Seisenegger. Vratislav of Pernštejn. Nelahozeves Castle (Bohemia).

188

189   190

191 Jacopo Pontormo. Portrait of Ugolino Martelli. Kress Collection, National Gallery of Art, Washington. The simple dark garment, fastened at neck and belt with two buttons and allowing the shirt to be seen, is typical of Florentine fashion, as is also the plumed cap.

192 Alabaster relief of Charles V and Isabella of Portugal. The Imperial pair are depicted in court dress, the Emperor in cap and cloak with broad collar and wide sleeves, with a heavy gold chain round his neck. The Empress's dress has richly decorated sleeves and a square décolleté, which is covered with a veil.

191

192

193 Michele da Verona. Brutus and Portia.
Museum Narodowe, Krakow. The classical
theme has prompted the artist to choose a
formal costume which only faintly
corresponds to contemporary fashion.

194 Raphael. Portrait of a young man (lost,
formerly in a Polish collection). The
exaggeratedly long hair and the large cap
worn slantwise are the characteristic
costume of the young nobleman.

195 Hans Holbein the Younger. Portrait of an unknown man in a red cap. Water-colour and chalk drawing. Kupferstichkabinett, Basle. The man with short hair is wearing a large cap, a gown and a cloak with slashed sleeves embellished with stripes.

196 Hans Holbein the Younger. Youth in slouch hat. Coloured chalk drawing. Kupferstichkabinett, Basle.

197 Hans Holbein the Younger. Theophrastus Bombastus von Hohenheim, called Paracelsus. Drawing. Kupferstichkabinett, Basle.

198 Giovanni Boltraffio. Le Belle Ferronière. Musée du Louvre, Paris. The sleeves of the low cut bodice are detachable. The band which adorns the hair of Francis I's mistress has been called *ferronière* after her.

195

196 197

199 Jean Clouet. Portrait of Francis I of France. Musée du Louvre, Paris. The court dress consists of a fur-trimmed cap, a doublet of patterned brocade and an embroidered jerkin.

200 Bernart van Orley. Isabella of Denmark. Museum Narodowe, Krakow. The front edge of the dark coloured bonnet is trimmed with a finely pleated ribbon and a row of pearls. Isabella is also wearing a brocade dress with a square neckline and jewellery.

201 Jan Gossaert, called Mabuse. Portrait of a young girl. National Gallery, London. On her curly hair the little girl is wearing a pearl-embroidered bonnet of the same material as the sleeves of her dress. Pearls have been sewn round the square neckline.

202 Gerard David. The Donor's Daughters. From Jan de Trompes' Altar of the Baptism of Christ, Academy of Fine Arts, Bruges. All the girls are dressed alike in dark French veils with a patterned border worn over fine white bonnets.

200

201 202

203 Albrecht Dürer.
The Cook and his wife.
Engraving.

The Reformation

The movement of the Reformation took hold of the whole of central, and a considerable portion of western Europe. The social and religious revolution, which brought about fundamental changes in the cultural and social life of the countries concerned, was bound to affect the costume of the people. In Bohemia and Germany, as well as in Switzerland, the Netherlands, England and France, the Reformation also meant reformation in dress.

Under the leadership of Jan Hus, the Reformation swept Bohemia a whole century earlier than the rest of Europe, with the result that in Bohemia the development of Gothic fashion came to an abrupt end. The Hussite movement profoundly influenced people's attitude to dress, since it condemned finery, gay colours and all manifestations of fantasy.

Jan Hus, the reformer who was burnt as a heretic in 1415 in Constance, in his writings denounced 'the women [who] wear their dresses cut so low at the neck and so wide, that almost half their breasts are revealed and anyone can see their glowing skin anywhere, in the temples of the Lord, before the priests and the clergy, as well as in the market-place, but still more in the home, and that portion of the breast which is covered is so prominent, artificially enlarged and pushed out, that it seems almost like two horns on the breast'. And in another passage: 'Then she makes two more horns on the breasts [earlier he had spoken of the horned head-dress] which are lifted up and artificially projected, so that even when they are not at all prominent by nature, at least by the shape of the shirt and by the addition of other garments, the horns of her breast stand up.' So thundered Jan Hus.

Although the basic shape remained unaltered, so that the silhouette was not markedly different at the time of Hus from that of the period of the Luxemburgers (from 1347 to 1437 Luxemburg Emperors ruled Germany), the dress of both sexes became firmer – it lost the lightness and elegance of the previous era. Delicate and costly fabrics were replaced by cheaper ones, which the burgher could afford

and which were more appropriate in view of the economic impoverishment of Bohemia. During the Hussite revolution the towns seized the political initiative and became representative of the advanced cultural currents. They could therefore not fail to have a decisive influence also in the field of fashion.

The Reformation exercised a similar influence in the other countries, but economically its range was far more limited. The religious and social battles in Bohemia had been of exceptional intensity; also, while the Hussite revolution had taken place in the first half of the 15th century, the rest of the reformatory movement fell into the epoch of the High Renaissance, when the greater part of the European nations had already adopted Italian Renaissance fashion.

An individual contribution to fashion was made in the first half of the 16th century by the Swiss and South German lansquenets; they were most probably the initiators of a curious novelty. Their costume seems to have been tight and uncomfortable and for this reason they cut it in the places where they found it most restricting. This was done in rather a primitive fashion by roughly cutting the material at the knees, the elbows and the shoulders. The openings made in this way revealed the white shirts beneath. Soon these openings were merely underlaid with lighter pieces of material so as to simulate fresh linen. When the tailors took over, these cuts or slashes were gradually extended to other parts of the garment until there was hardly any place left whole. Ultimately not even the Renaissance cap was left untouched.

One of the most eloquent preachers against trunk hose was the Superintendent of the Mark Brandenburg and Professor of the Holy Scriptures at the University of Frankfurt, Andreas Musculus. In a sermon, delivered on the Feast of the Assumption in 1555 he warned against the evils and the sinfulness of wearing trunk hose, which were possessed by the devil. The *Hosenteufel* (breeches' devil), a popular character of the widespread 'devil' literature of the time, earned further literary glory in Willibald Alexis' *Die Hosen des Herrn von Bredow*. The aristocracy and the upper middle class ignored this eccentricity of fashion until the time when the Emperor expressly permitted his soldiers to wear slashed garments. The male fashion during the period of the Lutheran Reformation consisted of a cap or barret, a comparatively lavish shirt, doublet, breeches which came to the knee, and hose. In cold weather a gown resembling the houppelande was added. Shoes were made of leather and rather large. Often they too were slashed. In Germany at the time of the Reformation it was fashionable to wear beards. Women's costume consisted of a bodice, which was separate from the skirt and had a small stand-up collar, and of a double skirt: the outer-skirt was beautifully decorated and always had a train, and the under-skirt, or petticoat, almost touched the ground and had to be decorative also, since the ladies, when walking or dancing, sometimes caught up the longer outer-skirt. In winter the women wore a long cloak which usually ended in a train. The ubiquitous barret formed part of women's costume also.

While the costume of the ruling courts, the aristocracy and the leading citizens showed no homogeneity and in its individuality approached the Italy of the Renaissance, the clothes of the rest of the population, not only through economic necessity but also because they were fired by the ideals of the Reformation, were plain and simple. The rich nobility was largely cosmopolitan in outlook and did not take the moral preaching of the Reformers nearly as seriously as did the burghers.

The fashionable colours of the first half of the 16th century were predominantly yellow and red; but in various countries certain preferences for other colours could be noticed. In France and England dress was generally brighter than in Central Europe; nowhere was white as popular as in France and in no other country could as many colour contrasts be found as in Italy.

The outer garments of the various professions, too, had their own colours: scholars preferred red, lawyers and theologians black. The costume of the clergy belonging to the various Christian churches was the most unvarying in all of European society, for it changed its colour even less than its form.

From the 1540s onwards new fashion influences, emanating partly from the court of the Habsburgs, partly from the region of the Lower Rhine, began to permeate Europe – influences, which clearly signalled the triumphal progress of Spanish fashion. Dress became ever stiffer, starting with headgear; the width gradually lessened, even beards became narrower; the costume appeared to get higher, which was most noticeable in shirt and collar; it became shorter, as could be seen in breeches and skirts.

204 Albrecht Dürer. Flagbearer. Engraving. This costume, consisting of a short, tight doublet, slashed sleeves, tight hose belted at the hips, and closed-in sandals, was the mark of the dandy of the period.

205 Albrecht Dürer. Three peasants. Engraving. Two of the peasants are wearing the typical late Gothic turban, the third a hat with the brim turned down in front. All three are wearing short belted doublets and tight hose.

206 Albrecht Dürer. Peasant and his wife. Engraving. The man is wearing the usual country garb, the woman a wide-sleeved garment; her hair is plaited.

207 Albrecht Dürer. Bagpiper. Engraving. The usual country costume: a jerkin with slashes on sleeves and hips, a turban embellished with a fringe, on the belt a purse.

208

208 Albrecht Dürer. Declaration of love. Engraving. The woman is wearing a bonnet with a veil, and a low cut dress with a wide skirt.

209 Albrecht Dürer. Dancing peasants. Engraving. A short dress with apron, a small bonnet and pointed shoes – the working clothes of country women.

210 Albrecht Dürer. Country folk at the Fair. Engraving. Rural garb: for the woman a veil which also covers the shoulders; for the man a short belted doublet and high turned-down boots.

209   210

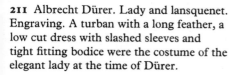

211

212

213

211 Albrecht Dürer. Lady and lansquenet. Engraving. A turban with a long feather, a low cut dress with slashed sleeves and tight fitting bodice were the costume of the elegant lady at the time of Dürer.

212 Albrecht Dürer. Lady and Scholar. Pen drawing. Hamburger Kunsthalle. The lady has a complicated hair style with braids, a dress with a square neckline, sleeves decorated with folly bells and a train and, of course, pointed shoes. The young man is wearing a cap on his curly hair, a pleated shirt with sash and tight hose – the typical late Gothic and rather dandified dress.

213 Albrecht Dürer. Promenade. Engraving. The costume of the German burgher: the woman is wearing a bonnet with a veil pulled low over her forehead, a tight fitting dress cut low over breast and back with slashed sleeves and train, as well as shoes with very narrow points; the man is wearing a plumed cap, tight hose and a cloak fastened on the right shoulder.

214

215

216

217

218

214 A Merchant. German engraving, from the 15th century. The short coat trimmed with fur reaches to the knees. With it tight hose and a cap are worn.

215 Nuremburg Merchant. German engraving, 1576. These are the clothes in which a merchant used to travel: a fur cap, breeches puffed above the knee and a short cape with hood, reminiscent of the cape of the *torero*.

216 Hans Holbein the Younger. The Family of Sir Thomas More. Pen drawing. Kupferstichkabinett, Basle. Typical English costume of the first quarter of the 16th century: the women are wearing Tudor headdresses, dresses with square necklines

and turned back sleeves; the men, caps, wide cloaks with collars, some with sleeves puffed at the shoulder.

217 Nuremburg Merchant. German engraving, 1610. The waistcoat, cut out in front shows up the pleated shirt. The cloak has been thrown asymmetrically over one shoulder. The sleeves, the breeches, which extend to the knees, and the cap are slashed.

218 Hans Holbein the Younger. Young girl. Engraving. The bonnet, richly adorned with plumes, and the dress with deep décolleté and pleated sleeves and skirt belong to the fashion image of the period. Attached to the belt, which falls to the hips, are an *aumonière* and a small knife, which was carried by women as well as men.

219 Peter Flötner. Lansquenet. Woodcut.
This costume of a lansquenet shows the
passion for slashing in the 16th century. With
it he wears a large feather-trimmed cap.

220 Hans Burgkmair. Mercenary.
Engraving. Even the lansquenets' armour
was embellished with slashed pieces of
material on sleeves and breeches.

219

220

XI Michael van Miereveld. Portrait of a Woman. Národni Galerie, Prague.

XIIa Juan Pantoja de la Cruz. Don Fernando D'Aragon. Nelahozeves Castle, (Bohemia).

XIIb Jakob Seisenegger. Archduke Maximilian. Castle Gallery, Prague.

221 Hans Baldung, called Grien. Portrait of a young Prince. Etching from the 'Karlsruhe' sketchbook. The cap is decorated with ribbons and plume; the pleated shirt has a small round stand-up collar.

222 Hans Holbein the Younger. Lady Ratcliff. Chalk drawing. Royal Art Collection, Windsor Castle. Typical Tudor headdress with the angular 'gable' hood, which completely hides the hair.

221

222

223 Engraving after C. de Passe.
Queen Elizabeth in
festive dress, partaking in
a ceremony at St Paul's Cathedral.

The Spanish Fashion
(1550-1618)

The dominance of Spanish fashion had a political basis. Its hegemony was bound up with the powerful position of the Spanish Empire, which reached its peak in the reign of Charles V. He became German Emperor (1519-1556) and he ruled not only over his native kingdom but also over the Netherlands, Austria and the immense Spanish possessions overseas, in America and Africa.

Philip II, Charles' son and successor in Spain, Burgundy and the Netherlands, well knew why he forced the subjugated people to wear the Spanish fashion, which seemed to make foreign ways of thinking conform to the Spanish will. The lands, which managed to throw off the Spanish yoke, soon threw off Spanish fashion as well. England's victory over the 'invincible Armada' in 1588 shook the political supremacy of the Spanish Empire (in which, according to a pronouncement of Charles V, the sun never set) as well as the supreme position of Spanish fashion in Europe, especially in England.

The Spanish power was the sworn adversary of all progressive and reformatory trends. The gulf between the fashion at court and the costume of the people was greater than ever; in the Renaissance the differences between the ranks had greatly diminished. The tendencies of the Renaissance and the Reformation to strive for greater freedom of thought were curbed with relentless severity in the lands of the Habsburgs.

The relatively free existence of the self-conscious burgher was suppressed, and the cold aristocratic reserve as well as the unapproachable exclusiveness of the complicated Spanish court ceremonial asserted itself wherever possible. In the forefront of the endeavours to introduce stiff court etiquette stood the Emperor Charles V himself; the greatest master of ceremony of all time, whose strict court formalities no one succeeded in overcoming - in this respect he can only be compared with Louis XIV.

In the severe and constricting Spanish fashion of the 16th century the Catholic Counter Reformation was given expression. The stiff, starched, uncomfortable and dark costume was the characteristic fashion image of the period. The high Spanish collar tolerated no lively movement or natural laughter.

The Spaniards moved rigidly; in their speech, manner, mode of life and dress they appeared forbidding. In Spanish fashion the functional purpose of dress was of secondary importance; what mattered was its decorative effect. Spanish costume was stiff - inside it the female form vanished completely.

The men wore high-necked doublets which were laced at the top and had high stand-up collars or ruffs, which became ever larger and stiffer, so that ultimately they were mockingly, though aptly, called 'millstones'. The stiff collar certainly helped to lift the head proudly, but at the same time it seemed to separate it from the body. The cuffs at the wrist and other embellishments of the garment matched the collar.

Later the upper part of the doublet was padded, above all on shoulder and chest; a particularly stiff piece of padding which started at the neck and extended to the waist with its end projecting over the belt was called the 'goose belly' or 'peasecod belly', from its shape. Aberrations of this sort were very popular early in the 17th century.

A book of historical anecdotes refers to the strange fashion of bolstering and stuffing: 'Under King Francis II of France (1559) arose a curious fashion for men. They found that their personal merits were infinitely increased by a fat belly. Those men who were unable to procure the necessary *embonpoint*, and through this a claim to greater respect, attempted to supply it from without. False bellies were produced and tailors had to supplement the empty kitchen.' The book continues: 'At the same time the ladies believed that the men's taste for large surfaces could be taken further, and now appeared the large posteriors (*culs*). This fashion lasted three to four years; one saw nothing but false bellies and swollen posteriors. The great confidence the ladies placed in their aspect from behind caused them to neglect their other charms.'

The men wore breeches which were extremely short, and puffed and padded to such an extent that the outline of the hips was considerably broadened. The barret was joined by a stiff velvet hat or by a small, stiff, silken head-dress with a narrow rim. This costume was completed by knitted stockings and decorated leather shoes.

Another typical item of Spanish fashion was the short, broad, stiffened, silken cape, the Spanish cloak, which usually was not buttoned and which did not cover the chest.

The writer on costume, Jakob von Falke, paints a telling picture of the Spaniard in this markedly masculine era of the Counter Reformation. This is how he describes the nobleman as we meet him in many contemporary paintings: 'The well supported head with mighty moustache is covered by a stiff hat or a high-crowned barret. A broad ruff surrounds the neck and forces the head to be held rigid. A small cape rests on his shoulders, but it is there just for show, for it neither warms nor protects; a stuffed doublet with pointed waist tightly covers the body and round the hips and thighs the breeches cling like thick pads, while elsewhere the hose fits most precisely and neatly; cuffs ruffled like the collar, gloves, fine shoes and the long rapier complete the affected costume.

'No crease is to be discovered anywhere unless it be one artificially produced with wire and smoothing iron; everything is round and tight, either exaggerating the natural shape or in direct conflict with it. From the excessive care which has been lavished on the costume we recognize the dandy; the haughty manner, which is shown in a stiff and straight posture and points to a reserved and taciturn temperament on the one hand and to a grave and serious nature on the other, is typical of the Spanish *grandezza*. One glance at this figure conjures up the entire court of the intractable Philip, the sinister, fanatical spirit, the joylessness and finally the unbending severity of the etiquette, which had been passed from Burgundy to Spain in a greatly intensified form.'

Women's costume closely resembled men's. The stiff corseted bodice with low waist also had cuffs and a stiff, high collar to match, which made it necessary to put up the hair. The sleeves were mostly narrow and often decorated with puffs at the shoulders. Women's hats, too, were very like men's.

The long skirts of wealthy ladies were encrusted with gold, silver, pearls and gems and were generally open in front in order to display the rich petticoat of equal length beneath. This was conical in shape and was further supported by another similarly shaped petticoat of stiffened linen: the predecessor of the crinoline.

At the end of the 16th century the farthingale came into fashion. This was a contraption consisting of a series of hoops made of iron or whalebone, which were sewn into the petticoat. Skirts of this nature appear to have been exclusive to the ladies of the aristocracy living in the towns. Trains and rich draperies were unknown in Spanish fashion. Etiquette strictly required legs and neck be completely covered. The 16th century Spaniards endeavoured to make men and women appear to be of equal height. Under their long skirts women wore high chopines of wood or cork. In Italy the chopines found unhoped-for allies in ecclesiastical circles. The clergy were full of praise for them because they saw in the uncomfortable shoes an effective means in the battle against worldly pleasures, above all against the dance – their wearers received indulgences.

The further development and spread of Spanish fashion to the rest of Europe brought certain changes with it. While the clothes in Spain were dark and monotonous in colour, in fact mainly black, in France and Germany lighter colours were preferred.

Germany resisted Spanish fashion the longest. The first Germans to take it up were the princes, who fought on the side of the Counter Reformation. For a time, at the Protestant courts in northern Germany, Reformation dress continued to be worn, but the Catholic South already wore Spanish costume. Ultimately the Protestants in the North, too, took up the Spanish fashion. The nobility came first, to be followed later and with certain modifications by the inhabitants of the towns and of the country. Italy declined to submit to

the exaggerated rigidity of Spanish dress.
At the beginning of the 17th century the
Spaniards themselves began to consider making certain changes, which would make their
clothes more colourful. As a result, not only
in the different countries but also in individual

224 Alessandro Allori. Francesco Medici.
State Art Collection in Wawel, Krakow. The
man with short hair is dressed in an
embroidered doublet with buttoned stand-up
collar and slashed sleeves.

225 Federigo Zuccari. James I. The boy is
wearing a fur cap, a short doublet with
pleated ruff and padded kneebreeches.

226 The portrait painter of the Family
Hohenemb. Detail from a family portrait.
The festive costume of a young girl, as
prescribed by Spanish fashion: a diadem in
the hair, ruffs at neck and wrist, decorated
with lace, a tight fitting dress of embroidered
material with sleeves of a different fabric.

224

225   226

165

227
228

towns, significant variations in dress became noticeable, even though the cut remained essentially the same.

France captured a direct share in the future formation of Spanish fashion, not only on its own soil but also beyond its boundaries. The French spirit acted as a leavening to the harsh dignity of Spanish costume and lightened it by introducing a greater variety of colour and style, and also some extravagances. Men's dress remained basically the same as Spanish costume but in women's clothes the Spanish characteristics actually became exaggerated.

The French did not persist in wearing the bizarre collar; the women often wore low cut dresses. The skirt became even broader and to begin with was bell-shaped, but later it assumed the form of a barrel or drum which was not, of course, possible without special supporting contrivances. The French for farthingale or verdigale is *vertugal(l)e*, which means 'French virtue' or *vertugadin*, meaning 'guardian or virtue'.

The dress of the ordinary citizens was always considerably simpler and as a rule lighter in colour than the costume of the aristocracy. Collars and cuffs were white also, but without lace trimmings. To a certain extent country people, too, adopted the Spanish fashion. While the legs of the simple women were concealed, peasant women and the poor women in the towns sometimes wore considerable

227 Diana Cecil, Countess of Oxford and Elgin. National Trust Regional Representative, Shrewsbury. The hair adorned with gems is combed smooth. Other characteristic features are the lace ruff, the wide embroidered cloak, the necklace, the lace-trimmed cuffs and the fur muff.

228 Jean Clouet. Portrait of Charles IX. Musée du Louvre, Paris. A doublet of the same striped bright silk as the breeches and a short cape of velvet made up the ceremonial court costume.

229 Peter Candido. Portrait of a German Duchess. The lace collar with ribbons, which in Spain only members of the royal family were permitted to wear, shows the influence of Spanish fashion in Germany.

167

décolletages. Children wore smaller versions of their parents' clothes.

In 1596 a book appeared in Frankfurt which bears the following title *Mme Isabella Cortese's hidden and secret arts and wonderful works in alchemy, medicine and chirurgy and other arts: above all how to make the ungainly body of man or woman appear young and beautiful (in the Italian manner) and at the same time how to make the face handsomely red and white, neatly dye the hair and drive away all kinds of warts and patches from face and hands. . . . All from the Italian language. . . .*

And these are the instructions of how to dye the hair chestnut brown: 'To dye the hair half red and in chestnut colour, take a solution of cabbage burnt to ashes and as much alum rock as you think fit and wash your hair with it, for after this liquid the hair will be prepared to take on the colour. In the same solution temper camphor and the hair will be white, take the leaves of a box tree together with shavings of its wood, put it in with celandine, barley straw, oakwood chips, lupins and pease-meal and when it has all been put into the solution as has just been described, the hair will turn red, but when one puts into the same solution sticados and gorse with skin and leaves, the hair will turn a chestnut colour.'

231

232

230 Titian. Portrait of a Nobleman. Staatliche Kunstsammlungen, Gemäldegalerie, Kassel. Charles V's court painter witnessed the development of the Spanish Power and paints a true picture of the fashion at the end of the 16th century which bears the imprint of Spain.

231 School of Clouet. Mary Stuart. Hermitage, Leningrad. Ceremonial dress in England in the Spanish tradition consisted of the Mary Stuart cap, high lace collar, dark velvet dress with gold chains, and a cloak with a stand-up collar of lace.

232 Federico Zuccaro. Sir Walter Raleigh. National Portrait Gallery, London. The bearded man is wearing a doublet of brocade with ornamental buttons sewn close together and a cloak, called *boemio*, which is embroidered with tapering rows of pearls.

234

235

236

233 Unknown master. James I. University Library, Cambridge. The sumptuous royal ceremonial dress of silk is lavishly decorated with lace, embroidery and jewels. The white stockings are held in place by embroidered garters. Buttons, belt and shoes are trimmed with jewels.

234 French school. Anne of Austria. 17th century, Versailles Museum. The Queen's festive dress has a bodice which is lavishly adorned with lace and pearls, with heart shaped flaps which continue from the bodice, and a broad collar, the millstone ruff; the skirt is the French farthingale. The coat is lined with ermine.

235 Unknown Master. Queen Elizabeth of England. The Duke of Devonshire's Collection. Festive court dress of embroidered material with stand-up collar of lace and jewels. In addition, gloves and a fan.

236 Frans Pourbus, the Younger. Henry IV. Musée du Louvre, Paris. Doublet with Spanish ruff and padded trunk hose, black stockings and black shoes with ribbons.

237

238

237 Unknown Master. Sir Robert Dudley. National Portrait Gallery, London. The English nobleman has subscribed completely to Spanish fashion: he is wearing a jewelled barret and a peasecod-bellied doublet.

238 Unknown Master. Queen Elizabeth. National Portrait Gallery, London. The English Queen, who is dressed in the Spanish fashion, is wearing a coronet and pearls in her hair, a round, stiff lace collar and a dark-coloured garment with satin sleeves which are richly decorated with ribbons, pearls and gems.

239 Courtesans. Contemporary engraving of the 16th century. Musée de Cluny, Paris. The Venetian courtesan is wearing knee length breeches underneath her long skirt, and high chopines.

240 Costume studies of the French nobility. Contemporary engraving. Here the pompous nature of the early farthingales is shown.

241 Costume studies of ladies of the Burgundian aristocracy. Contemporary engraving. The silhouette of feminine French fashion shows dresses with wide sleeves, bodices with the so-called goose-belly and wide skirts.

239

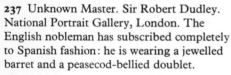

240

241

244

242, 243 Italian women's fashion. Contemporary engravings. The Italian fashion silhouette is freer than the French, the shoulders are narrower and the skirt folds softer.

244 George Gower. Mary Cornwallis. City Art Gallery, Manchester. The huge millwheel ruff lends majestic dignity to the garment. The sleeves of the brocade dress are decorated with a transparent pleated fabric. A medallion at the end of the pearl necklace, a second medallion hanging from a ribbon on the belt, a hair-net with pearls lend the finishing touches to the outfit.

245 Peter Paul Rubens.
Self-portrait with Isabella Brandt.
Alte Pinakothek, Munich.

The Thirty Years' War
(1618-1648)

In the first half of the 17th century Europe lacked the Ruling House which could give the lead in matters of taste and discernment, and for this reason the burghers in the Dutch towns temporarily became the guiding force in the world of fashion. The Court in Paris was presided over by two ecclesiastics, the Cardinals Mazarin and Richelieu; England was in a state of Civil War with Oliver Cromwell as the sober protagonist; Germany had become the battleground of the leading powers, and the Courts of Vienna and Madrid had receded into the background because they had become petrified in their cultivation of the unpopular Spanish fashion.

It was not by accident that the Netherlanders were the ones to go into the attack against Spanish fashion. It was not only because of the immense wealth of the Dutch burghers that this role fell to them; it was rather because of their deadly hatred of the Spanish Crown and all things Spanish. In Spanish fashion the body had been split up, as it were, with hips and shoulders clearly emphasized; Dutch fashion, on the other hand, gave preference to comfort and freedom of movement.

The doublet became longer and looser and gradually the padding and stuffing was omitted and the waistline rose a little. During the Thirty Years' War the great fashion boom in lace began. Sometimes lace was made into narrow collars, then again into collars so wide that they covered the entire shoulders; it was used not only for cuffs, but formed rosettes on shoes and decorated broad sashes. The breeches became wider and lengthened to well below the knee, and the feet were covered in a completely new type of footgear; top-boots. These were high leather boots with spurs and prominent heels, rather like the riding boot of today, with fairly wide tops which were turned down like a collar. A short cape, which was often worn over one shoulder only, completed the male wardrobe.

Since the Spanish collar was no longer worn, the men at the Court of Louis XIII let their hair grow and some even tied it into two plaits with narrow silk ribbons, known as *faveurs*; the plaits were called *cadenettes* after the Marshal Cadenet. The head was covered by a broad felt hat with feathers. This head covering, originally used by peasants, was also worn by the women. Women's hair, like men's, fell freely to the shoulders.

Women's costume was no longer held rigid with stays and padding. Outside Spain the corset and the farthingale disappeared, the necessary roundness and fullness was achieved by numerous petticoats. Around 1640 women's clothes lost all stiffness and tightness and became much lighter.

The typical collar was lower and instead of the Medici collar, which had been popular in the twenties, a broad lace collar was preferred, with the help of which the décolleté once again came into its own. With the progress of the Counter Reformation it had become smaller, while during the Thirty Years' War it increased appreciably and eventually became so low that the upper part of the breast was revealed. Around the year 1650 the square neckline widened to an oval, which also left the nape of the neck and the shoulders bare.

When the décolleté had become too low for decorum it was filled with yet another lace collar. Lace also decorated the wide sleeves, which gradually became shorter and left a large part of the lower arm bare. Decorative handkerchiefs too, were made of lace. The skirt fell loosely to the ground, sometimes it even trailed a little. The gold chain, which had been so popular in Spanish and Italian Renaissance fashion, was replaced by ropes of pearls in the hair, round the neck, sometimes also on the body. Flemish Baroque fashion required hair to be dark, and even blondes had to tint their hair with a special black powder. As it was fashionable at the same time to have a very fair complexion, elegant ladies, when going out and especially in winter, wore masks. In summer they protected their faces with broad-brimmed hats.

The Puritans prevailed in England in the first

half of the 17th century and lace, ribbons and embellishments of every kind were abandoned. In contrast to the Royalists, with their long artificially waved hair, they cropped their hair very short, which earned them the description of 'Roundheads'. Both men and women wore plain, drab clothes in dark colours.

The Puritans took their costume with them to America, and in the year 1776 Benjamin Franklin, as representative of the newly formed United States, brought the fashion back to Paris. The costume *à la Franklin* became in Europe the symbol of republican freedom.

During the period of the Thirty Years' War, Germany gave birth to a type of fop or dandy who slavishly imitated the affectations of French dress and manners: he was known as *Monsieur à la mode*. Since about 1630 the tendencies for which he stood provoked a special kind of literature, which bitterly attacked and satirized these 'foreign' ways. Friedrich von Logau, Germany's finest epigrammatist wrote: 'Alamode Dress, Alamode Sense; as it changes without so it changes within.'

Moscherosch, another German satirist, speaks of 'fops and monkeys' and mocks at German slavery to all things foreign. He pokes fun particularly at the frequent fashion changes, and in such an outspoken manner that his spiritual brother, the 19th-century aesthete Friedrich Theodor Vischer, only dared offer the pithy satirist to his own prudish contemporaries via a Greek translation! Here is a passage from the original, baroque-style text, dating from the 17th century:

'"Come hither," said Herr Teutsch Meyr. And, as I approached him, "Call yourself a German?" he asked. "Why, your whole appearance gives me to think otherwise. And I really do believe you have cast away your hat (which he pointed at with a great deal of merriment, for they had elected to make a spectacle of it by suspending it from a pair of antlers) just so that people shall not perceive its absurd shape."'

Elsewhere he cites the great variety of hats: 'pointed hats, cardinals' hats, floppy hats; hats with broad brims and with narrow; hats made

246

from the coats of goats, camels, beavers, monkeys, and the 'hair of fools'; some are shaped like Swiss cheeses, some like Dutch and some like German. And however foolish the costume is today, tomorrow it will be more foolish still.' These verses by Moscherosch may be freely translated thus:

Skirts may be short or long, till to the ground they fall,
Hats may be small and round or large and tall,
First sleeves are long, then short, then wide, then tight,
The breeches colourful and close or very wide.

One fashion suddenly leads to the next,
For the German spirit is never vexed.
Which shows what in his heart you'll find,
A fool is always changing his mind.

Fashion, it is clear, was almost as rich in vicissitudes in those far-off times as it is today.

246 Nicolaes Maes. Young Girl. Lord Ellesmere's collection, Edinburgh. A little girl with smooth hair lightly curled round the ears, and a rope of pearls. The sleeves of her dress are trimmed with fur.

247 Peter Paul Rubens. The Infanta Isabella Clara Eugenia with St Elizabeth. Detail from the right wing of the Ildefonso Altar, Kunsthistorisches Museum, Vienna. The Infanta is dressed in festive robes with a lace-trimmed, millwheel ruff and a brocade cloak edged with ermine.

248 Dirck Hals. Concert at home. Hermitage, Leningrad. The musicians are wearing the fashionable Dutch costume of the first quarter of the 17th century; broad Rubens hats, lace collars, doublet and knee length breeches, as well as cloaks.

247

248

249 Frans Hals. Willem van Heithuysen. Musée Royaux, Brussels. The man is wearing a barret and a doublet with lace collar, knee breeches and soft boots.

250 Jan Steen. The Coachman's Family. Museum of Fine Arts, Budapest.

251 Orazio Gentileschi. Lute Player (detail). Collection of the Duke of Liechtenstein, Vaduz. The girl's hair style is simple, with the plaits wound round her head. Her dress with shoulder-straps is laced above the hips.

252 Pieter de Hooch. Woman and Servant. Hermitage, Leningrad. The Dutch burgher's wife is wearing a white bonnet, a dark coloured dress with braid sewn to the lower edge of the skirt and an apron. The servant, in a dark bonnet, is dressed in a white, closely buttoned bodice, skirt and apron.

253 Louis Le Nain. Peasant family. Musée du Louvre, Paris. Traditional country costume: the women have veils on their heads, dresses with long sleeves and aprons.

249

250

251   252

253

254 Karel Skreta. Ignaz Vitanovsky of Vlčkovic. Castle Museum, Liberec, (Reichenau), Czechoslovakia. Costume worn by Bohemian nobility has a Dutch collar, slashed sleeves and a hat trimmed with feathers.

255 Karel Skreta. The Family of the Gem Cutter, D. Miseroni. Národni Galerie, Prague. Prague burgher's dress of the 17th century: white lace collar and slashed sleeves, through which show the white chemise.

254

255

256

257

256 Abraham Bosse. The Merchants of Paris before Louis XIII. Engraving. Conservative male dress of the middle class as worn by the merchants is contrasted with the fashionable clothes of the royal attendants.

257 Attributed to Georges de la Tour. The Card-Sharper (detail). Collection Pierre Laudry, London. The dress appears rather old fashioned: the woman's dress has slashed sleeves and a square neckline; barret and turban are trimmed with feathers. The young man's clothes are made from two kinds of cloth. Ribbons decorate neck and shoulders.

258-263 Engravings from the cycle *La Noblesse* by Jacques Callot.

258 The winter clothes of the elderly woman consist of a bodice, a wide fur-trimmed skirt, a cloak which also covers the head and a fur muff.

259 The man is wearing a broad 'Rubens' hat with feathers and a wide fur-trimmed cloak, breeches and high boots.

260 The nobleman with the beard *à la Henri IV* is wearing the Rubens style, floppy felt hat with feathers, a soft turned-down collar, gathered knee breeches with ribbons, a wide circular cloak trimmed with fur and shoes decorated with flowers.

259   260

261 Here the artist depicts the costume of the 17th century nobility: a fur-lined cloak, breeches with ribbons, decorated under-shoes, over which shoes with wooden soles are worn.

262 This nobleman is wearing a doublet shaped like a cuirass and long breeches.

263 The costume of the gentlewoman here consists of a dress with a double skirt, stiff bodice and double collar.

261

262   263

264

265

266

264-269 Fashion plates by Wenzel Hollar:

264 French burgher's wife, 1649. Over the skirt and apron the woman is wearing a short cape with a wide fur collar.

265 French burgher's wife, 1648. The woman is wearing a fine black veil, a tight-waisted dress with pleated skirt and broad collar, and a fur muff.

266 Paris Merchant's wife. In deference to the edict of 1633 the simple costume is without any kind of ornament.

267

268

269

le-woman
of France

267 Lady with hood and muff. Circa 1640.
The lady is wearing a mask very popular at
that period, and a cloak with hood. She has a
fur muff and a fan attached to the belt.

268 Irish Lady, 1649. The street clothes of
the Irish lady consist of a white bonnet,
which completely covers the hair and a
cloak with a broad shawl collar of fur.

269 French Lady. Circa 1645. The elegant
Frenchwoman's hair is arranged in a knot at
the nape of the neck, with the hair left loose
at the temples. The dress has a low neckline,
is laced in front and has a lace collar.

Fashion at the Time of Louis XIV (1646–1716)

There had been very little uniformity in dress during the period of the Thirty Years' War, and clothes had shown many variations from country to country and town to town, but from the 1660s onwards the Court of Versailles began to lay down laws of fashion – laws which hardly anyone resisted.

Paris strenuously publicized her fashion; each month life-size dolls dressed in the latest fashion were sent to London and later also to the other capitals of Europe. *Les Poupées Fameuses* thus accomplished an important mission and even the War of the Spanish Succession did not hinder them. French fashion not only unified the costume of the ruling classes of all European countries, but also influenced the dress of the ordinary people.

As in the days of chivalry, women were the ornament of the Royal Court and the centre of interest. Attention was not, however, focused on the 'highborn' ladies, but on the mistresses. The ruling aristocracy regarded conjugal fidelity as a middle class virtue. To be the king's mistress was regarded as the greatest distinction, and titled families vied for this honour, from which they expected – not without good reason – an advancement in their position. Fashion at the Court of the Sun King was led by Mme de Montespan who, from her dazzling vantage point, eclipsed everyone around her.

One of the most important elements of French fashion was the wig. Around 1640 wigs began to be worn, because long hair was fashionable and not everyone was blessed by nature with a plentiful growth. The young Louis XIV himself is said to have introduced the wig at the French Court in order to hide his baldness – but this is one of those apocryphal anecdotes which must be accepted with reservation.

In the year 1655 alone, Louis XIV granted licences to 48 Parisian wig makers. The wig was a symbol of the aristocracy of the period – it magnified, it stylized and it seemed to typify all that the ruling classes stood for.

After quite a short time the men no longer bothered to groom their own long hair. On the contrary, they had it shaved off or cut very short, for at home they wore a cap and the wig was regarded as the only fashionable headdress. The demand for wigs was so great that the cheaper ones were made of wool, goathair or horsehair. Poor people could not even consider high quality wigs. Women also wore long curls, but their hair styles never attained the splendour of the men's expensive wigs.

During this epoch the development of man's costume was more interesting than women's fashions. In the first half of Louis XIV's long reign the clothes of both sexes were characterized by a comparative lightness and freedom and looked rather picturesque. The men's hats had become somewhat stiffer and the wide breeches, which came to the knees and were edged with lace, were rather reminiscent of a short skirt. Numerous ribbons graced these 'Rhinegrave breeches' as indeed all the effeminate male clothing.

Women's clothes too were elegant but certainly not more so than the men's. The décolleté of the bodice extended to the shoulders and for this reason the flat collar had to be narrower. The cut and length of the skirt were not materially altered; the outer skirt remained open in the middle.

In the 1680s the waves of the Baroque became calmer and fantasy was replaced by noble splendour. At that time three of the most fundamental items of men's dress made their first appearance: the coat, then called *justaucorps*, the waistcoat and the breeches. The long waistcoat with narrow sleeves was generally made of coloured brocade. The relatively narrow breeches, known as culottes, were no longer so colourful and were usually made of the same fabric as the coat.

After 1690 it became customary to wear a cravat, made of lace or lace-trimmed linen, round the neck; this cravat or jabot was the forerunner of the tie. The outfit was completed by coloured stockings, usually red or pink; only fops wore pale blue. Silk stockings became so important that Colbert equipped a royal workshop for two hundred workers in a castle near Paris for the production of silk stockings; in 1672 he founded a technical school, so that this trade could be properly learned. The low-cut shoes had high heels in a different colour from that of the shoe.

The fiery-red or golden-haired wig reached the height of popularity at the turn of the century and was so bulky, that the tricorne became unsuitable as head covering and was condemned to be a mere ornament to be carried under the arm. The only masculine feature of this feminine fashion was the small moustache. At no period when the feminine element predominated were beards fashionable.

The great popularity of lace also made the shirt into a decorative garment, although it was seldom seen in its entirety. This was just as well for the contemporaries of the *Roi Soleil,* since the washing of clothes and personal hygiene were not regarded as important and were replaced by the lavish use of perfumes. Underwear was changed at most once a month.

Women's dress was the counterpart of men's. The high *fontange* was the ladies' answer to the wig. The bodice was cut very low and the sleeves at most came to the elbows. The lace chemise covered the rest of the arm, leaving half of the lower arm bare. The richly decorated bell-shaped skirt of moderate width was sewn on to the bodice. The slenderness demanded by the fashion was achieved by the tight corset, stiffened by a steel busk, half a yard long, which formed a straight vertical line from just below the breasts to the end of the trunk. This type of corset proved useful during court ceremonial which required long hours of standing.

The outer garment was the lavishly decorated *manteau,* usually in a contrasting colour and of a heavy satin or velvet material, the rich folds of which ended in a short train. In the home women wore a more comfortable house garment instead, which later became the *contouche.* On occasions a dainty ornamental apron was added. The French Baroque had a predilection for heavy, expensive materials and preferred darker colours, above all scarlet, cherry red or dark blue. The women were also permitted to wear pink, sky blue and pale yellow. Louis XIV's favourite colour was brown. The most popular gem of the period was the diamond, the King's favourite jewel. In the year 1669, at an audience with the Turkish ambassador, Louis XIV wore diamonds to the value of fourteen million *louis d'or.*

At the end of the 17th century the first court-plasters or beauty patches appeared on the faces of the ladies. In her memoirs Johanna Schopenhauer, mother of the great philosopher, refers to this strange fashion in somewhat sarcastic terms. She would be inclined to doubt the possibility of so absurd a fashion, she writes, were it not for the fact that she had often toyed with the flat mother-of-pearl box which was provided with a mirror inside its lid and which all the ladies carried filled with these objects, so that, in case a *mouche* had inadvertently left its position, they could immediately fill the gap with another.

These small patches, made from black silk, impregnated with an adhesive, were shaped like 'tiny full and half moons, little stars and hearts, which were intended, when attached to the face with taste and discernment, to increase its charms and enliven the facial expression. A series of moons increasing in size from the tiniest to the largest, affixed at the outer corner of the eye, served to make the eyes appear larger and to heighten their lustre; a few stars at the corner of the mouth were supposed to give the smile a roguish charm; a *mouche* in the right place on the cheek suggested a dimple. There were also patches of a larger size – suns, doves, cupids even. These were called *assassins,* presumably because of their devastating effect on the hearts'.

In due course edicts were issued in France forbidding luxury and waste. In Germany too, in the year 1667, lengthy instructions were laid down by the police of the town of Freiburg as to what was and what was not permissible in dress:

'And in the first instance we require all registered and other citizens, corporate members, dependants and related persons, male and female, young and old, married and single, without discrimination, truly and diligently

271

272

271 René Antoine Houasse.
Louis XIV on horseback.
Musée Nationale de Versailles.
With Louis XIV and his epoch
the lavishly decorated
justaucorps comes into fashion,
giving male costume a new
appearance.

272 Hyacinthe Rigaud.
Portrait of Count Philippe
Louis Venceslas Sinzendorf.
The gentleman is wearing a
white long wig, a satin coat
with jabot and wide sleeves,
and a cloak with embroidered
border.

to be warned from adopting sumptuous apparel lest they be led in the way of other indiscretions contrary to their inheritance and godly station, under which description are included the following frivolous and unworthy items:

'If wives, maidens, or other female persons possess unbecoming robes or overly low-necked dresses, which by the transparency of the lace-work or other manner inspire frivolous thoughts conducive to reprehensible behaviour; or if women display themselves in improperly high white boots, or other unseemly style, extravagantly coloured stockings and broad, flowing or otherwise ostentatious ribbons and garters . . .

'For the rest, each and every person shall henceforth dress in accordance with his or her station and the manner of their clothing shall be considered according to the requirements thereof. . . .

Edicts of this nature were known to have been published in Germany since the 13th century. They were issued by governments, municipalities, magistrates, feudal lords, etc. for a variety of motives: to preserve dignity and decorum; to curb excessive expenditure and luxury; to promote native industries; to protect the citizens from foreign influences; above all, however, to 'preserve class distinctions'. This last was the most important factor governing all German rules of dress.

273 Antoine Coyzevox. Bust of Louis XIV, Musée Nationale de Versailles. This is how the splendour-loving King had himself portrayed for posterity, with lace cravat and huge, long wig, which became the symbol of his epoch.

274 The state wig of Elias Bäck. *Il calloto risuscitato* or 'the resurrected grotesque figure'. A contemporary caricature of the giant wigs worn at that time.

275 Christian Philipp Bentum. Portrait of Count Václav Josef Lažanský with his sons. In Bohemia and elsewhere the powdered wig and jabot were taken up by the aristocracy only after some delay.

276 General's uniform in the 17th century. Engraving. Bibliothèque Nationale, Paris. Even high military dignitaries have accepted the wig, the satin coat with broad cuffs and the sash.

277 The Linen Seller, 1688. Engraving. Bibliothèque Nationale, Paris. In fashion pages the wasp waist is emphasized and formalized even more than was the case in reality.

278 Antoine Watteau. The Capricious Lady (detail). Hermitage, Leningrad. A street dress for the summer.

279 J. D. de Saint-Jean. Lady taking a walk. Engraving. The lady is wearing a street dress with variegated stripes, a light head scarf and is carrying a parasol.

280, 281 Male fashion in the period of Louis XIV.

282, 283 Female fashion in the period of Louis XIV.

284, 285 Male fashion in the period of Louis XIV.

286, 287 Female fashion in the period of Louis XIV.

288 Antoine Trouvain. Wedding dress of the Princess Maria Louise of Orléans, married in Paris in 1679 to Charles II, King of Spain. Engraving.

283   284   285

280-287 Fashion plates by Jean Bérain,
Bibliothèque Nationale, Paris. Under
Louis XIV, who as General often wore
soldiers' clothes, the coat acquired the special
significance for male dress, which it has
retained ever since. Reaching to the knees it
covered breeches and waistcoat, but its
turned-up sleeves permitted the lace cuffs to
be seen and it was decorated with all kinds of
ornament.

In female dress, during the 17th century, the
décolleté gradually became generally
accepted. The dress always had two skirts,
the outer one, which often ended in a train,
was made of a heavy material because it 'fell'
better. Embroideries made these dresses
often heavy and uncomfortable but lighter
fabrics gradually came into use. Lace was
very popular.

288

The Fashion of the 'Régence' (1715-1730)

The transition period between the styles of the Baroque of Louis XIV and of the Rococo of Louis XV has been called Régence after the regency, lasting from 1715 until 1723, of Philippe of Orléans on behalf of the infant King Louis XV. Philippe was husband to the jolly German Princess Liselotte von der Pfalz, and whereas in the last years of Louis XIV's life court ceremonial had become ever more formal, a new *joie de vivre* now made itself felt. The members of court society began to create a new style of living for themselves. It was only natural, therefore, that in fashion, too, attempts were made to get away from the stiff and pompous forms.

Formality in dress now began to give way to frivolity. The style during these fifteen years was gentler and lovelier than that of the Baroque, without, however, destroying its strict symmetry. Moreover, the period was influenced by the culture of the East.

In the same way as red and black lacquer were used to give furniture a Chinese flavour and the walls were decorated with Chinese landscapes, so the soft colours of Chinese silks characterized fashion. On the whole, costume in the 1720s was rather more practical and easy to wear than that which preceded it. The silhouette of the dress of both sexes was conical in shape, rather like the capital letter A. Male dress became tighter and the coat was almost never buttoned. The open part of the waistcoat and the ends of the sleeves were adorned with lace which was also the chief material of the narrow collar. The shoes were more dainty than before and formed the transition to the buckled shoes of the Rococo. Wigs no longer had such vast dimensions, the fiery red ones gradually yielded to white, which were sprinkled with powder. The question of wigs not only exercised the minds of the fops and dandies but also those of the worthy bishops. In 1725, for example, the Austrian bishops were much concerned with the question of whether they might read the Mass in a wig and so they humbly turned to

Rome for advice. The Holy Father's answer was in the negative, although documents are extant which show, that in individual cases the church did not oppose such a request, because the wig was generally regarded as a sign of dignity.

One noteworthy sequel to the wig fashion – according to the historian Hottenroth – was the custom of leaving the head uncovered in society, a custom which has remained in force until today (it is true, however, that in pictures of the more elegant coffee houses of the 19th century gentlemen wearing top hats may be seen sitting at the tables). In earlier days, even when dining with Louis XIV, gentlemen kept their hats on in the presence of ladies. But the large wigs obliged them to carry their hats under their arms. They continued to do so even after the wigs had become smaller. Because of the powder and the rolled curls, which were easily damaged, the hat could not again take its proper place. Since it was rather too high to be comfortably carried under the arm, a substitute was invented. It consisted of a hat with two points at opposite ends which could be folded flat. This was called the *chapeau claque* and remained in use until the French Revolution.

The outline and quality of women's dress changed even more. The high, important looking *fontange* and the *manteau* disappeared completely. On all occasions, when formal costume was not prescribed, the women wore the comfortable *contouche* which had evolved from the housecoat worn at home. A low, neat, powdered hair style replaced the complicated *fontange*. Necklines were even larger than those of the Baroque, the waist was laced only lightly in front and the dimensions of the hooped skirts, which had newly sprung to life, were not too unwieldy to begin with. The skirts were stiffened with whalebone. This was so much in demand that the Dutch States General in 1722 formed a company of whalers for the purpose of obtaining the material for the production of stiff skirts, called paniers –

literally wicker baskets. This is but one example of the way in which fashion is always creating new industries. Walther Rathenau mentions the whalebone boom in his writings: 'When first the hooped skirts became the fashion, the dress industry required enormous quantities of whalebone. Such a demand led to the foundation in Holland of a Company with a capital of 600,000 guilders, whose task it was to procure the necessary whalebone. This company employed a vast army of whale hunters, which in turn raised the demand for fishing boats.'

But what happens when fashion acquires new and different forms? This is a typical risk to which industries which are connected with fashion are exposed. Rathenau also reports the outcome of the whalebone boom: 'Twenty years ago the second Empire fell and with it its symbol – the crinoline. It is well known that the hard-pushed dealers in steel hoops managed to get out of their difficulties by inventing a new game with hoops. It was called *cricri* and satisfied the need for disharmony and mischief so well that it did not disappear from the face of the earth until all steel-hoop manufacturers had become rich men and all Europeans with weak nerves had died.'

290 Antoine Watteau. La Gamme d'amour. National Gallery, London. The dress intended for walks in the open air is much simpler than social dress. It is made of lightweight materials and in straightforward styles.

291 Antoine Watteau. Signboard of the art dealer Gersaint (detail). Staatliche Museen, Gemäldegalerie, Berlin. Street dress with laced bodice.

290

292 Hyacinthe Rigaud. Maximilian Kaunic. Castle Slavkov. Young nobleman in morning coat, lace chemise and barret.

293 Louis de Silvestre. Louis XIV receives the Elector of Saxony. Musée Nationale de Versailles. Ceremonial court robes of brocade, velvet and lace.

292

293

294 Nicolas de Largillière. Prince James Francis Edward Stuart and the Princess Louisa Maria Theresa Stuart. National Gallery, London. The children's dresses are imitations of grown-ups': the boy in a small *justaucorps* with chemise and lace jabot, the girl in a dress with train and the so-called *fontange* headdress.

295 Philippe Vignon. Mademoiselle de Blois and Mademoiselle de Nantes. Musée Nationale de Versailles.

294

295

296 Madame de Mouchy.
Engraving after
Charles-Antoine Coypel.
Grand evening dress in the
French fashion: hooped
skirt and overskirt trimmed
with pearls and
embroidery.

297-299 Antoine Watteau.
Fashion studies, circa 1715.

297, 298 Both gentlemen
are wearing *justaucorps*,
waistcoats, short breeches
and powdered, long wigs.

296

297   298

299

300

299 The gentleman is wearing a street suit, which is still reminiscent of the *justaucorps*, and the tricorne.

300 Pierre Imbert Drevet. The Duchess of Nemours. Engraving after H. Rigaud. Festive court dress trimmed with lace and a fine veil, which falls over the shoulders, a so-called hood, which became very popular at the beginning of the 18th century and was worn in all colours.

205

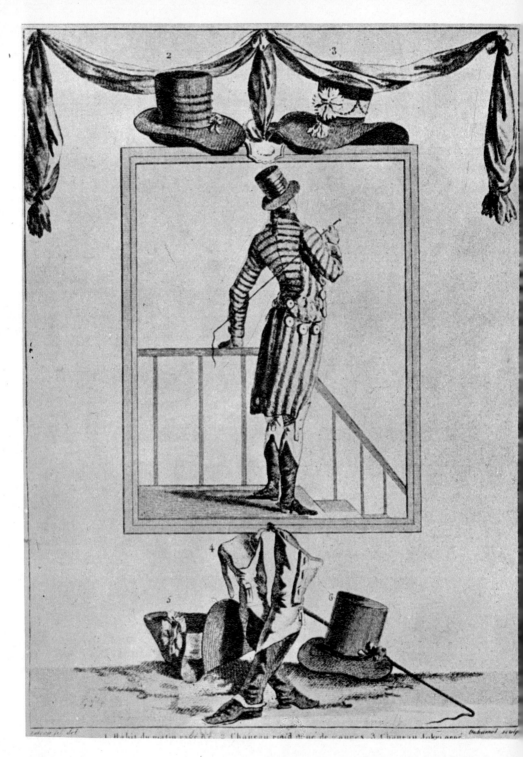

1. Habit de matin exécuté... 2. Chapeau raid digné de mauces. 3. Chapeau fabriqué

301 A. B. Duhamel. Men's Fashion.
Engraving. Suggestions for
morning dress and various hats.

The Rococo
(1730–1789)

A characteristic feature of the so-called 'gallant' epoch was its lack of moderation. An exaggerated realism, an exaggerated absolutism, an exaggerated cult of the aristocracy and an exaggerated militarism formed the picture of the period. The architects decorated their buildings rather too lavishly; eroticism was valued too highly and fashion over-shot its mark.

The width of the crinoline made walking almost impossible for the ladies of fashion; the candles of the chandeliers sometimes set fire to the high coiffures; make-up, powder and 'patches' were used too generously. In Prussia with its 9 million inhabitants, for instance, the annual consumption of powder was estimated to be in the region of 100 million lb., the greatest part of which was used for wigs. Make-up was applied so lavishly, that at a ball a husband often did not recognize his wife, even though she had had not the least intention of disguising herself.

The admiration for the art of the Far East, which in the period of the Régence had manifested itself particularly in the choice of its subtle colours, continued during the Rococo. But while the Régence had been attracted by the calm and simplicity of Chinese art, the Rococo turned above all towards its peculiarities, the bizarre and the capricious.

For the first time in the history of European costume the assymetrical ornament became acceptable. The Rococo endeavoured, wherever possible, to avoid straight lines and right angles. After a long period of neglect, flowers once again became the vogue and were now used more than ever. In Rococo fashion both real and artificial flowers were used as ornament for dress and hair.

The most remarkable object of Rococo dress was the dome-shaped skirt which was much broader than the conical skirt worn during the Regency of Philippe of Orléans. It was seen for the first time in 1718 at the Paris Opéra, became generally accepted in quite a short time and continued to be worn for almost 70 years. In the reign of Louis XV the framework of the skirt consisted of a series of five hoops which diminished in size towards the top and were fixed together with canvas or cotton or silk.

The idea was to contrast the bulk of the lower part of women's dresses with the narrow rib-cage and tiny waist. The overskirt was frequently left open in order to display better the sumptuousness of the material. The most popular fabric of Rococo fashion for both sexes was silk with flower motifs or heavy brocade. It was easy at first glance to see the fundamental difference between the stiff 'funnel' of Spanish fashion, which was combined with a high severe neckline, and the delicate panier skirt of the Rococo with its low décolleté. It was because of this that the guardians of morals attacked it so much more severely than its predecessor and for the same reason that it found many staunch defenders.

Already by the middle of the 18th century the outline of the skirt began gradually to become flatter and to form an ellipse. Its smooth and taut surface was embellished with ribbons, lace and artificial flowers in imitation of the stucco decorations on the walls of the salons. With these flowers the longing for nature of the Rococo ladies seems to have been satisfied, for their delicate high-heeled silk shoes would have made walking anywhere but on the parquet floors of the palaces exceedingly difficult. The daintily arranged hair, sprinkled with powder, completed the picture of the Rococo lady. Her white hair flirted with the grey hair of old age and at the same time blurred age differences. Only a little earlier it had been the incontrovertible rule to mask grey hair by dyeing or rinsing it rather than to allow oneself to appear older than one actually was. Since powdered hair needed a high colouring for contrast, even the men had to use make-up for, of course, they too powdered their wigs. The men's coat was the companion piece to the crinoline. Although cuffs and pocket flaps had now become smaller, it remained richly adorned with trimmings and embroidered ornaments, as did the waistcoat, which had become somewhat shorter and no longer had sleeves. The breeches were well fitting and came to just below the knees; stockings had lost their bright colours, and heels were a little lower.

In comparison with the Baroque period men's hair styles had undergone the greatest changes. The hair was combed backwards and held together with a silk ribbon, so that it formed the counterpart to the Prussian pigtail. This had first been ordered by Frederick William I 'for the convenience of the soldiers' of his army: it was taken up by the officers and became fashionable also with the burghers; eventually it crossed the frontiers of Germany. Gentlemen often had their hair carefully curled and they covered their heads with a tricorne.

The Rococo fashion spread quickly over the whole of Europe. The French ideas penetrated even into such artistically independent places as Venice, Rome, Vienna and Berlin, so that everywhere the salons and their frequenters were identical in appearance. The late Rococo fashion (1770–1789) embodied the wealth of a dying aristocracy, inclined to idleness, who lived on the income from their properties.

The political struggle for democracy mani-fested itself also in fashion. The costume of the young bourgeoisie became adapted to the requirements of any enterprising employer, whether master craftsman, merchant, banker or lawyer, and therefore it differed greatly from the cumbersome court fashion which was worn even at the smaller seats of the nobility. Already by the middle of the 18th century in England the costume of the burgher no longer had adverse connotations of class; on the contrary, the burghers took an active part in the further development of the fashion (in 1739 individual groups of young people in London imitated servants' dress in order to seem 'modern').

From the second half of the 18th century onwards the aristocracy began to lose the battle with the bourgeoisie for political and economic power in the state, and at the same time bourgeois fashion exerted an increasing influence on court dress. The comparatively simple garments of the English landed gentry together with the clothes worn by the bourgeoisie were gradually taken up everywhere in England and penetrated even to the court circles in London. Before and during the Revolution in France

302

the ballet and the ball were highly popular and to some extent influenced fashion. The dancers inspired not only the leading painters of the Paris Rococo, but also the creators of women's skirts.

When Louis XVI came to the throne (1774), ladies' coiffures had become so enormous that the strain for the neck had become almost too much. Cases are reported where the mouth was at a point halfway between the top of the hair and the soles of the feet. The ladies wore baskets with fruit or entire pastoral scenes on their heads including meadow and brook, two shepherds, sheepdog and shepherdess, or else windmills or three-masted frigates with hoisted sails.

In order to achieve greater height it was usual to fix a pad of horsehair to the back of the head, over which the hair was swept upwards. Quite a simple hair-style, however, sufficed to give shelter to the vermin with which most people were plagued.

In the same way that the Baroque had been a goldmine for the wigmakers, so the Rococo meant wealth for the hairdressers, who would spend hours arranging a single head of hair.

302 'Harlot's Progress'. William Hogarth. Engraving. The working clothes of men and women belonging to the artisan class are without ornament, although basically they are similar to the costume of the upper classes. The copperplate engraving clearly shows the differences between the social classes.

303 'Vanity'. William Hogarth. Engraving. The woman is dressed in simple working dress with apron and bonnet; the men in *justaucorps* and tricorne hats.

303

Their salaries achieved such proportions that even a rich lady could not afford the services of a hairdresser more often than once a week; those of lesser means only once a month. Before a grand ball the popular court hairdresser of the last of the Bourbons, Léonard, would work for days until he dropped.

His elegant customers, in the meantime, were sometimes unable to sleep properly for two days before a court ball, in order not to ruin the work of art which the hair artist had created on their heads. One can read about these never-to-be-repeated excesses of fashion in contemporary journals. In 1775 the *Haude-Spenersche Zeitung* printed 'a small contribution to the history of Paris fashion of which it could not possibly deprive its readers': 'At balls, which the queen attends twice a week, the Cavaliers are dressed in the fashion of the period of Henry IV. The ladies, in their turn, are distinguished by another peculiarity. They wear their hair piled very high and have it piled higher each day. A gentleman, who is a great admirer of England, has reported a new kind of headdress of this kind known as English Garden, and this is indeed an apt

description. Not satisfied with wearing a garden in their hair, the ladies go further and entire landscapes are now built on top of the head. Here one may see a lady wearing a village, there one with an entire wood, then again one with a large meadow, or with a great bridge, or with windmills. One must conclude that these edifices are very roomy because the artist has taken the opportunity to increase their value by adding some mechanical contraption; he has, where suitable, installed hidden organs, which from time to time play by themselves, or canaries which sing. What further limits such unnatural headgear may reach only time can tell.'

Traffic and transport arrangements were adapted to this fashion (*Vossische Zeitung* 1776): 'At Edinburgh in Scotland special sedan-chairs of enormous size have been constructed, intended for the female whose headgear has reached such a height that she cannot use an ordinary *portechaise*.'

Mightier coiffures were not possible. The tide turned. In 1779 one reads: 'Paris, 24th January. A local milliner has invented a type of headdress which is much lower than hitherto and

304 'Marriage à la Mode'. William Hogarth.
Engraving. The men in *justaucorps*, the
woman in the then very popular morning
dress, the negligé.

305 Johann Georg Ziesenis. The Countess
Schaumburg-Lippe. Staatliche Museen,
Gemäldegalerie, Berlin. A French evening
dress of brocade with lace decorating the
low neckline and the sleeves.

306 'Marriage à la Mode'. William Hogarth.
Engraving. English fashion of the period:
the men in *justaucorps* with rich embroidery,
the women in dresses with wide skirts and
deep décolletés.

305

306

307 Fashion drawing. Gallant pair in French court costume: the man in *justaucorps* with stiffened tails and wig, the lady in a skirt *à la polonaise* and feather hat.

308 Fashion drawing, circa 1775. Housewife and servant in dresses of the late Rococo period with hooped skirts: the lady's hair is dressed *à la circassienne*; the servant is wearing a bonnet, the *dormeuse*.

309 Thomas Gainsborough. The Morning Walk (detail). National Gallery, London. English fashion before the Revolution. The man in simple suit, the woman wearing a hat with feathers.

310 Dimitrij Lewizkij. Two pupils from the Convent at Smolny. Hermitage, Leningrad. The children's dress is, as always in this century, an exact imitation of adults' costume.

is intended only for theatres. This new fashion has found favour with all the ladies, who like to·be on good terms with nature, and each one wishes to be the first to possess a *Mignonne*, that is the name of the new fashion, obtainable for the sum of six to nine *livres*. Only a few beauties, who do not like to descend from their high pedestal and to whom it has occurred that the looks of the actresses under these *coiffures reformées* might have all the more effect on their lovers, are still opposed to them. One must hope, however, that these small pangs of envy will be silenced and that the menfolk, who are very interested in the matter, since hitherto, instead of the spectacle, they saw nothing but dark and fair hair, will manage to persuade their ladies to look upon this invention, which offers their eyes an un-impeded view, in a favourable light. The inventress is said to have sent to her clients in the most important cities of Europe models of these neat 'dwarf' bonnets called *carcasses à la nain* or *dormeuses racourcies*.

Another characteristic of the clothes worn in the last third of the 18th century was the hooped skirt with very strongly flattened outline: a woman wearing it would occupy an entire park bench and had to enter sideways through a double door. The corset on the whole retained its form, only the neckline be-came lower still. The décolleté was usually covered with a white triangular scarf known as fichu. The entire garment was over-

311 Diana Viscountess Crosbie. Engraving after Reynolds. Such 'informal street dress' of a young noblewoman can be seen in many contemporary portraits.

312 Thomas Gainsborough. Blue Boy. Henry E. Huntington Library and Art Gallery, San Marino, California. The boy is wearing a festive suit of satin. His hair is, of course, unpowdered and worn in the style of Van Dyck.

313 Johann Georg Ziesenis. Duke Schaumburg-Lippe. Staatliche Museen, Gemäldegalerie, Berlin. Festive suit consisting of *justaucorps* trimmed with braid, and tricorne.

314 François Janinet. Marie Antoinette. Engraving, 1777. With grand court dress a festive coiffure with pearls, ribbons and feathers is obligatory.

315 Thomas Gainsborough. Queen Charlotte of England. Royal Collection, London. Ceremonial ball dress with hooped skirt *à la française*, the so-called panier. The hair style was called *Pou au sentiment*.

313

314

Coiffure à la Flore

Pouf à l'Asiatique

Chapeau ou Casque Anglais orné de perles

Chapeau à la Nouvelle Angleterre

316

316–318 Nowhere are fashion's 'heights', not to say its drama, more apparent than in the chapter dealing with Rococo hair styles. Hundreds of fantasy names – with allusions which for us today are meaningless – were given to these increasingly foolhardy creations. The coiffures became ever more daring and bizarre – until the Revolution, and the hair *a la Titus*.

316 French hair styles after 1776. Coiffure *à la Flore*; coiffure with *Pouf à l'asiatique*; helmet type hat – *casque anglaise*; hat *à la Nouvelle Angleterre*.

317 'A Man's Trap'. Housedress from the period before the Revolution. Skirt and jacket, the so-called *caraco*; and a night bonnet, the so-called *dormeuse*.

318 French caricature of the giant hair styles, circa 1775.

219

319 320

embellished with embroidery, lace and garlands. These excesses of late Rococo fashion alone made it necessary to create a garment which could be worn at all times; the answer was a light house or morning dress – the negligé.

The arrogance and self-consciousness of fashion creators, who hitherto had been referred to simply as tailors, originated in this Rococo era. A little milliner, Rose Bertin, who had worked her way up, was called 'Minister of Fashion'. If the genuine memoirs of a time which seethes with spurious ones report correctly, then Queen Marie-Antoinette's passion for finery was the evil work of that Rose Bertin, who doubtless must have been gifted with a sure taste. A reliable witness is the Baroness d'Oberkirch, in whose memoirs this mischief-maker of the Rue Saint-Honoré is several times mentioned; in 1782 she describes a visit to that very famous milliner of the Queen: 'Mlle Bertin struck me as a strange personality, she was puffed up with conceit and regarded herself as equal in

importance to the Princesses. It is said that one day a lady from the provinces came to see her for the purpose of ordering a hat for an introduction to the Queen. It was to be something entirely new. The milliner arrogantly looked her up and down and, apparently satisfied with the result of her examination, turned round with a majestic air and said to one of her employees: "Show Madame the result of my latest work with her Majesty".'

By the end of the 1880s men's costume had begun to lose some of the excesses of ornamentation which the seventies had lavished on it: it became less colourful and decorative and the gold embroidery on coat and waistcoat became more restrained. The coat became simpler, with a somewhat higher collar, whalebone was dispensed with and the garment was frequently made of a delicately striped fabric. The waistcoat was shorter and came to just below the waist; breeches had undergone no significant change, but stockings were no longer so colourful and richly adorned – now they were mostly made of wool.

321

322

323

319–322 Paris fashions did not remain confined to France even when the Rococo excesses were at their height – this is the proof of France's supremacy. In Germany, too, the ladies endeavoured to keep up with the fashion in silhouette and accessories, as can be seen in these contemporary fashion examples. The man, on the other hand, appears modest and thus foreshadows the sobriety of men's clothing in the 19th and 20th centuries.

319, 320 German engravings from the *Modealmanach* 1786–1788. Rococo dresses with hooped skirts and flounces, and with matching hats.

321, 322 German engravings from the *Modealmanach* 1786–1788.

323 Engraving after Duhamel. In this nobleman's costume, *à la française*, one can see the predecessor of the *frac* or tail-coat.

221

324 From a French fashion journal. Evening dress. Feathers were much used even in day dresses.

The French Revolution and the Directoire

The French Revolution shook society all over Europe; it changed the political and economic situation; it had an effect on the reciprocal relationship of the sexes; and, not unnaturally, it was reflected in the costume of the period. Clothes became more comfortable and practical and fashion extended its sphere of influence to further sections of the population. Even before the storming of the Bastille hooped skirts and pigtails had disappeared. Rousseau's call for simplicity and Voltaire's rationalism were echoed in dress. The new fashion did not, however, hail from France, but came from England, whose citizens had earlier undergone a revolution, had quickly become strong economically and had expressed their matter-of-fact outlook also in dress. Besides the French Revolution, the formation of the United States of America in 1776, too, influenced clothing – some characteristic features were carried forward into the 19th century.

Although in France Rousseau's call for a return to nature and for a simple life in the country had no other result than to cause Marie Antoinette and the women of her court to play at shepherdesses in the royal parks, life in England developed on very different lines. Not only the climate of the British Isles, but lengthy sojourns in the colonies, life during long sea voyages and the Englishman's love of sport, led to a preference for practical clothes. The dominating role in England was played by the landed gentry, who managed their own estates, who were passionate lovers of hunting and race horses and who would hardly have fitted in with the tricorne-clad continental aristocracy. The English riding coat, which was something like the *frac* or tail-coat adapted for riding, the short waistcoat, the comfortable breeches, which were sometimes made of fine leather, the high leather boots and the round hat placed the Englishman for the first time in the history of costume in the forefront of men's fashions.

Mode à l'anglaise in the 1770s and 1780s was also an effective slogan not only in Germany (where this fashion was also known as 'Werther costume' after Geothe's famous hero) but even, after overcoming some initial resistance, in France. In 1768 Helferich Peter Sturz, a German writer, describes the contemporary Paris scene: 'To some extent we are avenged by the anglomania of the Frenchmen of today. Everywhere one meets wandering riding coats with fragile, sketchy and shadowy beings fidgeting in their folds; or coachmen evidently belonging to the race of Titans enthroned on English coaches and guiding their steeds with voices of thunder, with a few more giants at the back; not seldom a terrible cur jumps up and down beside the coach, in a corner of which you become aware of the wrapped-up remains of an old family – your heart is filled with pity for these pigmies surrounded by monsters.

'At the same time the place is crawling with Englishmen wishing to resemble Paris fops at any price. Nothing is more Hudibrastic than to behold a sinewy Briton, dressed *à la française* by his tailor, rearing and struggling in his unaccustomed trappings like an unbroken horse in sledge harness. It is strange that the sons of freedom willingly submit to any fashion and that the submissive Frenchman always adds a characteristically national touch. When dressed in riding habit he attaches a large bunch of flowers to his chest, and at the nape of his neck the small English 'catogan' swells to the size of a pudding. While the English Miss puts a chip-hat, decorated with a rose, on top of her curly brown hair, the *chapeau à l'anglaise* sits crookedly on the Frenchwoman's powdered head and the rose becomes a garland. Even the much praised costumes in the local theatre are so 'frenchified' as to be almost unrecognizable.'

Thus the French mistrust of English fashion was replaced by an absolute craze for all things English, with the result that in France coffee was replaced by punch and tea, French cognac by Scotch whisky, the Paris cabriolet by the London Tilbury, the traditional poodle by a bulldog, and even the characteristic French 'r' had to give way to the silent English 'r', so that

325

326

329

the average Frenchman could no longer understand a fashionable Parisian. All these fanciful notions continued until Napoleon made an end to them. He could not stand Albion and forced his subjects to adopt the same attitude.

Although the ground for a reform in dress had been prepared long before the Revolution, in May 1789 the Master of Ceremonies, Dreux de Brézé, produced an ancient order dating from 1614 which referred to the costume of the various estates and ordered, or rather attempted to order, the third estate to dress 'very simply' in black so that they might be distinguished from the prelates in their purple and the nobility in their gold-embroidered, lace-trimmed garments.

But in the same year the National Assembly abolished this antiquated law and the democratization of fashion became a legally established fact. The disdained, 'very simple' costume of M. de Brézé, according to a decision of the legislating Assembly, became the ceremonial dress of the victorious citizens at the inaugural meeting of the new Parliament. The splendour of court fashion was left to the

327

328

330

325 From a French fashion journal. Young lady in a *redingote à l'anglomane*, and a straw hat trimmed with feathers.

326 From a French fashion journal. Young lady in a hitched-up skirt, sleeves *à l'espagnole*, and a *turban d'amour*.

327 From a French fashion journal. The young lady of fashion is wearing morning dress and on her head a *toque à la couronne d'amour*.

328 From a French fashion journal. Young man in street suit and 'jockey hat'.

329 From a French fashion journal. Winter court dress with fur trimmings.

330 From a French fashion journal. Grand ceremonial dress.

servants and lackeys. The bourgeoisie of the Revolution had no objection to a simple and utilitarian costume, but it objected in principle to its arrogant enforcement by decrees from above.

From the beginning of the Revolution until the death of Robespierre (1793) women's costume remained faithful to the fashion of the *Ancien Régime*, while at the same time simplifying it considerably. This simplification was necessitated by economic considerations as well as by fear of a world, recently grown hypersensitive, in which it was not without peril to be seen in the street in delicate expensive fabrics and with powdered coiffures. Simplicity and a certain amount of *laissez faire* in dress were the expression of a progressive attitude. But the basic form of the costume remained unchanged. The revolutionary garment of the women was the dress *à la grecque*, which was widely worn only after 1793. It was reminiscent of Greece because it was light and comfortable, but the strong emphasis on the bosom and the train were uncharacteristic of Greek costume.

331

332   333

334   335

336

After the execution of Louis XVI radical views in fashion prevailed. Powder was considered royalist, so that having a powdered head was likely to bring one in danger of the guillotine. Before the October days of 1792 the extreme group of the Jacobins wanted to introduce a special republican costume which was to consist of the red Phrygian cap of the galley slaves, of a blue sleeveless waistcoat, reminiscent of the peasants' *carmagnole*, as well as of long

331 From a French fashion journal. Young girl in morning dress *à l'anglaise*.

332-335 Illustrations from the book *Modes et usages au temps de Marie-Antoinette*, which was the basis of the business journals of the Paris milliner Mme Eloffe. These illustrations give the reader a good idea of the eccentric luxury, especially in hats and hair styles, of the years 1787-1790.

336 A variation of the so-called bonnet *à la notable* which was worn over a white powdered wig.

white sailors' trousers. Pétion, the Mayor of Paris, was, however, too good a citizen to allow the young republic to be compromised by a tasteless tricolour costume.

Nevertheless, at the critical time many red caps could be seen in the auditoria of the theatres, for people with or without a hat were suspected by the radical elements. During a few performances of Voltaire's *Mort de César*, not only Caesar's murderer but also his bust wore a Phrygian cap. Even the fashion journals during the Revolution contained more political articles than reports on fashion.

The end of the 18th century saw one of the most important turning-points in the history of fashion; men's costume gradually grew less colourful, varied and ornamental; it became more sombre. Man seemed to have renounced his right to beauty and concentrated instead on the practical. The French Revolution changed men's dress far more than women's and from that time onwards variations in men's costume as compared with women's have become negligible.

To find the reason for this phenomenon we must examine the political and social happenings which culminated in the French Revolu-

337

338

339

340

337 Thomas Lawrence. Queen Charlotte. National Gallery, London. A white wig and a white fichu, edged with black lace, which fills the low décolleté, are part of festive court dress. The cuffs are of ruched lace.

338 Engraving after a drawing by Desrais. Promenade on the Boulevard des Italiens. Different kinds of outdoor dress: the ladies are wearing hats or bonnets decorated with ribbons, dresses with fichus, the skirts ending in trains. The gentlemen with top hats are dressed in tail-coats and knee-breeches.

339 Clergy, Nobility and Third Estate. Contemporary Engraving. The costume of the representatives of the three Estates was expressly laid down in 1789.

340 Francisco de Goya. Portrait of Signora Bermusedo. Museum of Fine Arts, Budapest. Richly adorned Spanish court dress.

tion. Hitherto the chief purpose of decorative clothing had been the differentiation and division of people according to birth and wealth, which the nobility between the 14th and 18th centuries had secured by numerous edicts. Such tendencies were totally opposed to the spirit of republican France. If the aristocracy wanted to stay alive in the future and to continue competing with the bourgeoisie, it would have to turn to the very activities with which the people had won their victory. So they took over the dress of the rich citizens.

The Third Estate determined fashion trends, in that the deputies at the National Assembly in Versailles in 1789 came in black tail-coats and top hats, though for the time being they still wore powdered wigs and short knee breeches. But the long pantaloons worn with a new type of low-cut shoe soon caught on. Elegant society looked askance upon these predecessors of our modern trousers and called the fashion 'sans culottes' – without breeches. Natural hair, too, soon became the symbol of a republican way of thinking, whereas wig, pigtail and hair ribbons were regarded as reactionary. The use of powder was condemned as anti-social, 'the flour necessary for the production of powder' was 'destined for feeding the people'. Hair became generally shorter, a hair style named à la Titus became popular. In 1793 a coiffure à la victime is mentioned, which imitated the head shorn ready for execution. With this fashion the aristocracy had originally intended to show their sympathy with their condemned peers.

As the political situation became more settled so the fashion stablilized. Republican feelings were no longer demonstrated by wearing clothes in the colours of the tricolour. The members of the Directoire regarded the Greek democracy as their model, the First Consul looked upon the Roman republic as the ideal and so the dress of both became the inspiration for the fashion of all Frenchwomen. Men's dress had nothing to do with classical costume. Under the Directoire women regarded it as modern to be able to put their entire wardrobe into one bag. Until 1797 fabrics became progressively more delicate and transparent. Ultimately the transparent muslin was replaced by the even more transparent tulle. In winter women wore something akin to the 'body-stocking' of today, as underwear. The bosom was exposed more and more, and the breasts laced higher and higher. Mme. Hamelin declared the garment to be a ridiculous sack and the shroud of beauty.

The queen of Paris fashion around 1795, Mme

341

341 Francisco de Goya. Game of Blind Man's Buff. Prado, Madrid. The young people's costume is a mixture of Rococo fashion and Spanish national dress.

342 Francisco de Goya. Comtessa del Carpio, Duchess of Solana. Musée du Louvre Paris. Spanish court dress of the 18th century is clearly influenced by national costume.

343 Jacques Louis David. Portrait of Mme Halelin. National Gallery of Art, Washington. This is the typical French Empire fashion; lightly curled hair, plaited across the forehead and a softly flowing garment with deep décolleté and high waist, the so-called chemise-dress.

344 *Journal des Luxus und der Moden*, 1791. The top hat with cockade is worn with a long coat – the 'garrick' – which has several layers of collars, tails, and ornamental buttons.

345 Jacques Louis David. Design for bourgeois dress, 1794. David, who always took a lively interest in political events – he was a Jacobin and follower of Robespierre – made this design for the *Nouveau Français*.

346 From a French fashion journal, 1791. Street dress from the Directoire period; a tight-fitting corset with fichu round the neck and a sash round the waist. Braid trimmings and flower motifs embroidered at the hem.

344

345

346

234

348

349

350

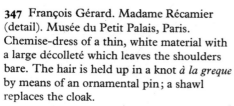

347 François Gérard. Madame Récamier (detail). Musée du Petit Palais, Paris. Chemise-dress of a thin, white material with a large décolleté which leaves the shoulders bare. The hair is held up in a knot *à la greque* by means of an ornamental pin; a shawl replaces the cloak.

348 Revolutionary with pike. Anonymous engraving of the year 1793. The revolutionary is wearing a Phrygian cap with cockade, a shirt, a short waistcoat, the *carmagnole*, long sailor's trousers the so-called *matelots*, and wooden shoes called *sabots*.

349 Flag-bearer. Copperplate engraving after Louis Boilly. Circa 1792. Instead of the Jacobin cap the flag-bearer is wearing a bicorne hat with cockade, a striped waistcoat with a jabot, a short jacket and *matelots*.

350 Jacques Louis David. Madame Récamier (detail). Musée du Louvre, Paris. Mme Récamier is again depicted in a chemise-dress with the typical Empire hair style *à la Titus*.

Tallien, née de Cabarrus, who was known as 'Notre-Dame-de-Thermidor', mistress of the Director Barras and secretary to the municipal council of Paris, was the centre of attention wherever she appeared. She had all the spiritual and physical attributes which enabled her literally not to have to hide anything, which in any case was never her intention. The basis of her sparse dress was nothing but a silk body-covering. In the autumn of 1795

351 Jacques Louis David. The Duchess of Orvilliers. Musée du Louvre, Paris. Simple dress of the time of the Revolution; a dark dress with large white collar and fichu; in addition a fine lace shawl.

352 Caricature by Vernet. *Les Incroyables.* The dandified fashion after the Revolution had many variants. The women wore large hats with ribbons and extremely wide skirts with many flounces. The men were proud of

351

352   353

their jabots which grew ever bigger and soon
– at least according to the caricaturist –
covered part of the face.

353 French caricature of 1796. *Incroyables
. . . !* 'Incredible . . . !' This word described
the dandy who exaggerated the fashion.

354 Jacques Louis David. Self portrait.
Musée du Louvre, Paris. While working,
the painter wears a house coat with white
jabot; the unpowdered hair indicates the
post-revolutionary period.

355 French caricature. Three Graces from
the Directoire period. The drawing alludes
clearly to the fact that the freely flowing
garments, worn without corsets, were not
created for all women.

356 *Gallery of Fashion.* London, 1797. The
fashionable silhouette is very clearly shown
in this illustration from the handsome
English fashion journal; when in profile the
face is hidden by the broad-brimmed bonnet.

354

355   356

357

359

358

357 *Journal des Dames*, 1799. Coiffure *à la hollandaise* and chemise-dress which has a train decorated with artificial flowers.

358 *Journal des Dames*, 1799. Fashionable Parisian costume from the turn of the century; peasant bonnet trimmed with gauze.

359 *The Ladies' Magazine*, 1800. These English chemise-dresses are decorated with ribbons and flounces.

360 From a fashion journal, 1801. Evening dresses, too, now have flowing lines and the girdle placed high under the breasts.

361 *Journal des Dames*, 1799. The London lady now wears chemise-dresses of a different type; the neckline is trimmed with lace; she wears long gloves and carries a fan.

362 From a fashion journal, 1803. Designs of hats and bonnets *à la mode* intended for wear with street costume.

360   361

362

363   364

she appeared at a ball at the Paris Opéra in a sleeveless tunic of white satin, entirely without underwear. The only 'covering' of her hands were rings, on her feet she wore antique sandals. Even Talleyrand expressed his appreciation of Mme Tallien's taste with the words: 'It is not possible to expose oneself more sumptuously.'

The composer Johann Friedrich Reichardt, whom Goethe admired and who had been musical director of Frederic the Great in Berlin, passed many an evening at her hospitable home after Mme Tallien's divorce. He noticed that 'Mme Cabarrus had wound her magnificent black hair in long thick braids round her head right down to her forehead and close to the neck. Ropes of genuine pearls ran through her shiny hair. She was dressed entirely in white satin with masses of magnificent lace'.

The middle of the 19th century produced two peculiarities of fashion: the *Incroyables* and their female counterpart, the *Merveilleuses*. It is clear from these names that the garments they wore gave the impression of self-caricatures rather than of solidly clad people.

The *Incroyables* exaggerated English fashion till it became totally absurd. The large white cravat not only covered the neck but the chin as well; its dimensions were more like those of a napkin. The apparently purposely, ill-fitting tail-coat in its obligatory blue, with high shoulders and broad lapels, and with tails which sometimes swept the ground, while the front barely covered the chest, stood in strong contrast to the yellow pantaloons, which came up to the chest and which made the tiny yellow waistcoat appear quite insignificant. The pantaloons terminated in a pair of high military boots.

The *Merveilleuses* wore long shift-like, sleeveless dresses of fine muslin, usually with a train; on their feet they wore sandals. The head covering varied but their hair was rather neglected and sometimes flowed wildly, exactly like that of the *Incroyables*.

363 *Hamburger Journal der Mode und Eleganz*, 1802. The dresses have double skirts; the lower skirt reaches to the ground and has a train, the knee-length overskirt forms a point at the back. The turbans are decorated with long feathers.

364 *Hamburger Journal der Mode und Eleganz*, 1803. The lady's shawl is laid in folds over her arm. The gentleman is wearing a tail-coat with white trousers and high boots.

365 James Gillray. Fashion caricature. The turban with its long ostrich feather is characteristic of the fashion *à l'anglaise*. The nursing mother is wearing a softly flowing dress without girdle, with oblong slits in the upper part; she has elbow-length gloves and a fan; the chambermaid's dress is old-fashioned and her bonnet is the *baigneuse* which used to be worn before the Revolution.

366 Francisco de Goya. The family of Charles IV. Prado, Madrid.

365

366

241

The Empire (1804-1815)

The Empire derives its name from the period during which Napoleon I ruled as Emperor after his coronation in 1804. During the preceding Consulate (1799-1804) costume had not been markedly different from that of the Directoire. In due course it had become clear, however, that clothing which was too scanty was unsuitable for the Paris climate. For this reason, and still more for reasons of commercial policy, the Emperor prohibited the import of Indian muslin, and this in turn gave a new lease of life to the silk industry at Lyons. Under Napoleon's rule warmer fabrics came back into fashion and taffetas, velvets and brocades were again in vogue. The neckline was raised and long sleeves were 'in'. In the case of short-sleeved dresses long gloves covered the rest of the arm. The train disappeared completely from everyday dresses and was retained only in official court robes.

By about 1810 dresses only came to the ankles and revealed the low, soft, heelless slippers. In the first decade of the 19th century the waistline slowly began to return to its natural place (from its position immediately below the breasts). Although women's dresses became more colourful, classic white still predominated.

The French court interrupted, at least where Paris was concerned, the natural progress of fashion. Napoleon wanted to carry on the traditions of the court of Versailles and ordered his court painters, David and Isabey, to make designs for ceremonial robes. Many of these designs were made for the Imperial pair personally, as well as for other high dignitaries of the court; the robes were worn at functions, the splendour of which was to symbolize the greatness and wealth of the huge new Empire and its ruler, who wanted to be the first in the history of the modern era to rule over the entire world.

Napoleon's ministers and marshalls were allowed to design their own uniforms according to their personal taste and discretion; it is not surprising, therefore, that their wives, mistresses and the rest of their female entourage regarded the creation of fantastic fashion products as the goal of their ambitions.

Sumptuous pelerines, short culottes embroidered with gold and silver, long trains, diadems, chains and necklaces of diamonds, ornaments made from the feathers of rare birds, Spanish collars and delicate lace once more briefly came to life.

Bonaparte carefully observed the costume of his courtiers. A lady who dared to appear twice in the same outfit was often made unpleasantly aware of the Emperor's disappointment. The great Corsican attached considerable importance to the magnificence of courtly fashion; he liked to see elegant women amidst the splendour of his court, for he knew that the people in the lands beyond the Rhine, the Alps, the Channel and the Atlantic Ocean followed current Paris fashion trends with keen attention.

Napoleon I thus takes his place among the ranks of French rulers who took an active interest in France's influence on fashion in the rest of the world. In her lengthy memoirs the Duchess of Abrantes describes the boost which Paris life had received under Napoleon: 'All members of the Congress came to Paris to take part in the sumptuous feasts which were given at the instigation of the First Consul, so that the people too could have their share in the rejoicing, and so that there would be a turnover in money, which would benefit more than a hundred thousand people in Paris who lived by the labour of their hands and were almost exclusively occupied with the production of luxury articles for the upper classes.

'The feasts given by the government were a signal for balls, banquets and festivities of all kinds not only for Paris but for the rest of France. The impetus which these activities gave to life in Paris only ended in 1814. Every day one might receive ten invitations for the evening.

'Madame Bonaparte, who understood to a high degree the art of being well-dressed, set an example of the greatest elegance. Nothing presented so handsome a picture as a ball at

Malmaison, at which were present so many graceful young women who had been introduced by the military household of the First Consul; they formed even then, though without bearing the name, the court of Madame Bonaparte.

'All were young, many pretty, and I only know one who deserved to be called ugly. When one saw them all in dresses of white crêpe, decorated with flowers, their hair crowned with garlands, which were as fresh as these youthful, laughing faces, full of charm and beautified by happiness, the lively dancing in these ballrooms presented a wonderful spectacle. A touch of piquancy was added by the fact that the First Consul, as well as the men who with him held the fate of Europe in the balance, strolled to and fro among the dancers. The costumes were frequently replaced and the first year of the Consulate had not yet gone by, when prosperity had come to the manufacturing towns of France, which flourished in honour of their fatherland.'

Under Napoleon there was a considerable widening of the gulf between bourgeois fashion and the romantic and traditional costume of the French court, which was largely the product of the Emperor's will. The Napoleonic wars had had such a devastating effect on the economic situation of almost all the European countries, that the citizens, for financial reasons alone, could not emulate the luxurious dress worn at the French court. Court dress stagnated into ceremonial uniform and only a few of its decorative elements were taken up on a large scale by the general public during the subsequent romantic epoch. For many European courts, however, the fashion at Versailles remained the guiding force.

English tailoring, which had made an impact on French fashion even before the Revolution, continued to influence the development of men's dress. As a result of the Emperor's militarism it lost the revolutionary characteristics which it had assumed in France at the turn of the century and acquired a certain military air. Trousers more and more resembled those of today. The most decorative feature in men's costume which, as is so often the case in fashion, was also the most uncomfortable, was concentrated round the neck. The collars of shirt and coat, together with the cravat, were so intricately arranged as to give the impression, that the wearer wanted to prove that it *was* possible to move his head, even under such trying circumstances.

Napoleonic ambition and the Wars of Liberation, together with the romantic movement, caused an upsurge of nationalistic feeling in the various countries and a desire to be rid of the tyranny of French fashion. But in Germany, for instance, the attempt to introduce a national fashion soon came to grief, in spite of the patriotic spirits who had demanded that the Germans should renounce fashion changes in the future in favour of a newly-to-be-created 'German National Costume'.

One of the instigators of this movement was Ernst Moritz Arndt. He wrote a paper entitled 'Manners, Fashion and the Power of Dress' in which he pleaded for a costume which would enhance man's dignity and humanity rather than one which suggested flippancy and frivolity. But although he gave detailed instructions, his 'eternal German national costume' stubbornly remained nothing but a regional fashion and he had to admit defeat.

A satirist named Th. H. Friedrich made fun of this abortive attempt: '. . . no doubt the desired goal would have been reached, had not a hostile chance, namely the arrival of the latest French fashion journal, nipped the well-meant revolution in the bud.'

The most notable result of the Napoleonic wars where clothes are concerned was the fact that, after the Congress of Vienna, Frenchmen completely adopted English tailoring, while English women took over an only slightly modified Directoire fashion.

It would seem that fashion was the field where the reconciliation of the two arch enemies was easiest to achieve.

368 Jean Auguste Dominique Ingres. Madame Devaucay. Musée Condé, Chantilly. Empire style evening dress of velvet with oval neckline and high waist; a broad shawl with embroidered edges, and a fan. The puffed sleeves are typical of dresses of the period.

369 Jean Auguste Dominique Ingres. Madame Rivière. Musée du Louvre, Paris. A chemise-dress of a white satin-type material edged with ornamental braid and a shawl of precious cashmere wool. The jewellery is simple: a smooth necklace and armbands.

368

369

370

370 Jean Auguste Dominique Ingres.
Monsieur Rivière. Musée du Louvre, Paris
With the dark tail-coat and light kneebreeches
a cravat is worn, knotted in the style of the
period.

371 From a French fashion journal, 1809.
The shawl worn with this softly flowing, high
waisted dress is permanently attached to it.

372 *Costume Parisien*. 1811. Court dress of
Napoleon's time has a deep décolleté, the
long skirt with train is of silk from Lyons
and decorated all over with artificial flowers
and twigs. Diadem, necklace and long gloves
complete the outfit.

373 From an English fashion journal. 1809.
The thin material of this ankle-length dress
makes a pelerine a necessity.

374 From an English fashion journal, 1809.
The style of this street dress is reminiscent
of ancient Greece.

375 *La Mésangère*, 1800. The Timid
Skater. Sports clothes of the Empire were no
different from ordinary outdoor clothes.

371 372

373

374

375

376   377   378

380   381

376-383 From the Paris fashion journal
Costume Parisien, 1810-1811.

376 Tall straight hat with a tuft of feathers hanging from one side.

377 Bonnet and dress of velour with lace.

378 Hair combed back, plaited into a knot.

379 The hems of the street dresses are trimmed with strips of fur and embroidered braid.

380 Around 1810 street dresses were generally decorated with flounces.

381 Dresses with frilled collars.

382 Street dress of Levantine cut.

383 Straw bonnet with feathers and dress with finely pleated frills.

384 From an English fashion journal, 1810. Dress with an antique air.

379

382 383

384

385 *Costume Parisien*, 1810–1811. Male dress-suit. The large hat is trimmed with feathers. At his side the cavalier carries a dress sword.

386 From a German fashion journal, 1810–1811. Street costume.

387 *Costume Parisien*, 1810. Percale bonnet edged with flowers. The low cut back is trimmed with ruches, as is the hem of the dress.

385

386

387

388 *Costume Parisien*, 1810. Overcoat and trousers which become gaiters at the bottom. The gentleman is carrying a top hat.

389 *Costume Parisien*, 1811. Outdoor clothes with an Italian straw hat. The fichu is set into the dress.

390 *Costume Parisien*, 1812. Lady and gentleman in outdoor clothes.

388

389

390

391

392

393

394

395

391 Antoine Jean Gros. Madame Récamier. Galerie Strohmayer, Zagreb. A street dress with lace bonnet.

392 From a German fashion journal, 1814. Sleeves *à la mamelouk*.

393 *Costume Parisien*, 1814. Ball dress of Indian muslin.

394 From a French fashion journal, circa 1815. This dress with lace flounces at neck, sleeves and hem, together with the tall hat, completely hides the natural body proportions. It is hardly likely that this design would find much favour.

395 Jacques Louis David. Madame de Tangy with her daughters. Musée du Louvre, Paris.

The Restoration (1815–1820

After the final defeat of Napoleon by the armies of the coalition the Bourbons wanted to wipe out all reminders of the past epoch and especially of the revolution. The government strove for a return to the political and cultural conditions which had existed before the revolution, and costume was to be a true reflection of the intentions of the newly restored rulers. But in this they were only partially successful. Women's dresses now barely reached the ankle and were much more decorative than during the Empire; trimmings were many and various. Although until 1820 the predominant colour remained white, exceptions were more frequent. The separate parts of woman's garments became more clearly distinguished and their rigid cone and cylinder shapes obscured the feminine form. As the plasticity of the clothes lessened so their properties of concealment increased.

The neckline came much higher and the sleeves, which were puffed at the top, extended to the wrist. Only evening dress remained as deeply décolleté as before. The modern distinction between day and evening clothes dates from this time. Once again the longing of women for a slender figure was demonstrated in fashion; even the shape of the hats sometimes supported their endeavour.

Between 1800 and 1830 was the hey-day of the English dandy. His chief characteristics were sangfroid, polite impertinence, cold sarcasm, irony, taste and elegance. He attempted to bring the outward forms of human behaviour – bodily movement, content and form of language, gestures and dress – into perfect harmony.

One member of this small tribe of arrogant and eccentric young men has been able to excite the admiration of several famous writers from Balzac to Virginia Woolf; this was George Bryan Brummel (1778–1840), the king of the dandies, whom his contemporaries called Beau Brummel. His biographer admiringly reports that the Prince of Wales would spend many hours watching him as he dressed, to fathom the secret of his impeccable taste.

Brummel's secret was simplicity. He avoided loud colours, jewellery and superfluous embellishments. The magic of his clothes was indefinable. His elegance lay in the unobtrusiveness of his attire. Since Brummel, this restraint has become the foremost principle in male clothing. It has been said that taste is almost as rare as genius. According to all reports of the period Brummel must have been a genius in all questions of taste. And with it he ruled men's fashion in London.

But in the end Brummel's impudence became too much for his royal patron, and the Prince dropped him. Eventually Brummel accumulated so many debts that in May 1816 in the depth of night he had to flee to France. Thus began the Brummel myth in London. Twelve years later he was back among elegant society in the form of a character in a best seller of the period: *Pelham* or *The Adventures of a Gentleman* by Bulwer Lytton. He was called Russelton in the book but everyone knew that it was Brummel.

'. . . the contemporary and rival of Napoleon – the autocrat of the great world of fashion and cravats – the mighty genius before whom aristocracy had been humbled and *ton* abashed – at whose nod the haughtiest noblesse of Europe had quailed – who had introduced, by a single example, starch into neckclothes, and had fed the pampered appetites of his boot-tops on champagne – whose coat and whose friends were cut with equal grace – and whose name was connected with every triumph that the world's great virtue of audacity could achieve – the illustrious, the immortal Russelton stood before me.'

One thing has remained with us from the era of the dandies: the black *frac* or frock-coat. It is the only article of clothing, apart from the top hat, which, with small modifications has survived the vagaries of fashion. It was the *frac* of Werther's day 'fully dressed with his boots on, in blue frock-coat and yellow waistcoat'. This is how Werther is found at the end of the book.

And in Goethe's *Dichtung und Wahrheit*

(Poetry and Truth) the clothes of another unfortunate suicide, Jerusalem, are described in even greater detail: 'He dressed in the traditional Low German style, which is an imitation of the English: a blue frock-coat, a chamois-yellow waistcoat and buckskins, and boots with brown tops.'

It is impossible to think of Brummel without this blue frock-coat. In the meantime long trousers had come into fashion. When in the summer of 1829 Felix Mendelssohn Bartholdy gave a concert in London he was dressed for the occasion: 'For Beckchens fashion journal: white, very long trousers, brown silk waistcoat, black cravat and blue frac.' Thus he writes in a letter. It was only the furore made by the book *Pelham*, in which Bulwer Lytton advocates black for frock-coats, which made black acceptable. And not very much has changed since 1840, when H. Hauff complained about the *frac* in his aggressive booklet *Fashions and Costumes*: 'the *frac* is a symbol of present day civilization; it is the uniform that the man of culture has to wear for all social occasions and ceremonies; we see it everywhere, where life is serious and where pleasure is taken seriously; it is worn by the supplicant, the communicant, the godfather, the mourner, and it is likewise worn by the man going to a ball, the ardent admirer of the leading lady and the fastidious tea drinker. It is the outward manifestation of a mystery, and while fashion may make occasional superficial modifications in its exterior it is inimitable at core. It has remained untouched in its basic form for more than two generations; and no dandy, intent upon setting the fashion, has been able to gain acceptance for the *frac* in anything but a serious and sombre colour.'

For this, however, the time was to blame. The gentleman of the 19th century, in the midst of the industrial revolution, worked in an office, where he accumulated the wealth with which his wife dazzled society. Solidity and sobriety were the order of the day, not gay colours. Here even the successor of the luckless 'First Gentleman of Europe', the pleasure-loving Prince of Wales, who later became Edward VII (1841-1910) could do nothing to change matters, and his inventive spirit – if anecdote is to be believed – had to be content with providing trousers with crease and turn-ups.

397 Henry Raeburn. Lieutenant-Colonel Bruce McMurdo. National Gallery, London. Even while fishing the gentleman is wearing the customary *frac* with high pointed collar, long trousers and low cut shoes.

398 From an English fashion journal, 1818. The thin chemise dress is decorated with narrow, dark braid, the turban with feathers. The gentleman is wearing the *frac*, a high starched collar, pantaloons and top hat. The side-whiskers were known as *favoris*.

399 *Costumes Parisiens*, 1819. The lady is wearing a dress lavishly trimmed with fur and from beneath it a ruff is visible at the neck. This is repeated in the bonnet. In her hand she carries a small bag, the reticule. The gentleman is fashionably dressed in the redingote – waisted and with revers on the collar.

398

399

400

401

404

405

406

402

403

407

400 *Modes d'Hommes*, 1819. The redingote *à la chevalière* has the highly fashionable shawl collar and bar fastening.

401 *Wiener Moden*, 1819. The hat richly decorated with ostrich feathers and the high-waisted street dress form a pretty ensemble.

402 *Wiener Moden*, 1819. Hat with ostrich feathers, street dress of a dark material, décolleté with short puffed sleeves, and the inevitable cashmere shawl.

403 *Wiener Zeitschrift für Kunst, Literatur, Theater und Mode*, 1819. For the evening or a ball: the *frac* with long tails, which come to the knees, starched, pointed collar, waistcoat with horizontal stripes and ankle-length trousers; a top hat completes the outfit.

404-407 Drawings by Eugène Delacroix. Musée du Louvre, Paris. They clearly reveal the silhouette of the man dressed in redingote.

The Biedermeier Style and the Romantic Era (1820–1840)

No other century was so much occupied with style – and no other century was so poor in style – as the 19th. Even as the machine age got into its stride the Romantics built Gothic parliaments and cathedrals, Renaissance palaces and banks; and fashion, too, had recourse to past glories. In the thirties it was often the least artistic features of the various styles which were selected.

Muddled aesthetic views contrasted with the mighty economic upsurge of industry. The number of consumers and would-be consumers rose, but the customer was not very discriminating. He was quite content with imitation goods and did not insist on originals. Beauty and quality of artistic craftsmanship were replaced by generally cheaper mass production. The bourgeoisie did not vaunt its wealth. The men were occupied with their business enterprises, their wives wished to avoid adverse gossip, and the daughters were sheltered from the world until the day of their wedding. It was not a time which encouraged excesses.

In the 18th century generals who had been lucky in war did not hide their decorations. They took general recognition for granted; they expected to receive the acclaim of their fellow men and they were not disappointed. But in the middle of the 19th century a general would have been considered arrogant indeed if he had stood out in any way from the other 'gentlemen'. Kings, whether Louis Philippe in France or the British monarch, doffed their uniforms and wore dark clothes with top hat and umbrella exactly like other rich citizens.

The more the bourgeoisie made plain their belief in a general levelling, the more fashion everywhere became independent of social status. Paris and London set the fashion trends which made only negligible concessions to regional character and taste. While dress in Paris favoured the town dweller, in London it was more suitable for country wear; what was decorative and gay in Paris became practical and sober in London; in Paris national costume influenced fashion, in London sport. Other differences might be due to different sources of raw materials or to different processes of dyeing.

A friend of Jean Paul and E. T. A. Hoffmann, a certain Baron Vaerst, set down in a book which has long been forgotten some observations on the atmosphere of fashionable Paris. Himself an ex-guards' captain, financial speculator, newspaper proprietor and theatre director, he wrote about the 'serene luxury' and 'tasteful elegance' which 'assails the spirit with its colours, shapes and fragrance':

'Who, indeed, has fewer cares than these people? They think little of the past or the future, seeking their pleasures in the present and fleeing from every kind of work or worry. His manner of idleness, the elegant person feels, is entirely beneficial to the human race; he engineers more in his way than is ever achieved by restless energy. An elegant person rises at eleven o'clock; his long and salutary rest enables the streets to clear themselves of the thousands of workers who had earlier made them virtually impassable. He goes to take breakfast at Tortoni's. There he appeases his desire for food, and by choosing ortolans *à la provençale* turns them into a fashionable dish; while the mere tone of his voice, when he orders truffles in Burgundy, becomes suddenly a fount of riches for all Périgord.

'For two hours or thereabouts he strolls along the boulevards. The aria he trills becomes a fashionable one; a remark, lightly passed, on the easy movement of a phaeton, or an expression of favour for English-style harness, sets whole factories in motion to supply the newly desired object. In the Jardin des Tuileries he nonchalantly awaits the hour for dinner, sprawled carefully over two chairs, and by his example he procures for the chair attendant a dazzling increase in the daily takings. Here he recounts a few amusing extracts from Aubry and Vernet, and, in so doing, fills the coffers of the variety theatres, for later everyone rushes off to them half-way through dinner, scorning dessert, fearful of not obtaining a seat. . . .

'More and more I came to feel myself a native of Paris, circulating with the fashionable elite – that harmless and noble youth which thought of nothing beyond balls, operas and pleasures of every kind. Each of them possesses his own considerable talent and each in his own right is an Odysseus in the art of discovery. One of my very closest friends conceived a beautiful design for men's open-worked silk stockings; another designed the embroidery for them. One of the greatest innovations was a method of cutting a coat which gave even a narrow-chested man an air of fullness and freedom, a style which, even today, after almost ten years, is still favoured by many. Equally important inventions included a lovely design for a cane-top and a quite exceptional nail-file which brought a fine, oval shape to even the flattest of finger-nails. One very refined man kept among his arsenal, or toilet-table, a cartesian devil; when tired after a bout of conversation, he would relax and draw

new strength from watching the amusing play of the devil as it rose and fell.

'Here fashions were determined and judged; with every moment a new one was born. I began to make a name for myself in Paris with the *femmes à la mode*; I was received into their boudoirs, a great mark of one's acceptance. I gossiped and passed sentence with them amid flowers and feathers, ribbons, shoes and shawls. Is there anything more charming, after the morning toilet, than helping a young beauty in her boudoir to choose a shawl to match her hat, her dress and her coiffure?'

In London the elegant world of 1820 gathered in Bond Street. The atmosphere there is fascinating to read: 'Here the topmost level of society, with its glittering vision of conceit, passes in a wickedly self-critical parade, up and down, all through the day until evening. Unlike ordinary folk, who change their wardrobe with the seasons of the year, these elegant people appear in new creations hour by hour, bringing to the eyes of the world the very latest offerings of the kingdom of *haute couture*. To do this they gladly pay twice or three times the price charged elsewhere in London.'

In the Romantic period the predominance of black for dress-clothes became firmly established. In addition to black, blue or brown frock-coats were mostly worn, together with short waistcoats in a colourful floral design and elaborately knotted cravats.

After the middle of the 19th century the *frac* disappeared as an item of everyday wear and was reserved for special occasions only. The trousers became a little wider. While in 1830 most men were still clean shaven, from then on it became fashionable to wear a beard, and this fashion continued until after the First World War.

The beginning of the twenties saw a return of

409

409 Carl Gustav Carus. Gondola trip on the Elbe. City Art Collection, Dusseldorf. The sports' dress of the young girl is of a checked woollen material with a wide belt. The broad-brimmed Florentine hat came into fashion at about that time.

410

411

410 From an English fashion journal, 1822.
Everyday dress of checked material with dark
belt and a hat with ostrich feathers.

411 *Wiener Moden*, 1822. Checked fabrics
enjoyed great popularity. The evening dress
is lavishly trimmed with ribbons and
artificial flowers, which form concentric
circles at the lower hem.

412

413

414

415

women's waistline to its natural position. This inevitably led to the cultivation of a slim waist and the reintroduction of the corset. After 25 years hygiene had once again to give way to looks; the contemporary ideal of beauty triumphed, as so often in fashion, over the verdict of medicine. To begin with, however, lacing was not quite so obvious and unhealthy

412 *La Mode*, 1832. Hair style by Maître M. Mulot. Crêpe dresses with appliqué work, and a reversible coat.

413 Fashion plates for the *Theaterzeitung*, 1831. Party dress for young girls.

414 Fashion plates for the *Theaterzeitung*, 1834. The *gigot* sleeves gave outdoor dresses an entirely new silhouette. Here they are worn with feather-trimmed bonnets and transparent veils, as well as with parasols and handbags.

415 From an English fashion journal, 1834. Morning dress for men: the *frac* is dark, the trousers light-coloured and long; a striped waistcoat and a new kind of cravat complete the outfit, with which top hat and walking stick were *de rigueur*.

416 Fashion plates for the *Theaterzeitung*, 1813. Street dresses of a thin material with broad epaulette-like embellishments attached to the upper part of the sleeves. The little girl is wearing pantalettes under her skirt. The boy's clothes are exactly like a man's.

417 From a Paris fashion journal, 1840. *Mantelet* or *mantelette* was the name given to the steadily lengthening sleeveless wrap.

416

417

as during the Rococo. The slender waist was emphasized also by the special cut of the sleeves and by the collar, which steadily became higher so that eventually, like a roof, it covered the shoulders entirely.

The fashionable silhouette was produced by the cone-shaped skirt which gradually widened as more and more petticoats were added and which took the place of the cylindrical skirt. In order to break up the large surfaces of the skirt, striped and patterned fabrics began to be used instead of plain ones. When around 1835 the circumference of the sleeve had reached its maximum, the skirt became longer and wider still. The sleeve was called leg-of-mutton.

References to this fashion often occur in reminiscences, as for instance in this extract written in the thirties: 'Especially striking was the circumference of the sleeves, which by and by grew to an enormous size, so that the back looked more than twice as wide as was compatible with the natural proportions of the figure.

418

419

418 From a Paris fashion journal, 1840. A waisted riding habit with white waistcoat and masculine cravat, as well as a top hat with veil attached.

419 Ferdinand Georg Waldmüller. Self-portrait. Austrian Gallery, Vienna. The at-one-time highly esteemed society painter has portrayed himself wearing a *frac* with a modishly striped waistcoat.

420

421

420 Ferdinand Georg
Waldmüller. The family of
J. A. Eltz. Austrian Gallery,
Vienna. Bourgeois everyday
dress: the women's dresses
have typically broad sleeves
and wide skirts with narrow
waists; the men are wearing
fracs.

421 Dietrich Monten.
Group from the
Feldmesse. Wittelsbacher
Ausgleichsfond, Munich.
The lady in street clothes
is wearing a bonnet on her
coiffure *à la Sévigné* and a
white dress, and carrying a
parasol and a shawl; the
gentlemen are wearing
fracs and holding top hats.

In order to see these sleeves, called gigots, in their entire fullness, they were stuffed with pads of feathers and later spread out by means of steel springs. At that time I frequently played four-handed piano with a lady. To make this possible the sleeve of her gown had to be held up with a steel spring and fastened to the shoulder with a pin, otherwise her fellow player would constantly have been pushed in the arm.'

The picture of the elegant lady was often completed by a cashmere shawl or the popular pelerine, which reached respectable dimensions since it also protected the wide sleeves. The lady's shoe continued to have a fairly low heel. The soft bonnet was slowly replaced by a stiffer and larger hat. A novelty in ladies' fashions were cambric pantalettes.

Hair styles, too, changed with the fashion, but almost everyone wore a plait which was fixed to the back of the head with a comb. This was usually made of horn. More elegant, but also far dearer, were combs made of tortoiseshell which were looked after with great care so that no teeth would get broken. A few people who had lost their hair wore false hair pieces, but the expensive trade in false plaits, which flourished later in the same century, was then quite unknown.

For a long time it was the fashion to wear ringlets at the sides of the face. These were curls of dyed red silk which hung in two thick puffs from the forehead and were fixed by means of a band tied round the head. Each lady chose puffs to match her hair from a selection in the shop. It was not a very attractive fashion but it was handy since one could make the hair look dressed with very little effort. This was the more necessary as very few women made use of the services of a hairdresser. Young girls wore a simple style, mostly with 'lovelocks' behind the ears.

The concept of *Biedermeier* came into existence only after the style had almost vanished. It takes the name from a political caricature in *Fliegende Blätter* and later featured in satirical poems by Ludwig Eichrodt. A *Biedermeier* is a philistine, but he is also a sober, upright man, and the style named after him is characterized by plain, simple forms.

422

423

422 Paul Gavarni. 'Friend, one must be reasonable'. Lithograph 1841.

423 Paul Gavarni. Two young girls. ca. 1850. Lithograph.

424 *La Mode de Paris*, 1839. These fashion sketches show various kinds of décolleté on day and evening dresses, an assortment of collars and lace trimmings – called 'Bertha' collars in the language of fashion – and complicated evening hair styles with feathers, artificial flowers and scarves arranged in the form of turbans.

425 Gustave Courbet. Sleeping Spinner. Musée Fabre, Montpellier.

424

425

Early Victorian
or the Second Rococo
(1840–1870)

In the middle of the last century the court of Paris once again instigated a fashion notable for its opulent splendour. It had some superficial resemblance to the Rococo, hence the name. The crinoline, called after the material from which the supporting skirt was made, namely horsehair (crin) and either cotton or linen thread (linum), now made its third appearance in the history of fashion. A certain remote analogy may be detected between the crinoline and the principles underlying the construction of a number of edifices which were built at that time, as for instance, the Crystal Palace.

The crinoline required enormous quantities of material, the more so since it was fashionable to embellish it with numerous flounces which replaced the garlands of the Rococo. In the year 1859 the Empress Eugénie wore a white satin ball-dress that had 103 such flounces. The consumption of hoops, too, was considerable. In the years 1854 to 1866 the largest factory in Saxony delivered altogether 9,597,600 crinolines. Since each one required on average about 90 ells (60 yards) of wire, this would have been sufficient to span the globe at the equator no less than 13 times.

The deep décolleté of the tight bodice left the upper part of the breasts, the shoulders and the arms bare. Hair styles were always small in order to provide the greater contrast with the voluminous lower half of the attire.

During the period of Napoleon III expensive fabrics were very popular. Silks, satins and fine worsteds were worn at any time of the day. Shimmering taffetas, rep, brocade, but above all watered silk (moiré), were much in demand. Summer dresses were of crêpe, tulle or muslin. In Paris the period from 1850 to 1870, which ended with the performances of Offenbach's bacchanalian operettas, was an era of grandiose splendour. It was *l'époque de Worth*. In 1853 Eugénie de Montijo had become the wife of Napoleon III. The Prussian Marshall von Moltke, who had seen her in Paris, wrote: 'The Empress Eugénie is a surprising personality. She is beautiful and elegant . . . neck and arms are supremely beautiful, the figure slender, her dress exquisite, tasteful and rich without being overloaded. She wore a white satin dress of such enormous volume that in future the ladies will need a few more ells of silk material than hitherto. In her hair the Empress wore a scarlet ornament and round the neck a double rope of magnificent pearls. She talks a great deal and displays a greater vivacity than is customary for one in such a high position.'

True, the era of the crinoline also had its dark side. In 1859 a Paris newspaper reported a tragedy: a young lady whom all her rivals had admired for her tiny waist, was dead two days after a ball. What had happened? 'Her family wanted to know what had caused her sudden death at such an early age and it was decided to perform an autopsy. The result was shattering: the liver had been pierced by three ribs!!! This is how one dies at 23 years old! Not of typhus, not in childbirth, but of a corset!'

There have always been reasonable men who have risen up in warning against the dangerous consequences of an unhealthy fashion – with what success can be imagined! There was at that time even a regular 'crinoline war'. The most eloquent fighter in the battle against the crinoline was Friedrich Theodor Vischer, a professor of aesthetics. He thundered: '. . . the crinoline is an exaggeration which does not add to the beauty of a slim figure, but distorts it, annihilates it and gives a completely false conception of the feminine, of the human build. When the contours from the hip downwards increase to an impossible size, the eye no longer seeks to compare the huge bulk with the small diameter of the waist; it is all the same, it does not matter whether one is slim or not, there are no longer any laws in this fantastic lie. And that is surely ugly, very ugly!'

And Professor Vischer continued his indictment. '. . . the crinoline is impertinent. Impertinent because of the large amount of room taken up by its wearer. But this is far too general, far too abstract a statement; no, it is impertinent because of its conspicuousness,

427 From an English fashion journal, 1849. Men's street costume showing several types of the traditional *frac* worn with top hat and walking stick. In the model on the left, the transition to the modern version, that is without tails, has already been made.

428 Gustave Courbet. Country Girls. Metropolitan Museum of Art, New York. Young girls, who pass the summer in the country, go for walks in dresses with softly swinging skirts, worn with shawls, parasols and hats.

427

because of its monstrous challenge to the man. "Would you like", thus the crinoline speaks to the individual of the male sex who comes near it, "to step down from the pavement, or do you dare to brush past me, to press against me? When you sit next to me in the stalls would you like to take my dress in your lap or to sit on it? Can you feel the iron hoops? Can you feel the impregnable castle, the Malakoff wreath, the terrible chastity belt which presses into your calves?"

'Are we being frivolous? Charming reader, you will not take even us dried-up scholars for such simpletons as to imagine that we do not know what dresses mean to the fair sex, or that we could possibly believe them ever to be anything other than a world of relationships, hints, a silently eloquent language, an arsenal of gentle questions, terrible snubs, touching requests, cruel threats, glowing confessions, cold reserve, or that we could have remained ignorant as to which of the weapons in your armoury are the more seductive, those that meet a man half-way or those designed to frighten him off; nor are we in any doubt as to what makes a man keener – to be encouraged or to be repulsed. "But, you immoral fellow, don't realize that a dress which stands so far away from the body that it gives you no hint of its real shape is the most modest of them all?".'

According to Professor Vischer the contrary is the case. He maintains that the more a fashion conceals the more suggestive it is. He concludes by saying that he would not dream of accusing any woman of being aware of the wicked thoughts a man might harbour at the sight of her in a crinoline, for 'we know the power of fashion, how it dazzles and compels'. Men's fashion was free from such discomfort. It lacked the variety of female fashion both in colour and style, and it was in no way reminiscent of the Rococo. On the contrary, it rejected fussy detail and superfluous embellishments. The man in the office had no use for a garment which would hinder his work and his movements. Even the complicated neckties vanished by and by; men's costume became ever more sober in appearance. At that time the plain and practical jacket came into existence, and ever since then it has remained a basic element in male clothing.

XIII Ferdinand Georg Waldmüller. Family in the park. Castle Gallery, Rychnov n.Kn. (Bohemia).

XIVa Spanish Master. The Infanta. Nelahozeves Castle.
XIVb Franz Fahrländer. Little girl with flower. Castle Kozel (Bohemia).

XIVc Unknown artist. Portrait of a young girl. Castle Kozel (Bohemia).
XIVd Auguste Renoir. Child with stick. Hermitage, Leningrad.

The waistcoat too lost its gay colours and the only bright spot in masculine attire was the cravat. The trousers always differed in colour from the jacket. In addition to the top hat, which remained an indispensable part of the male wardrobe, a somewhat lower hard hat began to be worn.

A well-tended beard of moderate size, side-whiskers with moustache, as well as a plain and simple hair style, graced the masculine head. A three-quarter length overcoat or weather-coat, shoes with low heels and a thin walking stick completed the picture of the correctly dressed gentleman.

In the sixties of the last century larger consignments of ready-made clothes reached the markets of Western Europe and the U.S.A. for the first time. The only advantage of these products was their low price; the quality remained doubtful for a long time to come. At that time – 1863 – the first mention appeared in the press of 'two smaller branches of industry which have grown to incredible size in quite a short time: the market in embroidery patterns

429

430

431

432

429 From a fashion journal, 1855. Street dresses of the middle of the century; both have crinolines; the dress on the left is of a striped material, the skirt has flounces and the sleeves are the so-called *mamelouk* sleeves; the dress on the right is checked, and worn with a mantilla and a bonnet, called *fanchon*.

430 From a fashion journal, 1862. Afternoon street dresses again have crinoline skirts, the one on the left is decorated with ribbons in a zigzag design, on the right it is interwoven with ribbon.

431 *Petit Courier des Dames*, 1864. Both street dresses have very wide crinoline skirts. Sleeves, bodice and skirt of the dress on the left are trimmed with a tightly ruffled frill; on the right a mantilla has been added.

432 From an English fashion magazine, 1864. The ball-dresses have imposing crinolines with trains.

433 From an English fashion magazine, 1865. The upper garment has now attained the form of the classical tailless coat, the collar, pockets and sleeves of which are edged with satin or fur. The top hat continues to be worn.

434 Edouard Manet. Concert in the Tuileries. National Gallery, London. The afternoon clothes of Paris men and women consist of various crinolines, bonnets and mantillas for the ladies and *fracs* for the gentlemen.

435 Gustave Courbet. Women sieving grain. Musée des Beaux-Arts, Nantes. Working dress of country women is traditional and does not follow fashion.

436 *Theaterzeitung*, Vienna. The emancipated woman of 1848. Gentleman: 'Do you no longer smoke cigarettes?' Lady: 'I prefer the pipe, since nowadays every shoemaker's apprentice has a Havana cigarette in his mouth!' At that time one spoke of Amazon costume.

433

434

435

436

and the so-called ready-to-wear trade in home-produced, ready-made coats and other garments. Berlin-made mantillas, wraps and *paletots* are sent to countries as far away as Denmark and Sweden and the far north, as well as south to the lands on the Danube and to Turkey, while the gracious Miss and the proud Lady, the women of London and New York do their embroidery with Berlin wool according to Berlin patterns . . .

'The reason for the boost received by these industries lies in local conditions, especially cheap labour. Many Berlin ladies, even of the better classes, do not disdain to occupy their idle hours in order to earn a little pocket money for small extra expenses, toilet articles and various hobbies.'

This, then, was the year of birth of the once so famous Berlin ready-to-wear trade.

437

438

439

440

437 Gustave Doré. Yellow Tiger.
Lithograph from the cycle *La ménagerie
Parisienne*. This sketch of women's costume
of circa 1860 shows a dress with crinoline,
pelerine and bonnet.

438 Gustave Doré. Rats. Lithograph from
the cycle *La ménagerie Parisienne*. Men's
working dress is traditional, like women's. It
consists of a shirt tied at the waist and long
trousers.

439 Honoré Daumier. Topicalities. From
Le Charivari, 1857. 'I would rather a
whirlwind went through my garden than that
accursed crinoline!'

440 Honoré Daumier. 'Natural Science
Lesson'. From *Le Charivari*. Even the
lower classes wear street dress consisting of
frac, tight trousers and top hat.

Mixed Styles During the Late 19th Century (1870–1890)

The rapid expansion in the economy was accompanied by great improvements in production techniques. But the aesthetic aspect of mass produced articles was neglected. After the Franco-Prussian War in 1870–71, and above all in the years of 'bubble company promotion' in Germany, the 'nouveaux-riches' ostentatiously showed off their flats, houses and clothes. They were concerned with effect rather than with genuine quality.

People who considered themselves important insisted on drawing and dining rooms in Renaissance style, a boudoir in the style of the Rococo and an oriental smoking room, not to mention the Turkish divan, which might be placed anywhere. An exaggerated feeling of nationalism further added to this chaos of styles; in the area between Memel and the Vosges it was considered good form to have at least one room in a Nordic or old German style. The deep folds of heavy curtains over windows and doors not only protected the home from the importunate intruder, but also from fresh air and sunlight.

With ladies' costumes it was much the same as with furniture. Fashion made use of every possible style. The resulting mélange was proof of the lack of direction which came about from too great a degree of freedom: each individual chose form, colour and fashion best suited to his personal taste.

By 1870 the crinoline had been replaced by the bustle. The *cul de Paris* and the *tournure* (the French for bustle) gave women's skirts an unnatural profile. A cushion of horsehair or a special spring sewn into the skirt served as padding. This enabled the tailors to produce dresses with draperies similar to those of curtains and furnishings. The tight corset gave an uplift to the breasts which added to the strange aspect of the female figure when viewed in profile.

Women's dresses as a rule had pointed necklines with lavishly trimmed collars. Hair styles varied; sometimes they recalled the *fontange* and at others the hair was cut short or pinned up. Most frequently the hair was combed back and tied in a ribbon at the nape of the neck.

Favourite accessories were fans and lace-trimmed parasols. Fans were carried not only at balls, in the auditoria of theatres and concert halls, but also on summer walks in the country. In her memoirs Maria von Bunsen recalls the important role parasols played in a woman's wardrobe:

'I was full of pleasurable anticipation of my journey to Cannes when I packed my bits and pieces. Packing then was a much more complicated business than it is today. I carefully considered how many parasols would be sufficient for my visit: a practical, solid one; a simple one; a brightly coloured one; a good one in coloured silk which would go with my best street costume; an airy one; and a decorated one to match my elegant afternoon gown. That would have to do.

'A whole pile of veils, both heavy and light, was prepared; a whole heap of gloves were needed for different occasions. The packing of each dress, with the exception of hard wearing sports clothes, was a highly complicated matter. Ruches, frilly wraps, flounces, full sleeves, skirts lined with stiffened gauze and underlayed with *balayeuses* (or dust ruffles) needed space; the hat boxes grew always more voluminous. But all that was necessary.'

Around 1870 fashion passed through a strange phase in which women dressed like expectant mothers. This was entirely contrary to the usual practice of concealing pregnancy rather than drawing attention to it. At that time *ventres à trois, quatre, six mois* were sold. (In 1913 there was a recurrence of this strange notion when, by suitable gathering, draping and pleating, the abdomen was made to appear larger.)

Before 1880 another important change in the feminine line took place. The dress enclosed the body from neck to knee as tightly as possible. The knees were actually tied together so that it was impossible to take large steps as these were considered detrimental to a graceful walk. It was only below the knee that the skirt flared out and formed a shallow train. When later on the skirt became a little shorter, fashion immediately decreed elegant shoes with really high heels. The narrow dresses demanded correspondingly small hats.

In the second half of the 19th century clothing generally speaking became simpler; its components were fewer. Even after the crinoline went out of fashion numerous petticoats, which had been indispensable with the crinoline, continued to be worn. As many as five to seven were customary and only in the last fifteen years of the last century did their number drop to one.

All the greater was the attention which both wearers and makers gave to the last remaining petticoat. From the time when very thin chemise dresses were worn, knickers had become a permanent item in the feminine wardrobe. Under the Directoire they were made of tightly clinging stockinette material, kneelength and quite unadorned; during the *Biedermeier* they became longer and had trimmings, but by the end of the century they were radically shortened.

All in all it may be said that ladies' fashion in the 19th century fed on historical reminiscences. Perhaps the rising bourgeoisie wanted to demonstrate in this way its desire to be set on an equal footing with the former ruling class. Only the flowing lines of Art Nouveau at the turn of the century indicated that the thorough-going economic, technical and political changes had not been without their repercussions on women's fashions.

The general uncertainty in the face of this jumble of shapes and colours led to a superabundance of counsellors on questions of dress, and advice was given in such an involved manner that it tended to confuse the questioner rather than clarify the position. The following answer to the question of how best to harmonize hair colour with the colour of ones clothes will illustrate this point:

'Blondes can, on the whole, always wear blue to advantage. Very pale delicate blondes, however, could easily look too insipid in blue and they might venture to emphasize their too soft colouring by the use of contrast. In their case a delicate shade of green is highly recommended. This gives the complexion a sweetly rosy hue. Should they wish to achieve a similar effect by the reflection from red tints, ruby or garnet red will be found to be the most suitable.

'If it is desired to enhance the whiteness of the complexion by contrasting light values, the soft gentle black of velvet will be found most advantageous. A fiery gold can take any contrasting colour, and green is especially becoming to it. A rosy face would lose by the use of bright red fabrics and look paler, but would gain by the contrast with dark red. If the complexion is highly coloured then neither green nor a strong red is recommended. Both would produce a scarlet effect – the former by making

442

442 Caricature from *Ulk*. Berlin, 1883:
Theory of descent – the development of
the bustle.

443 *Illustrierte Frauenzeitung*, 1874.
The street dress with bustle is lavishly
adorned with lace and elegantly draped.
The little girl's dress is a smaller version
of a lady's.

444 *Victoria*, 1871. Day dresses with
bustle: the dress on the left is embellished
with bows and worn with a polonaise – a
tunic looped up into scallops; the dress on
the right has lace trimmings. The ribbons
adorning the small hats fall to the
shoulders.

443

444

283

445 From an English fashion magazine, 1880. The everyday dress of the eighties, after the full styles of the previous decades, is very tight and constricting.

446 From a fashion journal, 1875. Both older women and young girls wear street dresses with bustles; skirt hem and sleeves are trimmed with tight frills. The little girl is wearing a coat with coachman's collar and high lace boots.

445

446

too strong a contrast and the latter by being too similar.

'The brunette may use stronger colours without hesitation and without fear that they would weaken the liveliness of her complexion, yellow and red are the colours preferred for a darker complexion. Whereas a strong blue enlivens the colouring of blondes by the creation of orange as contrast, in the case of brunettes it would tend to increase unfavourably the already existing sallow tints of the complexion. Even greater caution must be observed in the use of mauve, whereby any faintly bluish sections of the skin tend to acquire an ugly green tinge. The reason why yellow is so good for brunettes with a slightly orange complexion is because it makes the skin paler and clearer.

'Black, grey and white are colours which suit almost all complexions; only it should be remembered that tender, delicate faces are served better by the duller, paler shades, whereas lively and expressive faces do better with glowing and sumptuous shades. Black and white, which in reality are non-colours are

447 From a fashion journal, 1875. Outdoor clothes consist of a skirt with bustle, a short jacket trimmed with fur, and a muff. The loose house-dress has been widened to form a bustle and is trimmed with ribbons. Children's fashions are replicas of grown-ups'.

448 From a fashion journal, 1875. Street dresses for winter have bustles and are worn with short jackets edged with fur. Both ladies are wearing bonnets.

449 Henri de Toulouse-Lautrec. '. . . and the rest of the company consists of elderly English women . . .' From a *Cahier de zig-zags* produced during a stay in Nice, 1880–1881. This sketch by the then very young painter eloquently expresses the fashion silhouette of the English lady.

447

448

449

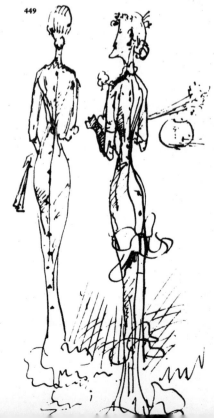

able, as no others, to lend their wearer, on suitable occasions, an aura of elegance and distinction; but no one should ever use them who knows from experience that they do not suit him. Just imagine the highly coloured, robust and coarse face of a cook in white Sunday clothes!'

By contrast men's clothing continued to develop in a logical and predictable manner, becoming always plainer and more practical so that it typified both the economic and political development and man's position in contemporary society.

Male dress undoubtedly overtook women's fashion in the course of the 19th century but in the present century women's fashion has caught up with men's and in many respects it has even taken the lead.

Jacket, tailcoat and *frac* remained the most important items in male clothing. The frock-coat on the other hand was replaced at the end of the century by the so-called cutaway coat, which had rounded corners in front. Later on the dinner jacket was added. The male wardrobe was more or less limited to these few styles. Only the cut changed from time to time

and in so far as it became more comfortable this was due to the influence of sport. One must not forget to mention the various types of overcoat, the double-breasted Ulster, the Chesterfield with concealed buttons, the tailored *paletot* and the comfortable and sporting raglan coat. All these garments were in muted colours, with black, grey, brown or blue shades predominating.

450 Edgar Degas. The Cotton Market in New Orleans. Musée des Beaux-Arts, Pau. The men's round hard hats are gradually replacing top hats and jackets are taking the place of *fracs*.

450

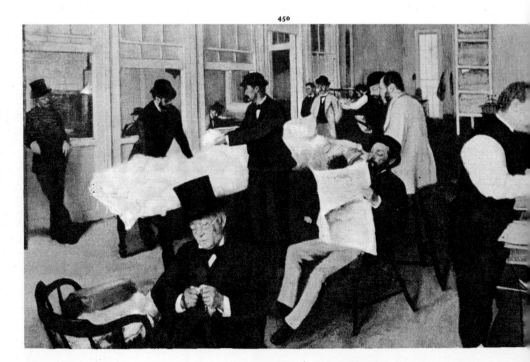

451

452

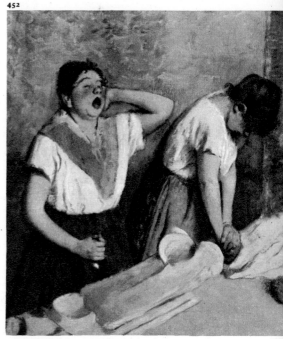

451 The Prince of Wales, later King
Edward VII, playing tennis. Contemporary
engraving, 1883. Men's sports clothes consist
of long trousers and a shirt. Boys wear
sailor's blouses and long trousers or
kneebreeches. Women's sports clothes do not
differ from simple street clothes.

452 Edgar Degas. Pressers. circa 1884. Musée
du Louvre, Paris. Working clothes have hardly
altered at the end of the century. They
consist of shirt with short sleeves, a long
skirt and a small fichu.

453

454

453 Photograph of Degas' friends. The house-frocks and everyday dresses in this contemporary photograph are made in the simple styles and plain materials familiar to us from contemporary fashion magazines.

454 Camille Corot. Lady in blue. Musée du Louvre, Paris. The blue evening dress with black ribbons is sleeveless; the skirt has a bustle.

XV Paul Cézanne. Lady in blue. Hermitage, Leningrad.

XVI Kées van Dongen. Madame Jasmy Alvin. Musée du Louvre, Paris.

455 Henri de Toulouse-Lautrec. Dance at the Moulin Rouge. Collection Henry P. McIlhenny, Philadelphia. The ladies visiting the Moulin Rouge are wearing feather boas with their evening dresses; the bustle makes the skirt wider at the back. The hats, too, are trimmed with feathers.

456 Henri de Toulouse-Lautrec. Doctor Tapié de Céleyran at the Comédie Francaise. Musée Toulouse-Lautrec, Albi. The tailcoat worn with light coloured waistcoat and top hat remains correct evening dress.

456

455

457 Auguste Renoir. *Le Moulin de la Galette*. Musée du Louvre, Paris. Afternoon dresses for summer are of a fine white or striped material. Skirts have bustles and are trimmed with ribbons and lace. The men are wearing flat straw boaters called *canotiers* in French.

458 Auguste Renoir. The painter Sisley and his wife. Wallraf-Richartz-Museum, Cologne. The house dress consists of a skirt with a polonaise, which has finely pleated edges, a white blouse and a bodice. The painter is wearing a long dark coat, a white shirt with dark tie and light coloured long trousers.

457

Renoir

The Turn of the Century

Fashion at the turn of the century was characterized by great diversity of styles and materials. Skirts, sleeves, hats and accessories varied so widely that no definitive fashion emerged. One might even say that this total absence of unity, where women's costume was concerned, was itself the fashion.

Never before had the theatre aroused such interest as at the end of the last and the beginning of the present century. First Nights were important social occasions and the popularity of actors rose as quickly as the income of well-loved authors. Plays were already being performed in period costume, which added to the profusion of styles.

The time was long past when the arbitrary taste of some ruler, his spouse or his mistress could dictate the course of fashion. In the last third of the previous century Worth, Doucet, Redfern and Drecoll, together with their staff of capable designers, fell into the modern rhythm of fashion changes. The most important salons in Paris became creators of a luxury fashion. During the International Exhibition in Paris in 1900 Haute Couture spared no expense in showing their creations to an amazed and admiring public. The following extract from a contemporary report gives some idea of the impact made by the exhibition's fashion section: 'For all who sacrifice on the altar of grace, brilliance, splendour and beauty, Paris was, is and always will be the seventh heaven of bliss. This is why so many artists, painters, sculptors and dressmakers make their way to Paris, which perhaps today more than ever stands under the star of woman.

'This, too, is the reason for the superb quality of everything which is part of that cult of which woman is the idol, or rather the ideal, especially of those products – and seeing them here one is almost tempted to say works of art – created for the purpose of making women look beautiful. . . .

'For this reason the *Palais des Fils, Tissus et Vêtements*, which houses everything to do

with dress, and especially the delightful section called *Toilettes de la Collectivité de la Couture* as well as the special tableaux by Worth in the *Salon Lumineux*, always draws large crowds.

'Among the most beautiful and charming of the creations are the *déshabillés* and *dessous*. The seductive *peignoirs*, the light and airy *négligés*, the coquettish *jupons*, the supple and becoming corsets and *combinaisons*, the lingerie and other items, which cunningly mould the figure and improve the stature, fire the imagination. . . .

'By comparison, the most elegant and expensive creations to be seen in Germany are, with a few isolated exceptions, hardly worth mentioning. In such matters the Frenchwoman is far, far ahead of us. She has a complete grasp of this self-worshipping cult, and carries all before her.

'How tasteful and pleasantly coquettish is, for example, the corset-jupon combination, in the Pompadour style, which bears the notice "Sold 22 times". The material is pink silk crêpe, covered with matching satin and embroidered with gloriously bright and eye-catching garlands of roses in white and green. A similar model in blue is embroidered with tiny sprigs of daisies, one of which, on the right breast, is surmounted by a diamond brooch. To lend them an extra something, the exhibitors have also added to some of the creations the names of the ladies who ordered and wore them. Regency princesses, duchesses, countesses, aristocrats, rich merchants, artists, the "jeunesse dorée" – who, incidentally, seem only to come of age in their fiftieth year – and many well-known and much-pursued women of the world. All, indeed, are peacefully assembled there. Such is life!

'And just as life itself intrigues us, so does that *tableau vivant*, the Worth department in the Salon Lumineux, reflecting a way of life which most people learn about through books and newspapers. Here the preparations for a court reception, bridesmaids going to fetch a bride, all are real dramas in which the leading players compete fiercely for the highest praise.

'The most pompous creation in this exhibition of costume-clad wax figures is surely the court-dress, whose heavy pink train was held up on the left shoulder and on the right hip with diamond and ruby brooches. Around the train, which was several yards long, there was a wide fixed flounce made of Flanders lace over pink gathered chiffon. Inside the flounce flower outlines are picked out in pink, white and green, their detailed fancy buds, flower-cups and filaments being made of gold and silver thread, pearls and dazzling jewels; under this was a short white petticoat, tied at the front. The shoulder straps of the sleeveless bodice were made from two thick strings of pearls.

In the first decade of our century no important fashion changes took place. Fashion continued on the lines laid down in the previous era. But the call for reform and innovation, demanding a natural silhouette, comfort, health, practical dresses suitable both for the street and the country, and lastly shorter skirts, could no longer be ignored. Practical considerations ultimately led to the fulfilment of these wishes. Right at the beginning of the second decade skirts became so tight that women could only hobble. The next natural stage in the development of the skirt was a shortening to compensate for the discomfort suffered in the previous period. Shorter skirts first came to England from the United States and only then gained acceptance in Paris. Communications in America could not keep up with the rapid growth of the towns and consequently were much worse than in Western Europe. Both the long dresses and their wearers suffered in the muddy and dusty streets to such an extent that the dress trade began to produce practical short skirts for wear on rainy days. These were called 'Rainy daisies' and were the starting point of fundamental changes in women's fashion, the most far-reaching since the time of the Directoire.

460

461

462

463

460 Claude Monet and the family
Durand-Ruel looking at the water lilies in
the garden of Monet's summer residence
at Giverny. Photograph. Everyday dresses
have become simpler, women's skirts
tighter; men's costume consists of jacket,
waistcoat and trousers.

461 *Journal des Demoiselles*, 1892. The
contemporary silhouette on the fashion
plate differs from that in the photograph.
The waist is more strongly accentuated,
the shoulder-line is raised and the skirt
widened towards the back.

462 *Journal des Demoiselles*, 1892.
Street clothes are similar in style and are
worn with small flower-trimmed hats and
a lace parasol.

463 *Journal des Demoiselles*, 1892.
Waist and hips remain slender but
shoulders are made more prominent with
flounces. One lady is wearing a pelerine.
Hats with feathers or ribbons make the
figure appear taller.

464

465

466

464 From an English fashion magazine, 1895. Travelling clothes – always in an English style – are simpler; usually they are two-piece garments of plain-coloured material.

465 *Journal des Demoiselles*, 1892. The silhouette of children's dresses is exactly like that of adults, with the shoulders similarly raised and accentuated.

466 *Journal des Demoiselles*, 1892. Street dresses for the afternoon – with hour-glass silhouette – are made of variously patterned fabrics decorated with ribbons. Small hats with artificial flowers complete the ensemble.

467 *Journal des Demoiselles*, 1892. Various types of hat, decorated with ribbons, feathers and artificial flowers. The sketch also shows the high collars which enclose the neck.

468 *Journal des Demoiselles*, 1892. The ladies' street dresses are two-piece throughout and are made from plain or unobtrusively patterned materials. The elaborately dressed hair is decorated with flowers.

467

468

469 *Punch*, London, 1890. The contemporary caricature illustrates the varying silhouette of women's dress, which here closely resemble men's, as has been the case several times in the history of fashion.

470 Henri de Toulouse-Lautrec. At the Moulin Rouge. *La Goulue et La Mome Fromage.* Lithograph, 1892. A fashion caricature from the nineties of the last century.

471 *La Vie Parisienne*, Paris, 1894. Caricature of the impractical clothes worn at the end of the 19th century.

472 Henri de Toulouse-Lautrec. *La Revue Blanche.* Poster, 1895. The poster shows the typical silhouette of women's dress, with broad feather-trimmed hat, coat with fur boa and muff.

469
470

471

La revue
blanche
bi-mensuelle
le n° 60 cent.
12 francs par An
1 rue Laffitte
Paris

Charpentier et Fasquelle, éditeurs
11, rue de Grenelle

The 20th Century
Innovation and Reform

An attempt was made in Germany to create a new type of clothing for women which was to be hygienic, aesthetic and practical. Clubs were formed for this purpose, and artists, doctors and tailors put their heads together to produce a suitable design.

The resulting costume, however, had little appeal, and it seemed for a long time that it would make only the smallest of impressions. The well-known Berlin architect, Professor Schultze-Naumberg, was not alone in his lack of success with his 'artistic clothes for ladies'. Reason, however, was on the side of the innovators and a newspaper article written at the turn of the century, more precisely in 1898, sets out with great clarity the aims of the reformers:

'The first thing to be combated is, of course, the corset – that female armour which is a threat to health, constricting chest and waist and endangering lungs, liver and heart. Numerous firms have attempted to replace the dangerous corset by harmless bodices, which unfortunately have been given clumsy names like 'platinum anti-corsets', but which, nevertheless, serve their purpose excellently.

'The principle underlying the design of both outer and underclothes has been to transfer the centre of gravity from waist and hips to the shoulders, which would seem to be the natural weight bearers; this aim has been achieved by various practical devices such as buttoning the underclothes to the topclothes, which in turn are supported on shoulderstraps. . . . In due course the costume will no doubt become more elegant and pleasing to the eye, since one must not forget that vanity is one of the chief factors to be taken into account. Feminine headgear is also in need of reform. The modern giant hats with their heavy load of feathers, ruches and flowers have been banished . . . and their place is taken by dainty and featherlight hats which can be folded and put into the pocket; for older ladies there are bonnets which cover the entire head and felt hoods for travelling and for bad weather. Everything is extremely light and due regard has been paid to sufferers from nerves and migraine.'

This endeavour to create a new type of dress was only one aspect of the general direction taken by visual art which wanted to get free from traditional forms. This trend manifested itself everywhere in Europe, where it was known by various descriptions. In Britain the name 'Arts and Crafts' gained general acceptance; in France one spoke of *l'Art Nouveau*; in Germany it received the name of *Jugendstil* after the Munich Journal *Die Jugend*; in Austria it was called *Sezession*.

Although Art Nouveau indicated a step forward which cannot be contested, its impact was more largely felt in the sphere of ornament than in structural matters. In fashion, the best expression of Art Nouveau is to be found in the creation of a straighter, more natural line.

473

473 Peter Severin Krøyer. Summer evening in Skagen. Den Hirschsprungske Samling, Copenhagen. This is what the champions of sensible women's clothes had in mind: a loosely fitting dress with flowing lines. The dress has a square neck, long sleeves and a skirt of medium width which falls to the ground. The man is wearing a light sports-suit and a soft hat.

474 Eugen Spiro. Lady in a Reform-dress, 1902. Although the dress is practical its silhouette is not very becoming since it conceals the feminine curves.

475 Capiella. Marguerite Moreno. Dress of the emancipated woman consisting of skirt and blouse which, like Reform-dress, does not require a corset.

476 Thomas Theodor Heine. *Simplicissimus*, Munich, 1904. Caricature of the supporters of Reform-dress being put forcibly into corsets by the police.

474

476

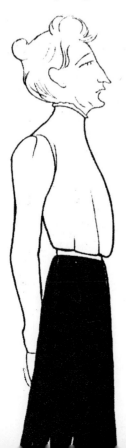

475

Incomparably more successful than the reformers in influencing fashion was the Russian Ballet, though this was certainly not its chief ambition. In the 19th and 20th centuries the French had made the acquaintance of many first-rate ballet ensembles, but the Russian Ballet was something entirely new, unique and revolutionary – it had the power to change general taste.

Blasé Paris went mad. Adverse criticism, however guarded, was drowned in the roar of spontaneous enthusiasm. *Sheherazade* above all was received with wild applause. Diaghilev, Fokine and Pavlova became the centre of interest.

The spectacular success of the Russian artists inspired Paul Poiret, many of whose creations had a decidedly oriental flavour. This famous tailor, great artist and astute business man altered the fashion silhouette. In the publicity

477

478   479

477 *The Ladies' Field,* 1903. The sports dress for the lady hardly differs from a dress for social occasions. It is edged with fur, has lace sleeves and is worn with a feather-trimmed hat – only the skirt is a little shorter.

478 *The Ladies' Field,* 1903. The material of elegant gowns is more sumptuous than that of street clothes; the dresses are embroidered and trimmed with lace and fur. The hats, too, have lace trimmings.

479 *The Ladies' Field,* 1903. The evening dresses have skirts of heavy satin combined with lace and tulle. The neckline and the skirt are embroidered with large star motifs.

480 Contemporary photograph. The lady visiting the races is wearing a two-piece dress with a fur stole, a hat with feathers, a handbag and a parasol.

481 Tailor-made costumes, 1912. The jackets of the ladies' costumes closely resemble the classical jacket of a man's suit.

482 Tailor-made costumes, 1912. Two versions of the simple, close-fitting ladies' costume.

480

481   482

483

484 485

486

487

previews of his fashion shows he allowed himself to be acclaimed extravagantly:
'To think that there is a man alive in Paris who one day realized quite suddenly what he must do to imbue feminine beauty with a new air of enchantment. . . . And somewhere in Paris or in London, in New York or in Berlin there lives a woman who yesterday only dimly felt the slavery of her unfashionable clothes, who yesterday knew and suspected nothing of the "Man in Paris" and who today will rejoice in her new-found freedom when she has seen his creations, when she has enveloped her body and at the same time revealed her beauty in the new and delightful garments which are Poiret's present to her. Poiret, who today will make her a queen. A queen of beauty . . . for the "Man from Paris" is more than a king of kings – he is a king of queens!'
In addition to Paul Poiret's models, the Russo-Japanese war (1905) intensified the influence of the Far East on fashion. In 1907 a new type of sleeve appeared in France, cut in the style of the Japanese kimono.

Between the Wars (1918–1939)

The First World War had as profound an effect on fashion as did all similar events in world history, even if the resulting changes were hardly noticed at first. The style of men's fashion remained much the same – at most it grew plainer and more uniform. But it became apparent in the course of the years that women's clothes had undergone radical changes.

While female emancipation had progressed slowly during the last half of the 19th and the early years of the 20th centuries, it took a leap forward as a result of the war. During the war women had been widely employed in auxiliary services and had taken the place of men in all kinds of public service, such as health and transport, as well as in the fields of industry and agriculture.

The equality of the sexes and 'free love' were a frequent topic of conversation among the young post war generation. Because of the war not only married but also unmarried women gained a certain amount of freedom in society. Many a single woman managed to achieve economic independence – the true emancipation. For to be able to do as one likes with the money one has earned by one's own endeavours affords a far greater degree of independence than any public proclamation of freedom.

The comparatively favourable economic position of many young women was also responsible for the shift of fashion in favour of youth – after all, fashion in our time has been chiefly created for youth. Physical movement at work, during sport and at dances determined dress styles, for it had long become clear how impractical the long skirt was for the active woman.

The reaction of fashion to these upsets and upheavals – aided and abetted by a far-reaching functionalism which dominated the twenties – was an exaggerated utilitarianism, a cult of simplicity. Dresses, even those created by the Haute Couture, were so uncomplicated that any manufacturer of ready-to-wear clothes, indeed any woman able to wield a needle, was able to copy them.

In the twenties the dress became a tube, wider or narrower as required, with a larger opening for the legs and a smaller one for the head, as well as two smaller tubes for the arms. All women wore dresses in this form whatever their walk of life. It must have been the first time since the dawn of human history that social differences in dress had dwindled to such insignificance.

Women now began to use make-up. Most of them confined themselves to lipstick and used powder very sparingly; only a minority painted their nails, cheeks, brows and lashes and bleached or tinted their hair. Women of the moneyed middle class had now taken the lead in fashion – the wealthy adapted themselves and the lower classes endeavoured to keep up. Fashion had become so democratic that it was hardly possible to determine a woman's social position by her clothes.

The greatest difference lay in the price-level of the clothes intended for the various social classes; the differences were also considerable in the quality of the material but were least in the style. The dress trade concentrated on the broad section of the middle class, for they had learned that the purchase of millions of smaller articles had a more decisive effect on turnover than a hundred large orders by the 'happy few'.

However, women's fashion in the twenties was too masculine; it paid no regard to the natural feminine shape, all curves were obliterated. Short hair was modern and all young women bobbed or shingled their hair; what had been woman's crowning glory fell victim to a pair of scissors. The female ideal of fashion had become an unreal creature, a hybrid of boy and girl, long-legged, flat-chested, with narrow hips and rather broader shoulders and an Eton crop.

The society magazine *Sport im Bild* stated: 'The dinner jacket (for the lady) has also become the elegant outfit for the afternoon, suitable for paying calls and going to the races. For this purpose woollen material is too stiff and unyielding; it is also too warm; therefore it is better to stick to silk, which neither crackles nor rustles, for the dinner suit of taffeta is among the latest contributions to this fashion-conscious season . . . there are even dinner jackets of velvet. These must be worn with a jabot of real lace which is far more becoming to the softly rounded female countenance than the stiff collar and masculine tie, which many an over-eager lady has chosen to go with skirt and waistcoat.' Surely the warning speaks for itself.

One might say that women were meant to look like somewhat girlish schoolboys. From the middle of the twenties they also frequently wore trousers which, until the beginning of the 20th century, had been an exclusively male preserve and which only after 1900 had found their way into the female wardrobe via sport. Jewellery and bijouterie were not popular and all accessories were of the plainest. Such extreme simplicity required that fashion – for a long time ill-disposed towards the machine-made article – no longer attempted to mar manufactured products by excessive ornament. Functionalism revealed the beauty of the delicate, faultlessly regular, machine-made textiles which exactly served the purpose for which they were intended.

One of the most striking and long-lasting features of this fashion were the short skirts and dresses. The shorter the skirt the greater was the attention paid to stockings and shoes. Never before had so much thought been given to female legs and never before had so much money been spent on them. Although the material of the stockings has since undergone a number of changes, the various flesh-coloured tones have remained fashionable.

The year 1925 for the first time in the history of modern European fashion exposed the knee. In fact for three years the feminine silhouette remained practically unchanged from morning till night. Only more elaborate materials and more intricate workmanship distinguished the evening dress, which around 1928 was also short – for the first time.

At the beginning of the twenties the corset disappeared. Immediately its place was taken for a number of years by elastic foundation garments which did not constrict the waist but above all flattened the chest, in order to produce a 'girlish' or rather 'boyish' figure. It was, of course, impossible to lace the waist tightly, because already by 1923 it was somewhere around the hips, and there it remained for several years.

After the First World War the passion for dancing became boundless. Dance-halls and bars sprang up like mushrooms and the whole world twisted and turned to the tunes of the early jazz bands. The modern type of social dances resulted in striking alterations in the cut of female dresses because the dance-partners were so close together that the back of the body was far more exposed to view than the front. Sometimes the back was left bare right down to the hips. Ornament, too, was concentrated on the back.

In the twenties the cinema had a great influence on fashion. The famous Swedish film actress Greta Garbo became the prototype of the modern woman. The blonde Scandinavian, with her wide mouth, flat chest, square shoulders, narrow hips, long calves and large feet would certainly not have been the ideal of beauty of every epoch but she became the idol of the twenties.

In the forties her place was taken by Katherine Hepburn, the typical representative of the

489

sporting and emancipated youth of the time. The rising importance of the film industry also increased the importance of the greatest film-producing country – the United States. The liberating influence of the practical, comfortable, hygienic and cheap ready-made clothes came from the States. They also deserve the credit for the increased interest in the pullover and sweater and in practical footgear.

It was now possible to put into practice what earlier had been quite impossible to achieve, namely to dress in comfortable, but at the same time fashionable clothes. Clothes, of which comfort, usefulness and simplicity were the keynote, were in harmony with the spirit of the machine age. Short skirts, open necks, sleeves of a length to suit the customer or none at all, light, low-cut shoes with medium heels, simple hats and hair styles were characteristic of a fashion which spelt progress.

From 1920 onwards both quantity and bulk of the material used for feminine attire was much reduced and fashion allowed complete freedom of movement. From then on the changes in fashion were due in large measure to the varying hemline. Most of the changes were a question of detail and affected colour and material more frequently than the basic cut. The fashion of the twenties bore the mark of the experimentation of the *avant garde* movement.

With the onset of the thirties fashion became stabilized – the broad lines of presentday dress had evolved. It was inkeeping with the economic circumstances of most women living in the industrialized societies of the first half of the twentieth century. The silhouette of the clothes, with few exceptions, harmonized with the natural curves of the female body.

At the end of the thirties the line of fashion again became somewhat more complicated. The coronation of King George VI and Queen Elizabeth in 1937 influenced fashion, as later on the coronation of his daughter Elizabeth II. In the leading London and Paris salons, stately brocade and royal purple once more for a time held the place of honour, and evening gowns for festive occasions were once again lavishly embroidered and trimmed with gold and fur.

Men's fashions experienced only unimportant changes in the years between the wars. Only the length of the jacket and overcoat fluctuated and there was some variation in the width of the jacket, the collar, the trousers and the turn-ups. Fashion only improved on nature when it was a question of correcting bodily defects or of bringing the figure of the individual male closer to the ideal.

489 *Le Rire Rouge*, Paris, 1916. 'The war is long but the skirts are short!' During the First World War short, wide, crinoline-like skirts became fashionable; these were singled out by caricaturists because of the incongruity of the arrival of an extravagant fashion in the very midst of shortages and deprivations.

490 *Gazette du Bon Ton*, 1924. The summer dress has no belt, the skirt flares out from the hips.

491

492

493

494

495

491 *Gazette du Bon Ton*, 1924. Cortège design, Worth. The evening dress has a deep décolleté, narrow shoulder straps and the belt at hip level. A fan of ostrich feathers forms part of the ensemble. The modern hair style is the shingle.

492 *Nos Loisirs*, 1929. The short skirt of the street dress barely reaches the knees and has wide flounces.

493 *Gazette du Bon Ton*, 1924. The figure-hugging winter coat, which tapers towards the hem, has a broad shawl collar of fur.

494 *Vogue*, 1926. Suzanne Talbot. This cleverly stylized creation has been inspired by the clothes of ancient Egypt.

495 *Gazette du Bon Ton*, 1924. Design by Poiret. This summer dress of a flower printed fabric must be worn with a sash and a Florentine hat.

496 *Gazette du Bon Ton*, 1924. The elegant dresses are cut like a chemise, have shoulder straps and are often worn with stoles.

497 *Gazette du Bon Ton*, 1924. Design by Lanvin. Cocktail dress of a richly patterned material worn with a stole. The young girl is wearing a short accordion pleated skirt and an embroidered jacket.

496

497

498 *Vogue*, 1926. Evening dresses are always getting shorter. They have a deep, pointed décolleté both back and front, are often pleated or trimmed with flounces. Instead of complicated hair styles the boyish Eton crop is worn.

499 *Vogue*, 1926. Design by Lanvin. The evening dress is cut asymmetrically, leaving one shoulder bare. The flounces on the skirt likewise are set at a slant. The flounces on the girls' dresses are similar.

500 *Vogue*, 1928. Diagonally cut evening coat draped in irregular folds and a long train.

501 *Vogue*, 1928. Draped evening dresses with deep décolleté and shoulder straps, made of fine, transparent materials.

500

The Fifties and the Sixties

Even a total war like the last can only thrust fashion into the background – it cannot suppress it completely. Even while bombs are raining down, hampered by clothes rationing and *ersatz* materials, the seemingly basic human need breaks through – not merely to exist but to be seen to exist.

There could not, of course, be any question of creativity in fashion until the war was over – but then it broke in upon us with a bang, marking both the end of an era and a new beginning – with the New Look. Christian Dior, its inspired creator, divining with a fine sensitivity the wishes and aspirations of women everywhere, in 1947 boldly conceived his new and utterly feminine line, with which he banished to the past the harsh memories of war and offered a glimpse of a future in which women would once again be beautiful and desirable.

In the following years 'lines', like A line, H line, Y line etc., succeeded one another with such rapidity that they almost cancelled each other out, so that everything became permissible in fashion. At this time it became clear that there were certain concessions women had retained from the war which they had no intention of giving up.

One of these concessions was trousers, an item which has become indispensable in the female wardrobe. Trousers may be seen anywhere – at home, in the street, at sport, in bars and hotels (with a few noteworthy exceptions) and even in the evening. The spread of the motor car is responsible for this development, as also for certain modifications in men's fashions, where it has produced new types of garments, found new uses for others and made some articles of clothing almost obsolete – such as the heavy overcoat.

Such tendencies are international. In the course of the twenty years or more which have passed since the end of the war, the standard of living in the industrialized countries of the West, having once recovered from the war, has taken enormous strides, and something like an international fashion has come into being, in which national and regional characteristics have faded into insignificance. It would not be an exaggeration to say that an internationally integrated mode of living of which fashion is a part characterizes our ever-shrinking world of the jet age.

The leading fashion centres, Paris, London and Florence, with the United States as their most powerful business partner, mutually influence one another and the style that emerges is wearable and worn everywhere. The 'provinces' in the old sense of the word no longer exist. Women's journals, with giant editions, and television swiftly acquaint the remotest villages with the latest styles both in dress and in the mode of living. The days of the 'backwoods' are numbered; the power of fashion in our lives is greater than ever.

The surplus in purchasing power, especially in the sixties, led to the ruthless commercialization of public idols – from James Bond to the Beatles. Never before were so many people able to afford so many fashion extravaganzas.

The wig, for instance, so indispensable during the Rococo and long since forgotten, turned up unexpectedly in America and immediately became a hit also in Europe. The boutique, a magic word of the postwar period, bears witness to the pleasure the consumer takes in nick-nacks, playthings, oddities and articles and accessories of all kinds, all delightful – and expensive.

Leisure time and sport, two mighty factors, have left their stamp on the fashion of our time, which has its accent on youth. Youthfulness is the ideal of our epoch; advertisers spend millions on wooing it in various guises. The old-fashioned flapper has become the self-assured teenager; she is taken seriously and spoken to politely; the teenagers show their gratitude by spending their not inconsiderable pocket money – and a great new market has been created.

But perhaps the greatest impetus received by fashion has been the post-war leisure-time craze for 'do it yourself' and hobbies of all

503

kinds; at any rate it has helped to free male fashion from the fetters of convention, and brought a little colour and variety into stale forms. Sport and sporting activities have become, not only in beach wear, a pretext for modish extravagances – après-ski fashions are a case in point.

Modern man, as innumerable tests have shown, readily and willingly accepts any comfort and labour-saving device offered to him. The textile industry has put this trait to good use. The advent of man-made fibres and with it light, hard-wearing fabrics needing only a minimum of care, has affected the habits of the individual and the work in the household. The ready-to-wear industry has now become respectable and 'off the peg' no longer means inferior. Thanks to developments in machinery and advances in processing techniques, the workmanship of ready-made clothes nowadays is excellent.

Twenty years of post-war fashions: at the beginning a throw-back to an almost forgotten feminine ideal – today skirts which are shorter than ever. Twenty years – a period which makes it possible to survey the development of fashion and which confirms the law of fashion's evolutionary character. The revolutionary topless dresses were bound to fail because they

504

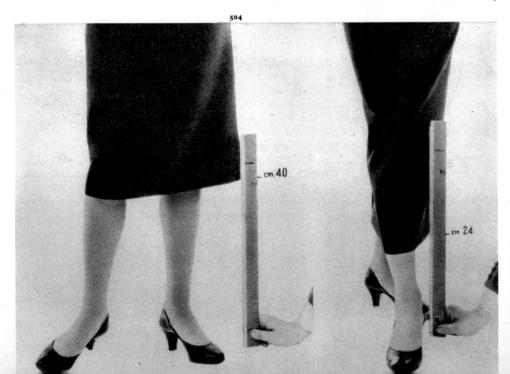

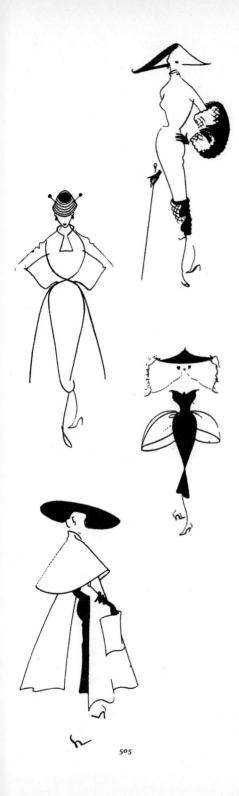

offended against the law, but slowly, as in all evolution, the idea is gaining ground in the use of transparent materials.

These last twenty years of fashion development have not differed greatly from past epochs: they have shown the same eclectic tendencies in their attempt to derive inspiration from historical sources; the same inclination to exaggerations and excesses, which are quickly forgotten and live on only in the fashion magazines, where they provide endless amusement for posterity; finally, the same sublime disregard for rational considerations by which women allow themselves to be persuaded to wear stiletto heels, to the detriment of both feet and floor-coverings – to cite one example among many.

503 This is the male fashion of the fifties in England: broad shoulders, loose jacket and baggy trousers with turn-ups.

504 This was the leap taken by Dior's New Look, measured exactly in centimeters. Even today one can easily imagine the sensation produced by this revolutionary drop in the hemline.

505 *Constanze*, Spring/Summer, 1951. In the Spring of 1951 the Paris designers discovered the geometrical figure and created their models accordingly – an interesting object lesson of fashion's formal possibilities.

505

317

506 *Constanze*, Spring/Summer, 1951. In his creations in 'geometrical style' Jacques Fath has kept to the silhouette of the triangle.

507-508 Courrèges in 1964 and in 1965. His ideas were something quite new in women's fashions and point to a fashion of the future – a space-age fashion.

506

507   508

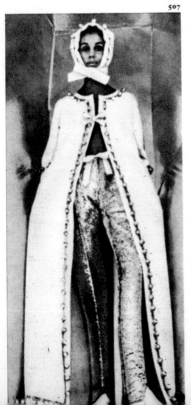

509 Trouser suits revolutionized fashion and helped usher in clothes which were easy to wear and comfortable. This trouser suit in a military style is by Lauer Bohlendorff, Berlin, 1966.

510 Mary Quant was the first British designer to jerk British fashion out of the doldrums and manufacture individual clothes at cheap prices. These 1967 designs are made of unbleached calico with a lace edging.

511 Another 'Space Age' couturier, Paco Rabanne, uses plastic and leather squares, linked together. This 1967 design is a dress of cut-out leather squares.

509

511

510

512

513

514

512 The conservative man's suit for which English tailoring is famed. This single-breasted suit is in a chalk stripe, worsted cloth.

513 The return of the dandy. 'Carnaby Street' clothes have had a profound effect on fashion for the young. Here a young man shows the 'kipper' ties on sale in a boutique.

514 Paper dresses first appeared in the mid 1960s. They are cheap, can be worn several times and then thrown away.

Glossary of
The Various Garments
and Accessories of Fashion

Hairstyles and their Accessories

Throughout the ages both men and women have lavished particular attention upon their hair. A truly artistic coiffure, declared Diderot, crowns the beauty of a woman's head and reveals the character of a man's features. Although the French philosopher was doubtless right, we must not overlook the fact that hairdressing follows the fashion and that it is fashion which decides what 'beauty' is. The ancient Assyrians, Persians and Egyptians loved splendid hairstyles and made up for any deficiencies of nature with the wig. They even dyed their hair, and the preoccupation with curls also dates from the earliest times. The Greeks wore their hair in loose curls framing the head and the women tied them up with ribbons. Unkempt, straight hair was a sign of mourning in Ancient Greece.

To the ancient Teutons and Celts on the other hand, long hair represented freedom and power. In medieval times long, unbound hair was the prerogative of young maidens; wives plaited their hair and hid it under a bonnet. The most extravagant period in hairdressing history was the Rococo period, when the coiffure attained the zenith of complexity and artifice with the aid of stiff wigs, ribbons, combs, lace, flowers and other adornments. French fashions led this trend.

A contemporary memoir paints a vivid picture of the craze: 'I had to have my hair dressed and assumed the grand style to go to Versailles. This dressing for court takes an age, and the journey from Paris to Versailles is most tedious, especially when one has to take care that one's petticoats and pleated hems escape ruin. I wanted to try a coiffure which is extremely incommodious but very modish: a few little bottles, shaped flat and curved to mould the head, hold a little water in which the stems of real flowers were then immersed. It did not always succeed, but when it did, it was indeed beautiful. The effect of spring on one's head amid the snow white powder was entrancing.'

Englishwomen had already renounced such hair adornments. Parisians would climb onto chairs to laugh at the spectacle of English ladies taking a stroll. 'Parisian ladies,' we read, 'wear high towers with an extraordinary number of flowers, pads, and ribbons. The English find such boundless display extremely ill-bred, and if any such lady comes to London, people hiss and throw mud at her.'

After the French Revolution, hair-styles became simpler and shorter, and wigs disappeared (to reappear in the 1960s). The Empire returned to the Grecian shorter hairstyle; in the early 19th century hair was smoothly combed from a centre parting and coiled in plaits or buns at the sides and back of the head.

A more complicated high-swept style came in towards the end of the century. In about 1920 came a radical change – the short-cropped style – which, with variations, has remained popular until the present day.

Ailes de pigeon. A male hair-style of the 18th and first half of the 19th century. They consisted of wide curls on the temples of winglike form. The hair was held at the back in a bow.

À l' Agnes Sorel. Evening hair-style popular in the 1840s, named after the famous mistress of King Charles VII of France. A parting in front was surmounted by a bow and the hair was coiled in a bun at the back.

À la chinoise. Ladies' hair-style of the 1830s. The hair was compressed into a roll on either side and coiled at the back into a bun secured by a decorative hairpin.

À la Hurluberlu (or **Hurlupée**). Female coiffure of around 1670 consisting of small curls which encircled the front of the head.

À la Maintenon. A style of the middle of the 19th century named after the Marquise de Maintenon. The hair was parted in the middle, piled high and curled.

À la Sevigné. Hair-style of 1650 named after Marie, Marquise de Sevigné, celebrated for her witty letters. The hair, drawn back from the brow, puffed out on pads, fell in waves or

516 Head of the so-called Tiber Apollo. Roman copy of early 5th century B.C. Greek original. Boy's hair-style with loose curls falling to the shoulders, a fillet encircles the head.

517 Head of a young woman. Thermal Museum, Rome. Her hair is parted in the middle and curls fall from her temples to her shoulders.

518 Dark-skinned woman. Pushkin Museum, Moscow. Curly hair-style with buns and hair-ribbon.

519 The 'Poetess' from the Casa di Libanio in Pompeii. Museo e Gallerie Nazionale di Capodimonte, Naples. Her hair is dressed in the style later known as *à la Titus* with little curls falling on the brow from a net of gold thread. She wears ear-rings.

516

curls on the shoulders and was held together by a bow at ear-level.

À la Titus. Introduced during the French Revolution. The hair was worn in short curls close to the head or rolled and combed over the brow after the antique style. The originator of this French fashion of the late 18th century was probably the actor Talma, who wore it in May 1790 for his role in Voltaire's *Brutus*. There was a revival of this style in 1946–47.

Bag-wig. Used by men in the reign of Louis XIV. The long hair (whether natural or bought) was placed in a longish taffeta bag decorated at the top with a ribbon or rosette. The bag-wig protected the clothes from the hair-powder and was more convenient than long, loose hair. It was not worn with dress clothes.

Bandeau. A band encircling the brow.

Bandeau d'amour. A coiffure of the 1770s–80s with high slanting and hanging curls.

Barbe. A lace or ribbon head adornment framing the face and neck worn in the 18th and 19th centuries round the hair or bonnet and, in the cinoline period, round the hat.

Beatle-cut. Hair worn long over the forehead and at the back by males in their teens and twenties; named after the English pop group from Liverpool who created a sensation in the early 1960s and which has been idolized by the youth of many countries.

Bob. Short-cropped hair-style for women which appeared circa 1920, sometimes called **Eton crop.** It belonged to the boyish style of the post-war period.

Cadenette (English – love lock). Hair-style of the time of Louis XIII named after Marshal Cadenet. The hair, curled or straight, was divided at the back or on either side of the head into two simple or plaited strands fastened with bows.

Catogan or **Cadogan.** Style named after Lord Cadogan, worn by men and women from 1760–90. Also called the **Club.** The hair, worn long, was tied back in a bow or plaited and held in a net. The fashion spread to Prussia, where it was worn by infantrymen.

Chaplet. Head ornament dating from the Middle Ages consisting of a jewelled metal circlet or a wreath of fresh flowers which is still

517   518

519

520

521

522

520 Germanic Bodyguard from the Missonium of Theodosius in Madrid. The soldier's hair is neck-length and curled upwards a little at the back. Their necklaces were called *torques*.

521 Codex of the 1st century. Christ is represented with long hair.

522 Albrecht Dürer. Self-portrait. Prado, Madrid. The painter has long curly hair and wears a turban-like cap.

523 Sandro Botticelli. Spring (detail). Accademia, Florence. Botticelli here represents Renaissance coiffures in such precise detail, that a hairdresser could easily copy them. The hair is plaited and knotted, and adorned with flowers and jewellery.

524 Sandro Botticelli. Young Women (detail from The Finding of Moses). Sistine Chapel, Vatican. It is easy to see that the Florentine lady's hairdressing consists of artificial hair.

326

523

524

525

526

527

528

529

525 Sebastiano Mainardi. Portrait of a
Young Lady. Mrs Huntingdon's Collection,
New York. The young Italian noblewoman's
hair is dressed in symmetrically arranged
plaits covering the ears but leaving the high
forehead bare. She wears a bonnet.
526 Domenico Veneziano: Portrait of a
Lady, Museo Poldi Pezzoli, Milan.
527 Joos van Cleve. Portrait of Queen
Eleonore of France. Kunsthistorisches

Museum, Vienna. The queen wears a
jewelled hair-net and a magnificent brocade
gown with a square décolleté and a necklace.
528 Francois Clouet. Elisabeth de Valois.
Museo de Bellas Artes, Toledo. The Spanish
fashion was also austere in hairdressing.
529 Diego Velasquez. Queen Marianne
(detail). Prado, Madrid. The Spanish queen
wears a helmet-like coiffure framing her face;
her hair is adorned with flowers and feathers.

530   531

532

533

534

530 Henry Raeburn. Marie d'Orléans, Demoiselle de Longueville. This hair-style with curls on the cheeks was named after Madame de Sévigné. The dress with oval décolleté is trimmed with ribbons and pearls.

531 Hyacinthe Rigaud. Dominik Andreas Kounic. The Castle Slavkov, Moravia. This curled wig is typical of the Baroque style; with it was worn a wide asymmetrically draped cloak.

532 Joshua Reynolds. The Waldegrave Sisters. The ladies as well as the men of the Baroque period had a preference for powdered hair. Ladies wore it raised from the brow and beribboned.

533 Fashion caricature of 1805. 'A difficult coiffure'.

534 Illustration from the book *Modes et usages au temps de Marie-Antoinette*, 1885. The period produced extraordinary coiffures, with even more ridiculous names.

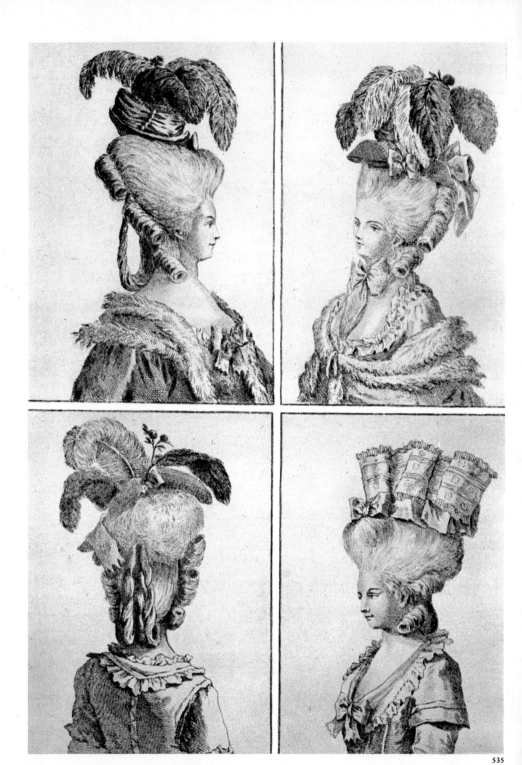

535

Bonnet d'un goût
nouveau et elegant
avec de perles

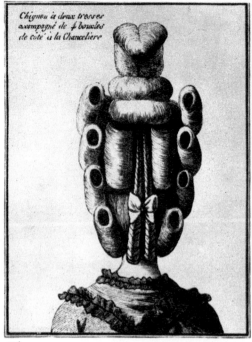

Chignon à deux tresses
accompagné de 4 boucles
de coté à la Chancelière

536

Petit Maitre avec un Cha-
peau a la Suisse et un
gillet à la Turque

535 Hair-styles of the end of the 18th century, from a fashion journal. The coiffures were intended to give height to the wearer; feathers, flowers and ribbons were perched on the crown of the head.

536 Designs for French coiffures, circa 1782. Above left: Bonnet in the 'latest style' with strings of pearls. Above right: Chignon with 2 plaits and 4 large curls on each side *à la Chancelière*. Below: Hat *à la suisse* and waistcoat *à la turque*.

537 Francisco José de Goya. Portrait of L. Correa. Collection Vicomtesse de Noailles. Spanish version of the Empire style. The short curls are held by a narrow ribbon to fall in graceful 'disorder' on the brow.

538 Antonio Canova. Paolina Borghese. Borghese Gallery, Rome. Empire fashions shared the tendency of the period to borrow from Greece and Rome. A typical Grecian hair-style.

537

538

539

540

539 *Costumes Parisiens*, 1811. The coiffure
à la Titus reappears in the Empire period
adorned with flowers or jewels.

540 Jean Auguste Dominique Ingres. The
Painter Granet. Aix-en-Provence. The male
hair fashion of the period with its careless
elegance corresponds to the female coiffure.
The loose strands of hair across the brow
were called *coups de vent*. The gentleman
wears a velvet coat, a stand-up collar and a
loose cravat.

542

543

541 Fashion-drawings from the Vienna journal *Theaterzeitung*, 1834. Early 19th century fashion reverted to elaborate coiffures, ignoring both the shape of the head and the natural waves of the hair, and was richly adorned with ribbons, flowers and little bonnets.

542 Fashion-drawings from the *Theaterzeitung*, 1831. Innumerable false hair-pieces and ornate combs went into the construction of an early Victorian lady's extravagantly heaped-up coiffure.

543 Fashion-drawings from the *Theaterzeitung*, 1831. Coiffures for balls and ceremonial occasions are ingenious combinations of tightly drawn hair and loose curls intertwined with ornaments. The dresses have typical wide sleeves, and flounced skirts, trimmed with artificial flowers, which emphasize the tiny waists.

544   545

546

544 Ferdinand Georg Waldmüller.
Austrian Gallery, Vienna. Young lady at the
dressing table.
545 Moritz Michael Daffinger. Portrait of
the wife of General Müllner von Marnau.
Austrian Gallery, Vienna. The early
Victorian hair-style looks natural here.

546 Edgar Degas. Monsieur and Madame
Edmonde Horbilli. Museum of Fine Arts,
Boston. A more austere Victorian hair-style.
547 *Magazine des Demoiselles* circa 1860.
The evening coiffure had become more
natural in the 1860s though many curls,
ribbons and flowers were still worn.

548 Henri de Toulouse-Lautrec. Studies of a head. Drawing. The silhouette is typical of the style worn at the end of the 19th century; the hair dressed high in front.

549 *Punch*, 1873. 'Who would fardels bear?' or 'The working classes'. The caricaturist satirizes the cruel burden of artifical hair imposed by fashion.

550 From a fashion journal, circa 1832. Decorative hairpins and richly ornamented haircombs such as these supported the early Victorian coiffure.

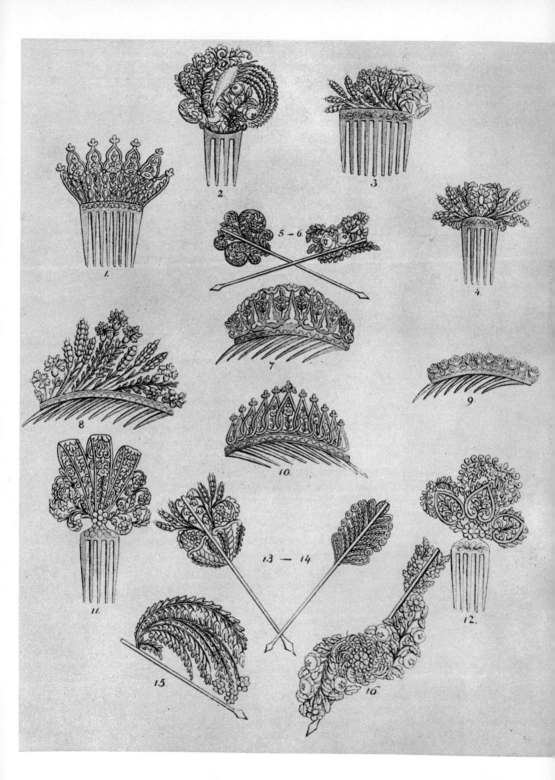

worn today at peasant or traditional weddings. The bride's chaplet which varies from country to country is often adorned with flowers, beads, precious stones and gold or copper coins.

Chignon. A coil of hair which is supported by a comb either high on the head or low in the nape of the neck, according to the fashion.

Comb: A tool for tidying the hair and beard usually made of horn, ivory, wood, metal or synthetic material. The earliest combs found in Europe are of the late Stone Age. The comb, however, is not merely a tool but also an ornament. The longer the hair and beard and the more elaborate their dressing, the more important became the comb.

Diadem or **tiara**. Circular hair-ornament of precious metal rising to a point at the centre of the brow, where a precious stone is usually set. It originated in the orient and betokened rank in all ancient civilizations. Fashion leaders borrowed it from the East as a festive headgear for women.

Dyes. Like wigs and hair-pieces, the dyeing and bleaching of hair was current in ancient times. It is well known that the Roman ladies were jealous of the Teutonic prisoners' long blonde plaits which were used to make hair-pieces. Fashionable Roman women already possessed all kinds of mixtures to change their naturally black hair to the desired blonde or reddish gold colour. The sun too was reputed to bleach the hair. The women of Germania and Gaul also knew certain bleaching agents. Medieval women not only bleached their hair, but, at fashion's dictate, also dyed it black. Red hair, however, was despised. Renaissance ladies unanimously preferred blonde hair and would sit for hours in the sun. When this and other means failed, they had recourse to wigs. In 16th century France, they took to powdering their hair. Until the Rococo period, fantastic quantities of rice and wheaten flour were used for this purpose. At the beginning of the Revolution, wigs and powder vanished with the aristocracy itself. But the many secret recipes for hair-cosmetics survived. At her wedding, in 1853, the Empress Eugénie not only created a new style in hairdressing but, with her reddish blonde hair, obtained with a secret herbal mixture, inaugurated a new

fashion-colour. Towards the end of the century, the custom of dyeing the hair became even more widespread. For bleaching the hair, hydrogen peroxide was used, as it still is today. In the 20th century the chemists took over the production of hair dyes, but it was not until after the Second World War that they succeeded in reproducing completely natural shades.

En dos de l'ane. Male hair-style of circa 1780 with side-curls and a long pigtail.

Escoffion. Female hair-style of the 14th and 15th centuries to be seen in paintings of the Italian Renaissance. The hair, simply combed, was rolled inwards and held in a net.

Ferroniere. A tiara with a single precious stone, named after the favourite of Francois I (1515-1547), 'la belle Ferronière,' who wears one in the famous portrait by Leonardo da Vinci. It returned to fashion in the early 19th century.

Fontange. Decorative hair-style consisting of ribbons and lace woven with thin strands of hair on the forehead, named after Marie-Angélique de Fontanges, a favourite of Louis XIV: 'A dainty little garter once inspired an important and lasting fashion' we are told. 'That charming and greatly beloved beauty, Madame de Fontanges, while out riding with Louis XIV, finding that the elaborate structure of her coiffure was collapsing, boldly and resolutely removed her jewelled garter and with it bound up her tresses. The incident created a hair-style which, thanks perhaps to the beauty of its initiator, found favour with the King and became universally popular.' Doubtless the lady would not have had recourse to her garter in her hour of need if it had not been a masterpiece of feminine coquetry. The fashion, immediately popular at the French court, soon spread to other countries and flourished for a quarter of a century, until circa 1710. The style, at first low and soft, was later materially reinforced and supported on a wire frame. It attained a dominating height, twice that of the head beneath it. A particularly high variant was known in England as the 'tower'.

Fringe or **bang.** Style in which the hair was cut short in front and combed over the forehead. It appeared at the end of the 19th century and is still very popular with young women.

Full-bottomed wig. Man's long-haired wig with ringlets falling to the shoulders. It first appeared in the 17th century at the court of Louis XIV and later became standard wherever French influence penetrated. It symbolized authority and dignity.

Hairpins. These ornaments are at the same time important accessories of the coiffure. The earliest known hairpins are Bronze Age finds. In ancient times, hairpins were favoured by the women of Egypt, Greece, Rome and Germania. They were frequently made of precious metals which were chased or set with jewels. Hairpins, grips and 'bobby pins' (U.S.) of wire, make an infinite variety of hair-styles possible.

Hairnet. A hairnet has been discovered among Bronze Age remains. It is appreciated both for its usefulness and its decorative effect. Medieval hairnets were sometimes of gold thread decorated with coloured embroidery. During the Renaissance they were usually threaded with pearls and precious stones, as we see from Italian paintings of the period. The hairnet, usually of wool, velvet or chiffon, re-appeared in the 20th century with the return to long hair. As well as these ornamental nets, entirely utilitarian, invisible nets made of human hair or nylon are used to keep the coiffure in place.

Hairslide. A both useful and ornamental object. It is usually of wire or a flexible metal. Decorative slides are often set with jewels.

Kolbe or **Kolbenschnitt.** In the second quarter of the 16th century men wore medium-

551 Antonio del Pollaiuolo. Portrait of a Lady. Howard Young Gallery, New York. Typical Renaissance hair-style with high shaved forehead, a knot of hair supported by a net and a light veil falling onto the shoulders.

552 School of François Clouet. Mary Stuart. Czartoryski Collection, Paris. A Renaissance hair-style with coils of hair and a net.

553
554

553 Leonardo da Vinci. The Lady with the Ermine. Museum Narodowe, Krakow.

554 Ornamental comb, circa 1824. Museum of Arts and Crafts, Prague. Ornamental combs were extremely popular in the 1830s.

555 Head of the Empress Theodora. Museo Archeologico, Milan. The Byzantine empress wears a wig surmounted by a diadem.

XVII Angelo Bronzino. Eleonora of Toledo. Národni Galerie, Prague.

XVIII Unknown Master. Franz of Lothringen. Archbishop's Palace, Prague.

XIX Unknown Master. Maria Theresa. Archbishop's Palace, Prague.

XX Unknown Master. Marie Anna, Countess of Stadion, née Schönborn. Castle Kozel (Bohemia).

555

length hair combed straight all round to an equal length, but cut horizontally across the forehead, above the ears and at the back of the neck. With it they usually wore a short beard cut horizontally below the chin.

Oreilles de chien. Nickname for the two long curls which framed the face in a male hair-style of the last decade of the 18th century.

Permanent Wave. The curling of hair with tongs or curlers was fashionable for both sexes even in ancient times. The effect was always transitory until 1904, when the 'permanent' wave, invented by Nessler, a German working in London, won rapid popularity. The 'permanence' was achieved by a chemical process, after the hair had been heated by electric current. Waves produced by this method lasted from 5 to 6 months. At first the hair forms tight ringlets which gradually loosen. Today it has been superseded by the cold permanent wave, in which the heating is omitted.

Plait. It consists of three or more interlaced strands of natural or false hair and was a favourite component of the male and female hair-styles of almost every period. In ancient Egypt the false plait was a mere ornament but the symbol of rank of a prince. Plaits were very fashionable for women in the Middle Ages and for men's wigs in the Rococo period. Artificial plaits of dyed silk, wool and other fibres form part of certain national costumes. In this century they are mainly used in elaborate evening coiffures.

Splendone. Decorated band of woven material or leather which completed the hair-dressing of Grecian ladies. It was wider in front, gradually narrowing towards the back.

Stephane. Headband in the shape of a half-moon set with brilliants. The ceremonial headdress of Grecian ladies.

Tonsure. Clipped or shaven circular area on the crown of the head of a Roman Catholic priest or monk.

Toupet. 1. Tuft or roll of hair combed high in front in hair-styles for both sexes in the second half of the 18th century. 2. False front of hair used mainly by men. The modern technique is to 'sew' or 'tailor' the toupet with natural, chemically cleaned, untinted hair which matches the existing hair exactly. The hair-piece, which allows air to the skin, is secured on either side by filmy adhesive strips.

Vergette. Style of wig worn circa 1730. The bag was of rubberised black taffeta and the number and arrangement of the side-curls varied with the fashion.

Wig. A covering or transformation of the head of hair consisting of human hair or similar material from horses' manes, sheep's wool, vegetable or synthetic fibre, silk, etc. The hair is sewn onto a base usually of woven material, sometimes of thin skin. Wigs were worn by the Egyptians, Sumerians, Assyrians, Persians and Romans. They reached the height of their popularity in the 17th (Louis XIV) and 18th centuries. In 1794 the following report was sent from Paris. 'The extravagance of the fair sex increases daily. The ladies of Paris trim their dresses with lace worth 2000 *livres*. Their hair-style is changed three times a day and consists of three different wigs, black for the morning, brown for the afternoon, and blonde for the evening, when they walk out on the boulevardes. A blonde wig costs 600 *livres*. In the evening they paint their eyebrows black. Commissioner Payan took occasion to remark in the Chamber of Deputies that a new sect had arisen in Paris which openly venerated and paid homage to the victims of the guillotine. Women who affected solemnity, lest a smile reveal their toothless mouths, bought the blonde hair of the decapitated to bedeck their bald and grizzled heads. Thus a new kind of masquerade, a new branch of commerce and a new religion had arisen.' Today the wig is part of the official dress of English judges. Since 1962 there has been a growing demand for female wigs. The trend originated in America. Many special boutiques have appeared in Europe, and large stores have opened special departments.

556 The last funeral rite before entering the tomb. Tomb of Nehamun and Ipuki, 18th Dynasty, Thebes. Wigs were fashionable even in ancient Egypt. The lady (*centre bottom*) wears a dark, flowing wig; her brow is bound with a fillet.

557 The Toilette. English engraving, circa 1780. Wigs attained their maximum circumference before the French Revolution. The bonnets or *dormeuses* were in proportion and were trimmed with ribbons and ruching.

556 557

558 The coiffures of the second half of the 18th century became more and more elaborate; their increasing height involved the addition of false hair-pieces. The towering, dome-like Rococo hair-styles were a favourite target for the whimsical wit of contemporary caricaturists.

559 An engraving after Moreau. 'Great Heavens! All that glorious hair. . . . !'

560 *Cabinet des Modes et les Modes Nouvelles*, Paris, 1785. The fashion for wigs died down even before the Revolution. Men's hair was no longer cut short but dressed in roll-curls and plait-like pigtails at the back.

561 William Hogarth. The Judge. Engraving. The subject of Hogarth's biting satire wears a full-bottomed wig which has remained the symbol of his office to this day.

558

559

560

561

562 Maurice Quentin La Tour. Self-portrait. Amiens. This hair-style was worn by men in the last third of the 18th century. A powdered wig, it was called *ailes de pigeon* and consisted of rows of tightly rolled curls. The pigtail is tied with a bow.

563 William Hogarth. 'Taste in High Life.' Caricature of a man wearing a tight-fitting, stiff-skirted coat, knee-breeches and a pigtail of exaggerated length.

564 J. Kramp, Master of Ordnance Joseph, Baron Alvinz von Berberek. This 18th century male hair-style, in which the long pigtail was tied with a bow and enclosed in a net, was known as a *catogan*.

565 Engraving by Caldwell after Brandoin, London. 'Now, sir, you're the perfect "macaroni".' "Macaroni" was one of the many nicknames for a foppish dandy.

562

563

564

Beards

A well-shaped beard is said to impart character to the male physiognomy. It was esteemed in by-gone centuries as a sign of strength, virility, freedom and wisdom. 'Who dares deny that our forefathers seem wiser to us than we ourselves with our hairless chins?', demands the author of a long-winded book published in 1797 entitled 'History of the Masculine Beard throughout the World'.

The shaving off of a man's beard was once regarded as a shameful punishment. A man swore by his beard; he expressed mourning by having it shaved off – or by letting it grow. The shape of a man's beard was not merely dictated by fashion, but sometimes expressed fundamental attitudes and beliefs or political convictions.

Razors found among prehistoric remains have proved that men shaved from the earliest times. In ancient Egypt the bearded chin was the prerogative of kings, who wore false beards especially designed for them. (The custom of shaving and wearing a false beard seems to have been revived later, for tradition has it that, in 1351, the Spanish king expressly prohibited the wearing of false beards: 'Let no man dare to wear or to make any false or contrived beard' ran the edict.) Our earliest evidence that the Assyrians and Babylonians shaved dates from the reign of Nebuchadnezzar II (605–562 B.C.).

The Jews cultivated their beards as symbols of freedom and piety. In Greece, the habit of shaving was not widespread until the time of Alexander the Great. The Romans imitated the fashion, which soon became a social convention with them. Not until Hadrian's reign (A.D. 117–138) did the beard begin to reappear. In the Middle Ages, the beard was not shaved but simply clipped to the shape currently in fashion.

The Russian *Brada* contains an interesting, though unverifiable, story. Although the Slavs had learnt the habit of shaving from the Greeks, a long beard remained a sign of saintliness in Russia until the time of Peter the Great, who introduced Western fashions. The Eastern Church pronounced the shaving of the beard to be a heathenish custom. At the famous ecclesiastical congress of 1551, the Russian clergy decided that it was 'impossible for a beardless man to enter the Kingdom of Heaven'.

The opposite prejudice obliged the French King, Henry II, to issue a special order in council because a diocese, upholding its statutory rights, refused to recognize its newly appointed bishop on account of his long beard. In 1551, the king wrote to the Chapter: 'We have learned that you have brought reasons why you should not receive our loved and trusted uncle, M. Antonius de Carraccioli, as your Bishop into your Church except he . . . shave his beard. It pleases us to send you these present letters to pray you not to withold his right for such a reason, but to hold him absolved from your statutes, and the more readily since we shortly intend to send him out of the realm on a matter close to our heart whither we should not desire him to go beardless. . . .'

Beards began to go out of fashion in France at the court of Louis XIV, whose courtiers appeared clean-shaven to flatter the young monarch. In any case, beards were out of keeping with the luxuriant wigs. The wearing of a moustache was a privilege of the court elite. After the Restoration, which aimed at the revival of the aristocratic army tradition, moustaches were worn by officers only. Relics of this custom survived in Central Europe until the beginning of the present century.

Rulers or leaders often set the fashion in beards, as is witnessed by many of their names, for example: the 'Henri Quatre beard' (though that monarch never wore it!), 'Franz-Josef' side-whiskers, the 'Kaiser William' moustache, etc.

Beards became a symbol of political conviction among the democrats of 1848, as was the pointed beard for the followers of Garibaldi in 19th century Italy and for the Fascist groups of the 20th century; the unkempt, shaggy 'existentialist' beard was adopted by Fidel Castro's revolutionaries. In the course of the 20th century, various artistic groups have distinguished themselves by characteristic beard-styles. Rulers no longer inspired the fashion in beards, moustaches or imperials; now it was the turn of the filmstars: moustaches were named after Adolphe Menjou, Clark Gable or Charlie Chaplin.

English Moustache. A small close-clipped moustache, a favourite style in the 20th century. Variants were made popular in the 1930s by Clark Cable, Adolphe Menjou and Charlie Chaplin.

False Beard. A long narrow chin-piece consisting partly or entirely of woven or plaited false hair and tied by strings behind the ears. It was worn by the ancient Egyptians, Babylonians and Assyrians. In Egypt it was worn only by royalty.

Favoris. Long, narrow sideburns framing the cheeks, which were particularly popular in the first half of the 19th century.

Franz-Josef. Thick side-whiskers worn without beard or moustache. If the chin was not completely shaven and the side-whiskers pointed downwards, the typical 19th century beard in the shape of a 'W' resulted.

Fräse. Apart from the full beard, this was the earliest form of beard; it was introduced into Babylon by the Semites. It was worn with sideburns framing the face, but the lips were cleanshaven.

Full Beard. A natural beard and probably the earliest form of beard. Since it was commonly considered a sign of virility and freedom, slaves and prisoners of war were often deprived of their beards. It was worn in the 19th and 20th centuries as a mark of liberal or revolutionary convictions.

Henri Quatre Beard or **Goat Beard.** A French version worn in the 17th century was named after King Henry IV of France. The beard was cut to a point and was always worn with a moustache; the latter varied in size.

Knebelbart or **Twisted Moustache.** A moustache worn with a small beard which was particularly fashionable in Spain. It was revived by Napoleon III.

Moustache. A beard grown on the upper lip. Its size varied with the fashion. It was popular at the court of Louis XIV. In the army this adornment was reserved for officers.

567 568

569

570

571

567 Assyrian mural
painting (detail). After
Perrot-Clipiez.

568 Syrian chieftains
paying tribute. Painting
from an Egyptian tomb.

569 Etruscan sarcophagus
from Cervetri. Villa
Giulia, Rome.

570 Egypto-Roman
Master of the 2nd
century. Portrait of a
Mummy from El Faiyûm.
Metropolitan Museum of
Art, New York.

571 Albrecht Dürer.
Portrait of Johann
Kleberger.
Kunsthistorisches
Museum, Vienna.

355

572

573

574

572 Hans Holbein the Younger.
Self-portrait. Palazzo Pitti, Florence. The
hair cut in a short fringe above the forehead
and the short-clipped beard was the
conventional masculine style in the
Renaissance.

573 Hans Baldung, known as Grien. Portrait
of a Man. National Gallery, London. The
hair is long in the late Gothic style. He
wears a flat cap or barret and a full,
untrimmed beard.

574 El Greco. Julian Romero de las Azanas
(detail). Prado, Madrid. The Spanish
nobleman wears a short haircut, a small
moustache and the beard known as an
'Henri Quatre'

575 Diego Velazquez. Portrait of King
Philip IV of Spain. Kunsthistorisches
Museum, Vienna. The Spanish king
(1621-1665) wears uncurled hair falling to
his collar and a moustache.

576

577

576 Aert de Gelder. Esther and Mardochai (detail). Museum of Fine Arts, Budapest. The man's hair is covered by a cap and his full beard is untrimmed.

577 Théodore Géricault. An Officer of the Carabineers. Rouen. The hair is worn short. The moustache and side-pieces suit the young officer well.

578 Contemporary caricature. The various types of beard and side whisker here depicted, together with the top-hat, the tail-coat and the crinoline represent the typical Victorian style.

579 J. W. Zinke. Lithograph (detail). The Housewife: 'My husband's in agonies from the colic. What have you been giving him?' – The Neighbour: 'A homemade remedy.' The husband is wearing 'mutton chop' whiskers.

578

579

Peak. Originally a full beard cut to a point; the name was later applied to a small beard covering the chin only.

Pencil. A small beard or moustache. The beard, worn with a moustache, was popular in the 16th and 17th centuries.

Roman T Beard or **Hammer Cut.** A 17th century style consisting of two narrow strips of curling hair along the upper lip, the rest of the upper lip being cleanshaven. It was always worn with a small pointed beard.

Senator Beard. Side-whiskers which were parted and brushed outwards. They were worn without beard or moustache.

Sideburns or **Side-whiskers.** A style which originated at the end of the 18th century in England. The beard was grown in a narrow line from the hair-line to the lips. Two beard-styles developed in the 19th century: one was a continuation of the neo-antique style of the first half of the century and was particularly popular among the French Bonapartists; the other was the English style; it was longer with projecting points and was worn with 'mutton chop' whiskers.

580 Bust of Queen Nefertiti.
New Dynasty, 1370 B.C.
State Museums, Berlin.

Headgear

Headgear has a protective and decorative function. As it protects the head from the effects of the weather, it changes completely according to the season, geographical latitude and location. Its etymology often indicates its purpose: the basis of the well-known word sombrero is 'sombra', shade.

In tropical Africa, headgear ceases to give shade to the face and the upper half of the body; the turban may be taken as an example, i.e. it protects the skull only. The Bedouins also protect themselves against the glare of the sun by means of a cloth covering the back of the head. Because of their dark skin, many natives in countries on the equator need no protection at all against the rays of the sun.

Agrarian and pastoral peoples were content with a simple headgear, which was sometimes edged by a wide brim (China, Japan, India); tribes of warriors and hunters paid more attention to their head covering, as here protective and decorative functions were united. For example, the American Red Indians decorated themselves with birds' feathers as if they wished to indicate the speed of their movements thereby.

In ancient times, headgear was mostly practical. The exception was the soldier's helmet which not only gave protection from the enemy but also symbolized manliness. It was not until the Middle Ages that headgear was given different shapes, such as hemispheres and cylinders, cones and pyramids. At that time hats became predominantly objects of decoration, indeed of luxury. They were decorated with feathers, fur and ribbons, and rich people also used pearls and diamonds.

The effort sometimes put into headgear at certain periods can most appropriately be apprehended from the objurgations of the clergy. According to the words of the Augustine, Gottschalk Hollen, it may be imagined that the head decoration of 'fashion conscious' ladies was as follows:

'First of all, a vain woman places a man's hood over her veil; secondly, a costly, folded veil; thirdly, a three- or four-layer silk net; fourthly, gold and silver hair pins; fifthly, a piece of jewelry on the forehead (or bosom); sixthly, shining hair from the body of a dead woman; seventhly, a rosary of coral around the neck. All this a woman needs for decorating her head. She can scarcely buy this for one hundred guilders.'

Symbols of state or church authority or of academic honours are also worn on the head. Crowns are considered to symbolize steadfastness, firmness and nobility. The hat of our day will always be decoration and at the same time protection. This applies to ladies' as well as to gentlemen's wear.

Baigneuse. Bathing cap, corresponds to the *dormeuse*, sleeping cap. Originally a cap with a purpose, intended for sleeping or for bathing, it became part of a citizen's everyday wear with variations in its style, particularly in the last decades of the 18th century.

Balzo. Turban-like Italian cap of the 15th and 16th centuries. The base consisted of a metal plate or leather covered with a coloured fabric, usually silk.

Barret. Soft, flat headgear of various sizes, round or square. Part of ladies' and gentlemen's fashionable wear; popular primarily in the 15th and 16th centuries. It was often made of velvet and decorated with embroidery and feathers. In more recent times, particularly during the Romantic movement, it was very much favoured among artists.

Basque beret. The small, soft round headgear of the Basques. The French made this cap fashionable everywhere in the twenties. Today, children and men use it as casual headgear.

Batwat. A small padded cap worn by knights in the Middle Ages to relieve the pressure of the helmet.

Bicorne. A two-pointed hat with the points towards front and rear; Napoleon wore similar headgear at the beginning of the 19th century.

Boater or **Canotier.** Stiff oval straw hat with a flat crown and straight brim which established itself in gentlemen's fashions around 1900. It was soon taken over by ladies also. It became the indispensable gimmick for many a film star: most notably for Harold Lloyd,

Buster Keaton and Maurice Chevalier.

Bonnet. It appeared in the Middle Ages and the original medieval bonnet continued to be worn in many versions into the 17th century. A later form of bonnet came into fashion in the early Victorian era.

Bowler. It appeared in about 1850 during the period when the top hat, as part of street dress, became unfashionable. It is actually a compromise between the top hat and the felt hat. It has a narrow, curled brim and a stiff dome-shaped crown. It is usually seen in black; only rarely in grey. In the City of London, the bowler hat, together with the umbrella, is the typical uniform of many. In France and Germany it is called a 'melon'.

Butterfly. A lady's cap from the second half of the 18th century, with added wing-like side pieces.

Byssus. A fragile, transparent veil with which the Egyptians covered their mummies at the time of the Pharaohs. It was also worn by Egyptian women. Their moral code forebade its being worn without an underskirt.

Calabrian hat (also called the **Carbonari hat** after the 19th century Italian secret society). A felt hat with a wide brim and high crown, originally worn by the inhabitants of the Italian province of Calabria. Later it became an article of ladies' fashion, particularly as a summer straw hat.

Cap. Of ancient origin it has been headgear of varying shape. Today, to distinguish it from the hat, we know it as being soft without a brim, also sometimes stiffened by inserts. With a peak, it forms part of many official uniforms and has also been rediscovered at intervals by fashion, as in 1964/65.

Capote. A small lady's hat, set high on the head, with a brim framing the face and very popular around 1850. About 1890 it was predominently worn by older women. (Also the name of a gentleman's coat with a turn-down collar and cuffs at the end of the 18th century).

Castor (hat) (Latin – beaver). A felt hat, not always made from beaver hair, and primarily used in the 18th century.

Chapeau bras. This was the name of the three-cornered hat carried by men under the arm in the 18th century.

Chapeau-bonnet. A mixture of a hat and a cap. This was the name given to large, usually richly decorated ladies' hats of a bonnet-like appearance, over which was often worn a veil tied under the chin. It became fashionable towards the end of the 18th century.

Chapeau Claque, crush hat or **opera hat.** A top hat with a collapsing mechanism, invented in 1835 in Paris. Also called the **Gibus hat** after its inventor. Up to the year 1914 it was part of the evening outfit of a gentleman and was worn with tails. When indoors, it was carried under the arm in its collapsed state.

Chimney-pot hat. Top hat from the period of around 1848; sarcastic name for citizens who always wore this conservative headgear, as opposed to the revolutionaries who wore the rounded liberty cap.

Coif. Lady's bonnet of white linen which covered the head completely. Very popular in German medieval fashion.

Coronet. Originally a wreath of laurel or olive branches placed on the heads of deserving personalities among the ancient Romans, particularly victorious warriors. At the time of the Emperors the round crown developing from the wreath or coronet gradually became the symbol of ruling power. It is now a symbol of the peerage. The rim is usually of gold, studded with pearls and jewels. The upper part is crossed by arches in the case of kings and high nobility. In the various monarchies, the shape and size of crowns are prescribed for the various ranks of nobility.

Cowboy hat or **Stetson.** Originally the wide hat of the cattle herdsmen in the American West. From time to time various versions of this headgear have appeared in ladies' and gentlemen's fashions. For some time, the well-known Parisian dress designer Pierre Balmain also tried to popularize the cowboy hat by wearing it personally.

Cowl. Medieval hood with a collar-like shoulder piece which became popular headgear for gentlemen in the second half of the 14th century and which characterized the fashionable silhouette of the Gothic period. It is the predecessor of the fool's cap and fell from fashion on the appearance of the hat.

Deerstalker. A sportsman's helmet-shaped cap, made famous by Sherlock Holmes.

Fez. Red hat of felt, popular in the Near East,

particularly in Turkey, the Arabian states, Cyprus, Albania and Greece. A gentleman's fez has a black or blue tassel. The tassel on a lady's fez is often decorated with gold or pearls.

Gefrens (Gefrenns). Fringe-like lady's head decoration which was worn at the back of the head. Fashionable in the second half of the 15th century.

Helmet. A hide or leather head-covering, first found in ancient times, used as protection against weapons, or sun in the tropics.

Hennin. A high, cone-shaped headgear for ladies. The three- to four-foot high cone of stiff paper or starched linen was covered with silk or other precious materials. Across the whole of the back of the hennin, and sometimes also across the face, fell a transparent veil which often reached as far as the floor. Hair protruding over the edge of the hennin was shaved off, apart from a small triangle in the middle of the forehead. In the middle of the 15th century, the hennin was introduced to the court of Burgundy by Isabella of Bavaria. No other lady's hat has ever dominated fashion as this did for half a century. Later, hennins

were worn in the shape of a crescent or two-pointed hat. Until this very day a modified form of this hat is worn by the Jews of Algeria and Tunis as well as by many citizens of the Lebanon.

Homburg. A man's felt hat, with narrow brim and crown, dinted in at the top.

Kruseler (Middle High German – kriuseler). Typical headgear of ladies between about 1340 and 1430. It existed in various shapes as head-scarf and bonnet. It gets its name from the tightly-frilled trimming.

Leghorn hat, flap-hat or **Florentine hat.** A hat plaited from Italian straw; hence its name. It has a flexible brim and was modern in the 19th century at the time of the crinoline. It is still used to-day as a sun-hat.

581 Isis accompanies the queen into the next world. The tomb of Queen Nefertiti, 19th Dynasty, Thebes. The goddess wears the symbol of the orb of the sun on her head, the queen a high crown, symbolizing the power of the state, set on a metal helmet.

Liripipes. In the 15th century, strips of material falling on to the shoulders on both sides of the face and often decorated by being slit or with fringes, were fixed to hoods and caps.

Paon (Peacock hat). A narrow gentleman's hat with a high crown of the 14th century. The brim is bent upwards at the back and increases in width towards the front, protruding far beyond the forehead. It is often thickly covered with sewn-on peacock feathers – hence the name. It remained popular well into the 16th century.

Petasus. Part of the Greek travelling outfit of the Ephebes. A hat with a flat crown and a flat broad brim, tied at the back with a strap (the god Hermes is usually illustrated with a winged petasus). The Romans also wore it and later, in the Middle Ages, the Jews wore it as part of their prescribed dress.

Phrygian cap. Cone-shaped headgear with a forward point. Originally worn by the Phrygians and taken over from them by the Greeks. During the French Revolution it became part of the Jacobin dress.

Pilos or **Pileus.** A cap-like hat of felt, straw

582

or skin worn by the Greeks and Romans. Among the emancipated it was considered a symbol of freedom.

Pleureuse. The trimming for ladies' hats of the beginning of the 20th century, consisting of joined and curly ostrich feathers.

Plumage. The feather trimming which framed the brim of the three-cornered hat at the turn of the 17th and 18th centuries.

Riding hood. A hood covering head and body forming part of the middle-class town lady's dress in the 18th century.

Rubens hat or **Rembrandt hat.** Large felt hat, popular in the 17th century, particularly in the Netherlands. It was given its name because of the many portraits by Rubens and Rembrandt in which it appeared again and again.

Skull cap (French – calotte). A net-like, plaited hair bonnet which appeared during the penultimate and last decade of the 15th century. Later, it often only covered the back of the head.

Sombrero. Straw hat with a wide brim.

Straw hat. It was known already in ancient times. (The Greek petasus was made of straw). The Franks wore straw hats in the 9th and 10th centuries, and they remained a protection against the sun, particularly among farmers, in Germany and France right into the 16th century. It was not until the middle of the 18th century that it became an item of ladies' fashion. The Florentine hat, the Panama hat and the *Canotier* became classical straw hats.

Stuart bonnet. This is a bonnet-like hat forming a widow's peak on the forehead and slightly curved at the sides. It gets its name from the Scottish queen, who did not invent it but liked to wear it.

Top hat. This tall hat was made generally popular by the English shortly after the French Revolution, when tail-coats were worn during the day and the top hat became part of this manner of dress. Since those times, there have been changes in height, shape and colour. Empire and Early Victorian times loved the coloured top hat, particularly in light grey. It is still worn today on ceremonial occasions and at weddings.

Toque. A brim-less beret with a pleated crown forming part of men's and women's dress of the second half of the 16th century. Since the 20th century it has re-appeared in ladies' fashions in different versions.

Tricorne (three-cornered hat). A hat with the brim pressed together into three points which was fashionable among men at the time of Louis XIV. During the Rococo period, it was also worn by women. In the 17th and 18th centuries it formed part of uniforms and at the end of the 18th century it was replaced by the two-cornered hat, or bicorne.

Trilby. A soft, felt hat, which originated from George du Maurier's novel, *Trilby* (1894).

Trotteur. Generally the normal name for a small hat worn with street clothes.

Turban. The Persian word denotes the veil-material from which the Persians make their coiled headgear. The Arabs and other oriental people took over the turban from them. It came to Europe with the Crusades. In French-Burgundian fashion, the ladies and gentlemen of the court wore turbans. Liripipes also are a European variant of the turban. Similarly, the *Balzo* of the Renaissance is a stiff, unwound variation. Caps of the 15th and 16th centuries often reveal their links with oriental models. In the 17th and 18th centuries, the turban disappeared from European fashion and did not reappear until the time of the Napoleonic campaign to Egypt (Empire fashion) and later once again during the Second World War.

Veil. A fine, transparent fabric of silk, cotton or wool worn by women, partly to cover their face and partly as a head decoration. Originally, however, it formed part of the clothing for the whole body.

The veil probably originated in the orient where it has held its ground until modern times. In Middle Eastern countries women concealed their faces with quite a thick veil not only in the street but also at home when strangers were present. From ancient times until today, the veil has had various sizes, shapes, colours and decorations.

In ancient Egypt, the women covered themselves in a fragile veil called a *Byssus*. From Asia Minor or from Egypt, the veil reached Greece where it was worn richly and artistically folded. At the time of the Roman Emperors, the veil (called flammeum or recinium) was a favourite item of decoration.

As from the 4th century, the white veil – the symbol of purity – became the indispensable ornament of the Christian bride. The black veil, on the other hand, is the symbol of mourning in Christian religion. In the 10th and 11th centuries, veils which also covered the shoulders were worn.

In the late Middle Ages, the veil once more came to Europe from the orient as a hat decoration. In the 14th and 15th centuries nothing less than a veil cult prevailed at the court of Burgundy. The women wore veils attached to their hennins; the men, attached to their hats. The medieval veil was also perfumed. In the 16th century, the veil disappeared together with the bonnet, except on Spanish women

582 Statue of Rameses II, 19th Dynasty, Turin. He wears a blue crown of war with the regal symbol, the *uraeus*.

583 Greek clay figure from Tanagra (detail). The cloak is pulled over the head.

583

who wore a black lace mantilla. The veil was rarely to be found in the Baroque and Rococo periods.

The fashions of the Directoire period brought in ladies' dresses made from thin, light materials. During the early Victorian period, the veil decorated ladies' hats once more, particularly top hats for ladies, worn as part of their riding habit. As from the beginning of the 19th century, tulle veils appear. These have also remained an essential part of some ceremonial dress, in particular wedding gowns. Veils were very fashionable at the end of the 19th and the beginning of the 20th century, right up to the First World War. They were attached to the brim of the hat and covered the face either completely or in part.

Whatever criticism was levelled at the veil – it damaged the complexion, it was said; it was the cause of red noses; it reduced the vision – nothing was able to harm this 'visor' until its time was up, at all events in fashion. A fashion report from the period before the First World War reads:

'. . . thus, for the *grande dame*, the veil is just as important for street dress as is the hat. In the same way as the latter, the former is also subject to fashion; it can be worn well or badly, be becoming or the opposite. Each year has its special 'veil moods'. Since the spring of 1911 we have been under the spell of lace design. Sometimes, the lace pattern is used only as trimming, a specially clever fashion which leaves the eyes free under the fine *tulle craquelé*, while any small defects on the nose and mouth are kindly veiled by the lace trimming. . .'

Wimple. Typical headgear for ladies of the 13th century (the statue of Uta in Naumburg Cathedral). It was constructed of a linen band, wound firmly around the chin and head, and a head band of starched linen. In addition, a head ring or an indented crown was often worn on top of this.

584

585

586

587

584 Three Tanagra figurines. National Museum, Athens. The typical Greek headgear is the round hat, the *petasus*, placed on the head as protection against the sun. All the figures are dressed in short or long tunics, over which the woman to the left wears a *himation*, the men the so-called *chlamys*.

585 Madonna from a triptych, about 1420. Flössnitz village church. The crown of the Madonna is similar in its form and structure to the royal crown of the time.

586 Isabella de Bavière. End of the 14th century. Palace at Poitiers. The crown of the French queen is supplemented by a net concealing the hair.

587 Hans Suess of Kulmbach. St. Catherine. Museum Narodowe, Krakow. Richer variation of a royal crown, decorated with pearls and jewels.

367

589

590

588 Mitre, 17th century. Kremlin Museum, Moscow. The mitre of the Moscow patriarch has a rounded shape, decorated with pearls and jewels as well as with the figures of saints in relief.

589 French Master of the 15th century, Mourning Christ (detail). Hermitage, Leningrad. Mary here wears the white veil of the married woman, completely covering the hair.

590 Giotto. Woman's head. Museum of Fine Arts, Budapest. Lightly folded veil above the forehead forming small pleats under the chin.

591

591 Unknown Master of the 16th century.
Agnes Sorel. Duc de Mouchy Collection.
The Renaissance veil serves more as
decoration than for concealing the hair. It
was usually made of fine, transparent
material, and here falls as far as the back.
This portrait of the mistress of Charles VII
of France is famous for the low neck of the
dress.

592 Hans Memling. Portrait of Marie
Mereel, called Sibylle Sambertha. Musée
de l'Hopital Saint-Jean, Bruges. A
conical hennin of the Netherlands with a
transparent veil.

593 Rogier van der Weyden. Portrait of a
lady. National Gallery, London.

594 French School of the 16th century.
Antoinette d'Orleans. French-Renaissance
veil placed high on the temple over the hair
built up into a kind of diadem, with the ends
falling to the shoulders. With this is worn a
decorated stand-up collar of lace.

595 Master E. S. Detail from the Austrian
coat of arms. A hennin sewn with pearls and
a veil which reaches to the deep décolleté
dress, with a shawl collar round a brocade
insert.

370

592

593

594

595

596

597

598

599

372

596 French School of the 15th century. The wife of Jacques Coeur. Musée du Berry, Bourges.

597 Geertgen Tot Sint Jans. St. Sippe in church (detail). Rijksmuseum, Amsterdam.

598 Jan van Eyck. Portrait of the artist's wife. Academy of Fine Arts, Bruges.

599 Pisanello, 1410–20. Courtly lady. National Gallery of Art, Washington. The Italian lady wears a turban decorated with precious stones, a dress of brocade with a high collar and a double string of pearls.

600 Leonardo da Vinci. Madonna Litta (detail). Hermitage, Leningrad.

601

602

601 Jean Fouquet. Charles VII, King of France (detail). The French king wears a wide-brimmed hat decorated with embroidery. The coat is trimmed with fur.

602 Master of Messkirch. Crucifixion (detail). Pushkin Museum, Moscow. Top hats already existed in the 16th century, although it was not until the 18th century that they became an indispensable part of male dress.

603 Hans Holbein the Younger. Cardinal Fisher, Bishop of Rochester. Drawing, Royal Art Collection, Windsor Castle. The barret, set low on the forehead, with ear flaps, is one of the numerous forms in which this favourite, and for a long time popular, headgear came.

604 Hans Holbein the Younger. Thomas Parrie. Drawing. The barret of the English nobleman is wide and adorned with a feather, and is worn over short cut hair.

605 Albrecht Dürer. Friedrich der Weise, Elector of Saxony. Engraving. The barret, set low on the forehead, with wide flaps which are buttoned together on the crown, is worn over richly curled hair.

Thomas Parrie

603   604

605

607

608

606

609

610

606 Bernart van Orley. Portrait of Emperor Charles V. Museum of Fine Arts, Budapest. A jewel-adorned barret on smooth hair. The Emperor wears a pleated shirt, a fur-trimmed cloak and the Order of the Golden Fleece around the neck.

607 Hendrik ter Brugghen. Flute player. National Art Collection, Kassel. The wide barret is adorned with feathers, the doublet is slashed on the back and in the shoulders.

608 Lucas van Leyden. Card players. Collection Earl of Pembroke and Montgomery, Wilton House, Salisbury. Various types of Renaissance barrets for the men, plain or decorated with feathers. The women wear veils.

609 Jan van Eyck. Portrait of a goldsmith. Museum of Art, Bucarest. The Dutch artisan wears a barret with liripipes, decorative strips of material flowing down to the chest.

610 Master of the Lower Rhine. Konrad von Lindenach, circa 1500. Museum Narodowe, Krakow. The German nobleman wears a jewel-decorated barret and a triple gold chain around the neck – nothing unusual at a time when men dressed considerably more splendidly than to-day.

The Lady Eliot.

611 Hans Holbein the Younger. Lady
Margaret Eliot. Drawing. Royal Art
Collection, Windsor Castle. The English
lady's bonnet is worn deep on the brow and
covers the hair and ears.

612 Hans Holbein the Younger. Lady
Parker. Drawing. Royal Art Collection,
Windsor Castle. The young English lady's
bonnet covers only the crown of the head
and forms a kind of raised diadem.

613 Hans Holbein the Younger. Unknown
Lady. Drawing. Royal Art Collection,
Windsor Castle. The many different types of
bonnet – including towering types supported
by wire frames – were interesting variations
on the fashion of the 16th century.

611

612   613

Parker.

614

615

614 Jan Steen. The Idlers (detail).
Hermitage, Leningrad. The man has long
hair and wears a barett. The woman wears a
white cap with a narrow lace edge, a
stylized form of the head scarf.

615 Peter Paul Rubens. Suzanne Fourment.
National Gallery, London. The wide,
feather-or flower-decorated hat was
fashionable in a number of periods.

616   617   618

619

616 Wenzel Hollar. Lady promenading in Munich. Copperplate engraving. The middle-class German lady wears a wide hat, a ruff, a dress with laced bodice, a skirt with an apron and a short *pelerine*.

617 Wenzel Hollar. English woman. Copperplate engraving. The fashionable outfit of a lady in the middle of the 17th century – a ruff edged with lace, a bodice reaching to below the waist in front, a double skirt with a bell-shaped flare at the bottom – is made complete by a hat with a high crown and a fan of feathers.

618 Wenzel Hollar. English burgher's wife. Copperplate engraving. The middle-class English woman wears a bonnet covering her ears under a wide hat with a cone-shaped crown.

620

621

622

619 Wenzel Hollar. The Turk with the flowered waistcoat. Copperplate engraving. The classical type of Turkish turban has appeared in many different guises at all periods.

620 Joshua Reynolds. Nellie O'Brien. Wallace Collection, London. Wide, flower-decorated hats were very popular in the second half of the 18th century. With the hat, the noble lady wears a décolleté dress decorated with lace.

621 Portrait of Friedrich Wilhelm of Seydlitz (detail), Ohlau Church. He wears a feather-trimmed hat.

622 Fra Yittore Ghislandi. A nobleman in grey. Museo Poldi Pezzoli, Milan. Originally the three-cornered hat was part of military uniform, but it was also worn with civilian clothes. It was made of black felt decorated with gold braid.

623

624

623 William Hogarth. The House of Commons. Copperplate engraving. The men wear three-cornered hats over their wigs.

624 Jacobin. Engraving from a painting by Fragonard. The Phrygian cap returned with the Revolution.

625 Engraving by John Finlayson. Elizabeth, Duchess of Argyll.

626 Thomas Gainsborough. Miss Catherine Tatton. National Gallery of Art, Washington. The wide hat completing the summer dress was very popular towards the end of the 18th century.

627 Army Beauty. Anonymous engraving. About 1781. At the end of the 18th century the young lady wears a feathered hat on top of her wig and a bodice with epaulettes.

628 Johann Heinrich Wilhelm Tischbein. Portrait of Goethe in the country. Stadelsches Kunstinstitut, Frankfurt on Main.

625

626

627

628

629

630

629 Francisco José de Goya. Carlos IV.
Prado, Madrid. The dark tricorne was also
worn in Spain at the end of the 18th century.

630 Francisco José de Goya. Duke Fernan
Nunez. Prado, Madrid. The wide,
feather-decorated hat was also worn
at the end of the 18th century.

631 From an English fashion magazine,
1818. Victoria and Albert Museum, London.
Following English fashion, the ladies wear
large sun hats decorated with ribbons and a
veil with their street dress.

632 Christoph Haller von Hallerstein. The
hats of 1810. A caricature engraving.

384

631

632

634

635

636

637

633 Hats from a fashion magazine, circa 1806. At the time of the French Empire bonnets were low and oblong and decorated with ribbons, small ruches or artifical flowers.

634 *Costumes Parisiens* 1810. A straw hat, a white dress of Indian calico and cotton stockings are part of the trousseau of a lady of the French Empire.

635 *Costumes Parisiens*, 1810. Bonnet with ribbons tied in a bow at the top, complete this dress *à la Ninon*.

636 *Costumes Parisiens*, 1809. A transparent veil with lace completes this loosely flowing dress with a lace stole.

637 *Costumes Parisiens*, 1812. The lady wears with her dress a large sun bonnet decorated with ribbons and ruches.

638   639   640

641

638 *Wiener Moden*, 1821. The lady wears a wide-brimmed sun bonnet with lace, a dress with a wide collar reaching to the waist and sleeves widened at the shoulders.

639 *Wiener Moden*, 1823. The sun bonnet of gathered material is decorated with flowers and smartly tied under the chin.

640 *Wiener Moden*, 1822. The wide Florentine hat with the indispensable flowers and ribbons.

641 From a fashion magazine, 1827. With street dresses, the wide Florentine hats were worn in the 1830s.

642 Eugène Delacroix. Detail of a painting 'Freedom leads the people to the barricades'. Musée du Louvre, Paris. The Parisian student wears a tail-coat with a dark cravatte and a top hat with a very extreme turned-up brim.

643 *La Mode*, 1832. With the moiré dress, the lady wears a turban decorated with gauze and topped by bird of paradise feathers.

644 *Wiener Moden*, 1836. In the 1830s the sun bonnet was still part of the street dress with wide sleeves and a narrow waist. The man wears a tail-coat and top hat.

642

643   644

645 *La Gazette des Salons*, 1839. Street dresses with frilled skirts worn with a parasol, the so-called *Sylphide* parasol. The young girl wears her hair *à la Sévigné*; the lady has a sun bonnet on her head.

646 *Allgemeine Modenzeitung*, 1837. A bonnet, sun bonnet or feather covered turban was worn also with evening dresses in early Victorian times, and hair styles with flowers and ribbons plaited-in.

647 Gustave Doré. Wolves. Lithograph from the series *La ménagerie parisienne*. The gentlemen talking are illustrated in the classical fashionable dress: tailcoat, overcoat or cape and, of course, the top hat, which has now become very tall again.

648 *Allgemeine Modenzeitung*, 1840. Street dress with bonnet and stole. Never again has the cult of headgear been so great as in early Victorian times. Suggestions for dresses in fashion magazines were always accompanied by imaginatively decorated sun bonnets.

645

646

649 From a fashion magazine, 1862. Fashionable figures in dresses with crinolines, flounces and lace borders.

650 From a fashion magazine, circa 1860. The doll-like costume of the Victorian period had many forms of bonnet-like hats, which framed the face.

651 *Magazin des Demoiselles*. An innovation to the street dress in the 1860s is the bonnet edged with lace on the forehead, called the Stuart bonnet.

652 Ferdinand Georg Waldmüller. Portrait of an old woman. Austrian Gallery, Vienna. The old burgher's wife is wearing a soft, lace bonnet above a satin dress with wide collar, also trimmed with lace.

653 Degas in the year 1885. Etching. Bibliothèque Doucet, Paris. The tall top hat with narrow brim was still essential in the 1880s.

652

653

654

654 *Charivari*, 1875. Paris. Hat with bells on the end of streamers. A fashion loved by the late-Gothic it reappears in the 19th century in caricature.

655

655 From an English fashion magazine, 1886. Victoria and Albert Museum, London. In summer both men and women wore straw hats, called *Canotiers*. The sailor suit worn by the women is in two parts.

656 Antonio Mancini. The model. Chiaranda Collection, Naples. Ladies' hats at the end of the century became even wider, and were decorated even more richly with artificial flowers, ribbons and feathers.

657 Boldini. Portrait of a lady. Etching. Muff, fur collar and feather hat form an elegant ensemble.

656

657

658

659

658 Auguste Renoir. The Luncheon of the Boating Party. Collection Duncan Philipps, Washington. A party in a garden restaurant wearing headgear of the most varied styles. The ladies wear small flower hats or bonnets, the men top hats, *Canotiers* or bowler hats.

659 Aristide Maillol. Head of a young girl. Musée H. Rigaud, Perpignan. The black lace hat is reminiscent in its shape of the sun bonnet from the 1830s, almost completely covering the face.

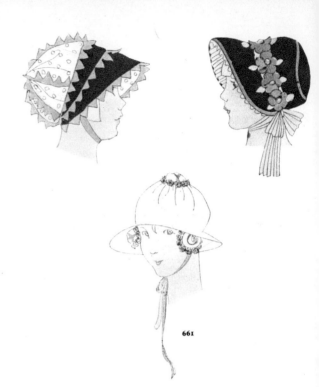

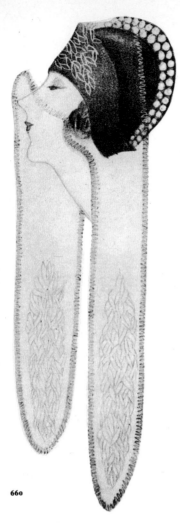

660 *Gazette du Bon Ton*, 1924. Jeanne Lanvin model.

661 *Vogue*, 1928. Elegance for our children.

662 Pictorial Comedy, London, 1908. Fifteenth and twentieth centuries. The artist caricatures the eternally uncomfortable female fashions.

663

664

663 *Nos Loisirs*, 1930. Models Jeanne Lanvin and N. Groult. In the thirties, hats were worn fitting closely to the head and generally provided with only a narrow brim bent downwards.

664 *Nos Loisirs*, 1929. Several variants of hats and handbags as launched by French fashion in the thirties.

Collars and Collar Ornaments

Until the late Middle Ages clothes were made without collars. It was only in the 13th century that a narrow strip made its appearance at the neckline, evolving gradually into the stand-up collar. In the 14th and 15th centuries the narrow stand-up collar was a characteristic of the doublet and the Burgundian style of men's coats.

Bertha: Collar-shaped border to the wide neck of a woman's dress, about 1830 to 1860.

Betsy Ruff. A ruff which returned to fashion between 1820 and 1830.

Buffon. With the bustle, women's fashion during the last ten years of the 18th century evolved a highly unnatural, S-shaped silhouette, causing the fichu above the bust to form a huge roll into which the chin frequently disappeared. This neckerchief supported sometimes by a framework was called a buffon.

Byron collar (*Schillerkragen*). Since hiking began at the beginning of the 20th century, men have worn sports shirts open at the neck, often described in this manner. Its name derived from the careless, open collars of contemporary pictures of romantic poets.

Falling Bands. A collar, elongated and divided into two, used from the mid 17th century, and still preserved in the bands of Protestant ministers.

Fichu, Neckerchief. Women's fashion accessory, a neck or breast cloth made of cambric, silk or lace, concealing the décolletage of the bodice. Worn mainly during the second half of the 18th century and the first thirty years of the 19th.

Folette (French). A triangular neckcloth of soft, light-coloured material. During the first half of the 18th century it was worn as a loose scarf with the ends tucked into the neck at the front.

Frill. Pleated or folded strips of material, flounce. A standard feature of 18th century undergarments, visible at the bust when worn beneath a coat open at the front.

Golilla (French, *collier*). A Spanish term for an upstanding and circular collar.

Halshemd (German). Cloth mentioned at the turn of the 15th century covering the shoulders and neck to diminish the neckline.

Kerchief. A small cloth used especially in country and informal dress, similar to the fichu.

Partlet. From the beginning of the 16th century, a bib covering the low neckline of a woman's dress. It was also used in men's clothing of the period and may still be frequently seen in traditional costume.

Römerhals (German). Since no collar adorned the clothing of ancient Greeks and Romans, the present fashion of the collarless neckline is described in the men's trade as a 'Roman neckline'.

Ruff (Fraise, Frill, Duttenkragen, Cartwheel, Millstone, Kalbgekröse Tripe, Pulcinello). Wide white collar fitting close to the neck, originating in 16th century Spain, where it was worn by men, women and children. After 1575 it became in its own right a regular feature of fashionable dress and attained such a size that in 1586 it became known as a cartwheel, a description frequently exploited by caricaturists. It was made of fine linen, stitched, folded and starched, and frequently stayed with wire. In Germany and Flanders, where it was commonly known as a *Duttenkragen*, the ruff was worn up to the early part of the 18th century. Until well into the 18th century it was preserved as an essential feature of Jewish traditional dress. Today it survives in folk costume and in the traditional costume of the pierrot. It was sometimes supported by a supportasse or underpropper.

Stomacher. The stiffened bib of women's bodices at the turn of the 17th and 18th centuries, worn over the front piece of corsets.

Vatermörder. A Biedermeier (early 19th century) collar attached to men's shirts, having stiff, protruding points. It survives as the butterfly or wing collar worn for formal dress today.

Wisk or **Standing Band.** Square collar, supported by underpropper or supportasse.

666 Giotto. Virgin Mary, detail from The Annunciation. Chapel of the Arena, Padua. The early Gothic fashion was collarless.

667 Hans Memling. Donor of the Portinari Altar. Metropolitan Museum of Art, New York. Not until the Middle Ages did women begin to wear low cut necklines, trimmed, as below, with an ermine, shawl collar, and worn with an expensive necklace.

668 Nuremberg Merchant. Anonymous woodcut, 1610. The wide, flat and completely plain coat-collar goes with the simple style of the clothes.

669 Ascribed to François Clouet. Louis de Béranger de Guast, Bibliothèque Nationale, Paris. He wears a small pleated ruff.

670 Diego Velasquez. Portrait of Philip IV. Prado, Madrid. He wears a square standing band or wisk.

671 French School of the second half of the 16th century. Louise de Lorraine. Musée du Louvre, Paris. The French lady is in a décolleté dress with pleated stand-up collar, probably supported by wire stiffening or supportasse or underpropper.

666

667

XXI Anton Machek. Lady in a blue dress. Národni Galerie, Prague.

XXII Anton Machek. Ondřej Pech. Národni Galerie, Prague.

668 669

670 671

672

673

672 Peter Paul Rubens. Portrait of a lady-in-waiting. Hermitage, Leningrad. She wears a large ruff with a fragile lace border.

673 Jan Cornelisz Verspronck. Portrait of a Young Woman. Hermitage, Leningrad. As time went on, the stiff white collar assumed vast proportions, being called a millstone ruff. This one, like the little cap edged with lace, is part of the clothing of a young Dutchwoman.

674 Antony van Dyck. Family Portrait. Hermitage, Leningrad. Cartwheel ruff on the woman's dress; the man, as also the little girl, wears square, lace-edged standing bands or wisks.

675   677

676

675 Juan Pantoja de la Cruz. Portrait of Donna Juanna of Aragon, née von Pernštejn, wife of Ferdinand of Aragon. Nelahozeves Castle (Bohemia).

676 Jan Vermeer van Delft. Portrait of a Woman. Museum of Fine Arts, Budapest. The big, conical collar of the young Dutchwoman is held together by a bow. The cuffs are made of the same material as the collar.

677 Duke of Buckingham. Engraving after Peter Paul Rubens. The stand-up collar is edged with fine serrated lace. The portrait of the nobleman is completed by the waved hair, moustaches and pointed beard.

678 Portrait of an Unknown Man. Ascribed to François Clouet. Hermitage, Leningrad. Stand-up collar with starched ruff in the Spanish fashion of the second half of the 16th century adorns the doublet with slashed sleeves.

679 Bartholomäus Spranger. Epitaph for the Goldsmith Müller. At this time ruffs were characteristic of the clothing of men, women and children alike.

678

679

405

680 Wenzel Hollar. Noblewoman with big double lace collar. Engraving.

681 Wenzel Hollar. Spanish Lady. Engraving. The collar of the gown is wired to frame the large ruff. An example of regional dress.

682 Wenzel Hollar. Woman of Zürich taking a stroll through the town. Engraving. A white hood covers the head. In the mid 17th century a ruff is worn round the neck – another regional survival.

680

681   682

683

684

685

683 Wenzel Hollar. English woman in winter dress with a light-coloured muff. Engraving. As time went on, fashion decreed an increase in the size of wheel collars. Hats followed suit.

684 Wenzel Hollar. A Woman of Amsterdam. Engraving. The ruff survives in Flemish middle-class fashion. Here it is part of clothing consisting of bodice, shirt and apron.

685 Wenzel Hollar. Woman with semi-circular collar or standing band. Engraving. The collar conceals the woman's shoulders and the upper part of her arms.

a Merchants
of Franckfo

Wentzel Hollar

686 687

688

686 Wenzel Hollar. Gentleman Bowing. Engraving. The cavalier is wearing the falling band typical of 1630. Termed the 'Swedish collar' in Germany, after that worn by Gustavus Adolphus. With it he wears a doublet and wide trousers and turned-down boots. In his hand he holds a Rubens hat adorned with feathers.

687 Wenzel Hollar. Woman of Frankfurt. Engraving. The Frankfurt merchant's wife wears a fur hat, a wide, upstanding collar, the wire support for which can be clearly seen.

688 Wenzel Hollar. Wife of the Lord Mayor of London. Engraving. The Englishwoman wears a ruff with a lace edge over her kerchief.

689 Hans von Aachen. Portrait of a Young Man. Národni Galerie, Prague. By the second quarter of the 17th century the ruff was small, worn drooping and without starch.

690 Karl Skreta. Portrait of a Middle-Aged Man. Národni Galerie, Prague. This elongated, rectangular collar appeared in the 17th century and had developed from the semi-circular collar in the 1660s. This was first called falling bands. As two rectangular pieces of cloth, held by a tape, they are retained as clerical bands.

689

690

691 Portrait of Prince Metternich. Engraving after the painting by Michèle Benedetti. At the beginning of the 19th century the complement of the frock-coat was the *Vatermörder*, a tall, man's collar with prominent points.

692 *Le monde élégant.* The wedding-dress is in the fashion of about 1878. The low necks are filled with lace and the bustle skirt is richly adorned with lace and embroidered flowers.

693 Supplement to the *Allgemeine Muster-Zeitung*, 1852. A selection of necklines and collars of the mid Victorian era. The day dress is high-necked with a small collar; the evening dress is characterized by a deep décolletage and bare shoulders.

694 *Vogue*, 1928. The collar in the twenties varied; there were small draped collars and also low, stand-up collars with a V-neck.

691

692

693

694

695 Antoine Jean Gros. The Young
Napoleon. Musée du Louvre. He wears
a black military stock.

Cravats and Ties

The first neckband was worn by Roman legionaries for whom, no doubt, it was a protection against the cold. It also absorbed the sweat of the neck. It was worn once again by Louis XIV's soldiers, especially by his Croatian regiment, and from this the term was originally derived: the Croats, in French, Croates, were miscalled 'Cravates' in the 17th century. In 1692 there was a bloody battle at Steinkirchen, described by Voltaire in *The Age of Louis XIV*: 'The Duke, the Prince de Condé, the two Messieurs de Vendôme, and their friends, upon their return discovered all the roads crowded with people whose expressions of joy and admiration exceeded the bounds of reason, the women seeking to attract the glances of the victors. At this time, men wore lace cravats which required some time and patience to put on. In their haste to prepare for the battle, the princes had carelessly twisted these cravats round their necks; women now began to wear an article on the same model called *Steinkerque* or *Steinkerk*.'

The history of the tie starts in the 17th century. The cravats with their knotted ends were precursors of ties in the modern sense as an appendage of the collar. They were sometimes made of lawn or muslin and sometimes of lace. Some preferred the stock, a gathered band placed around the neck of the shirt and fastened with a buckle at the back. By the end of the 18th century it had become very high and stiff.

At the time of the Revolution and the Directoire, men wore wide neck cloths made of white material. As a protest against these white cloths, the French revolutionaries wore a black cravat ('black as eternal damnation'). The method of tying cravats during the first half of the last century was very complicated. In the middle of the century, a number of manuals on the art of tying cravats appeared (one of these was written by the novelist, Balzac). The more sober men's fashions became in the 19th century, as compared with the 18th century, the more interest became centred, understandably enough, on the tie, one of the

last decorative elements of men's attire. The donor George (Beau) Brummell's skill in their arrangement is famous. The writers of the manuals accordingly demanded that the way a man tied his cravat should reveal his personality as clearly as did the folds of a man's clothes in classical times. The cravat of a genius must therefore have an ingenious line, and the *petit bourgeois* was held to be recognizable from the unimaginative form of his cravat. The *Cravate à la Byron* possessed something of the spirit of the great poet, if the author of *Cravatiana oder neueste Halstuch-Toilette für Herren* is to be believed; this little book appeared in 1826 in Ilmenau, aping of course the great works on the subject of London and Paris. 'Everything', we are told, 'that issued from Lord Byron's eccentric genius, bears the stamp of a certain originality. Hence we cannot expect, in the manner of cravats assumed by the famous poet, either the studied nicety nor the petty fussiness generally to be observed in the neckcloths of the fashionable.

'The slightest restriction to which the body is subject is nearly always reflected in the mind. Who can say to what degree a more or less stiffly starched and tightly bound neckcloth can restrain the springs of fantasy or throttle thought?

'The bard of the corsaire has thrown off all restraints. The neckcloth to which he has given his name, however, differs in one very important respect from all other neckcloths. The difference lies in the way one begins to put on the neckcloth, for instead of beginning at the throat, the start is made, on the contrary, at the nape of the neck, both ends being then brought to the front, immediately below the chin where a large knot is tied that should be at least four inches across and terminate in two great points. This neckcloth is especially suitable to summer travel because it is only wound once round the neck, which is thus left wholly free. Its colour, in harmony with the sombre flight of fancy of its originator, is that of the scabious.'

In the last thirty years of the 19th century, the dangling ends of the bow eventually became the long tie as we now know it. Today it reigns supreme in men's fashion, abetted by the industry's remarkable ingenuity in design. 19th century forms of tie have survived in the Ascot cravat and the stock worn for hunting. Bows were sometimes worn with sports clothes in Germany called 'Lipton bows' after the English tea magnate, Thomas Lipton.

The cut of the tie and the type of pattern are dependent on the current fashion in collars and also on the cut of the suit – whether high or low buttoning. The shape of the knot changes accordingly. Connoisseurs are always very particular about choosing the right design of tie – anything from classical to sporting – to fit the time of day and the occasion of wearing.

696 Jacques Louis David. Barère denouncing Citizen Capet (on 4th January 1793). Engraving.

697 Adélaide Labillé-Guiard. Maximilien Marie Isidore de Robespierre. Robespierre is wearing wig and frockcoat together with white stock and white ruffles.

698 Francisco José de Goya. Marquis Caballero. Magyar Memzebi Galeria, Budapest. The Spanish nobleman's stock is made of fine lace and disappears under the gold-embroidered waistcoat and frockcoat.

696

697

699 Abraham van den Tempel. Family portrait, circa 1660. Hermitage, Leningrad. The wide knotted cravat of the Dutch nobleman is made of plain, broad, white cloth, his companion's of lace, and fills the neck opening of the doublet. The doublet was ornamented with numerous buttons on the front and sleeves.

700 'Venal Love'. Anonymous engraving of 1793. The neckcloth of the men's fashion in those days was a much-discussed expression of wild political feelings.

701 Wenzel Pobuda. *Incroyable* and *Merveilleuse*. Lithograph. A characteristic article of clothing of the French *Incroyable* was a broad cravat that virtually covered the mouth. The frockcoat of unusual cut was worn with a flowered waistcoat with wide revers, and knee stockings with tassels. The girl, a *Merveilleuse*, wears a hat with a soaring brim.

699

700   701

416

XXIII Thomas Gainsborough. Duchess of Beaufort. Hermitage, Leningrad.

XXIV Anton Machek. Lady with a letter. Národni Galerie, Prague.

702 Peltro William Tomkins. Trying on Shoes, English-fashion. Engraving after a painting by Charles Ansell. The 18th century frockcoat and wig are worn with a stock and lace-frilled shirt. The dress is low-cut.

703

704

703 Hyde Park. French etching. The over-emphasis on neck and bosom by the collar and stock and shirt-frill is underlined in this picture.

704 Jean Auguste Dominique Ingres. M. Cordier (detail). Musée du Louvre, Paris. The Empire style frockcoat is worn with a *Vatermörder* with stiffly starched points.

705 From a fashion journal. *A la Byron, Primo Tempo, Irlandaise* and *Orientale* are the far-fetched names for the different methods of tying cravats, which had grown to a considerable cult around 1830.

706 *Petit Courrier des Dames*, 1838. The frockcoat and the cutaway of the 1840s are sometimes worn with a stock (*left*) instead of a cravat, which either blends or contrasts with the colour of the clothing.

418

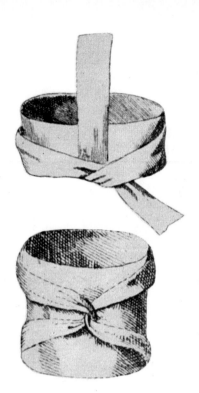

705

706

707 *Petit Courrier des Dames*, 1837. The tailcoat (*centre*) is worn with a black cravat; the morning suit consists of a cutaway, spongebag trousers and a stock.

708 Fashion plates from the *Theaterzeitung*, 1831. The gentleman in tails and a flowered waistcoat wears a wide cravat that covers the whole neck. Over her dress with balloon sleeves, the lady wears a draped shawl, wound loosely round the neck.

709 Fashion plates from the *Theaterzeitung*, 1831. The gentleman in the redingote wears a short-ended cravat wound twice round the neck, and also an eyeglass on a ribbon.

710 Fashion plates from the *Theaterzeitung*, 1842. Tails are worn with a white cravat or a stock. The lady's dress leaves the shoulders bare; she also wears a hat trimmed with feathers, and a stole.

707

708

709

711　　712

713

714

711 Domenico Morelli. Portrait of the
Painter Celontana. The frockcoat is worn
with a white waistcoat, a black cravat tied in
a bow and a top hat.

712 Eugène Delacroix. Self-portrait.
Musée du Louvre, Paris. The painter has
portrayed himself with a moustache, and
wearing a frockcoat with velvet collar
and a cravat wound twice round the neck
and tied with a small knot.

713 Cham (Amédée de Noël). The
Ill-Natured Necktie. Cravats with starched
and pointed ends were often the object of
satire and caricature.

714 Edouard Manet. The Balcony. Musée
du Jeu de Paume, Paris. The double-breasted
jacket which, at the turn of the century,
gradually began to oust the frockcoat, is here
worn with a loose-ended tie in the modern
fashion, presaging those of today.

715 Statue of Mary Magdalen.
Notre-Dame, Montlucon. The Gothic
dress had long, narrow, flowing sleeves,
usually plain. The cloak worn here was at
the same time a hood.

In the history of clothing, the sleeve is an interesting example of the pattern along which fashion develops, in the sense that fashion, with its unswerving passion for experiment, will exhaust all the possibilities of shape within a comparatively restricted range. It will go to extremes and then swing over as far again in the opposite direction. Variations of sleeve are now, as always, important to the fashionable line, and the great store of invention, still evident in much traditional costume is a continual source of inspiration for creators of fashion. So too the shoulder line, in men's fashions for example, varies from natural to padded – as has been the case throughout the centuries.

Even though sleeves are known to have been worn in earlier civilizations, examples being found among the Egyptians, Persians, Assyrians and in the portrayals of Minoan culture, it can be assumed that the earliest clothes of most races were sleeveless. In any event the garments of classical antiquity which influenced European clothing for hundreds of years, were sleeveless, as were coats in the West until the Middle Ages.

Medieval clothing derived its sleeves from Byzantium. In the 12th century and particularly the late Middle Ages, a huge number of variants was created, often evolving into fantastic styles of great charm. Only then did the standard make of the permanently sewn on sleeve appear. There were many different kinds: hanging sleeves, wing sleeves, funnel-shaped sleeves, sack sleeves, bag sleeves, purse sleeves, stuffed sleeves. In the late 15th century sleeves were padded at the shoulder. Slashed and stuffed sleeves became very popular in the 16th century, especially amongst the mercenaries.

The 15th and 16th centuries were the great era of the pin-on or tie-on sleeve, usually an expensive and richly decorated article. Clothing, particularly in noble circles, was most luxuriously furbished, so people restricted themselves to a few splendid garments and a number of interchangeable accessories. Moreover sleeves fixed in this way are easier to fit and allow movement at shoulder and elbow.

As extravagance increased, sleeves being eventually slashed to reveal yet another sleeve beneath, an attempt was made to control such luxuries by sumptuary. In Regensburg the council restricted the wife of each citizen to three pairs of sleeves. During the 17th century the sleeve returned to the natural shape of the arm. A typical feature of women's clothing in the 18th century was the half sleeve with frilled cuffs and lace ruffles. Quite short sleeves were worn around 1800. The Early Victorian period saw the return of wide, opulent sleeves bearing many descriptions.

But, as often happens in fashion, the cut was varied. In the 1830s, for example, several forms of sleeve were in fashion. 'At one time' writes Hottenroth, the costume historian, 'the *gigot* sleeve became narrower immediately at the joint of the arm so that it was baggy above the elbow and tight below. At other times sleeves were cut to fit the shoulder closely, being secured at the wrist by a broad, tight ribbon. The remaining portion was puffed to such an extent that the bagginess tended to subside, the whole sleeve resembling an inverted *gigot* sleeve. . . . The name 'Amadis', which at one time was given to the sleeve with a puffed top, later came to mean one that was tight over its whole length; indeed, at one time or another, various sleeves and their cuffs were called by this name. Tight sleeves, when simple and unadorned, were also called 'Quaker' sleeves. By 1836 the *gigot* sleeve had almost disappeared. . . .' Such is the great diversity of fashion in sleeves. In the 1840s sleeves became tight, but the cuffs broadened into the pagoda sleeve. The wide puffed sleeve of the 1830s was revived in the 1890s.

Although the 20th century returned in general to the natural line of clothing and experiments with sleeves have been kept in check, repeated attempts are made to give greater variety to garments by the expressive use of the sleeve. In men's coats particularly, and sometimes in jackets, there has been a return to the padded shoulder which first made its appearance on the 17th century jerkin. The sleeve is a particularly clear example of the power of fashion.

716 Titian. Man in Blue. National Gallery, London. The Renaissance nobleman wears a jerkin of satin with exaggeratedly padded sleeves.

717 Jan van Scorel. Mary Magdalen. Rijksmuseum, Amsterdam. This young woman of the Renaissance is wearing sleeves ornamented with beads in a criss-cross, diamond shaped pattern.

718 Bernhard Strigel. Bianca Maria Sforza, Maximilian's second wife. The sleeves of the ceremonial court dress are decorated with what are known as puffs. They are slashed at shoulder and elbow. The slash is filled out with white gathered undersleeve material which is kept in position by bows. The rest of the sleeve is decorated with embroidery and bows.

716

717

427

719 Michelangelo da Caravaggio. *La Bonne Aventure* (detail). Musée du Louvre, Paris. A variation on the Baroque slashed sleeve: a strip of different coloured material is sewn down the length of the sleeve. A white cuff is set on the wrist which is similar to the collar. The costume is set off by a barret with two-coloured feathers and brim.

720 Karel Skreta. Portrait of a lady. Rožmberk Castle, Bohemia. The lady wears a lace bonnet, the corners of which fall onto the forehead. The wide slashed sleeves are edged with fur.

721 William Hogarth. Bishop Hoadly. Engraving. Ceremonial bishop's dress: the Baroque sleeves are tied with a ribbon; over them falls a wide mantle with slashes for the arms.

719

720

722

723

724

722 Johann Kupecky. The wife of Merchant Haberstock. Národni Galerie, Prague. Up to the end of the 18th century men's and women's sleeves did not differ.

723 From a Fashion Journal, 1830. During the 1820s the cut of women's clothes changed. Sleeves became wider at the shoulder, waists grew smaller – and this was the beginning of the many different kinds of puffed sleeve.

724 *Wiener Moden*, 1832. The *gigot* sleeves are set straight into the wide neck-line; they fall full from shoulder to wrist where they again become narrow.

726

727

725 *La Mode de Paris*, 1833. Wide sleeves are emphasized by the two tiered lace frill half covering them.

726 *Petit Courrier des Dames*, 1836. In this instance the line of the sleeves is given emphasis by the use of striped material.

727 Lady's evening dress. Lithograph, 1872. Amsterdam. The dress retains the wide sleeves of the 1860s.

728 *Simplicissimus*. Thomas Theodor Heine: 'No, madam, no! You won't be able to get through this narrow gate with those wide sleeves.' Contemporary caricature made fun of big sleeves for which the gate of heaven was not big enough.

729 *Le Rire*, 1896. Man at the turn of the century. Women's wide sleeves were still being caricatured. 'Leg of mutton' and *gigot* sleeves were once more in fashion in the nineties.

728

729

730 Unknown Master. Ladies' Concert (detail). Hermitage, Leningrad.

Cuffs

In Germany the word 'cuffed' (*Manschetten haben*) has established itself in the language as a synonym for being afraid. It derives from 18th century student's slang and described a man, under threat of bodily assault, who thought it expedient to spare his gorgeous and expensive cuffs by refusing to come to blows with his adversary. The French word *manchette* reached Germany by the end of the 17th century and then meant the lace ruffle which had been fashionable since before 1600.

Germans called them hand-ruffles or *Hand-blatter*. *Manchette*, a diminutive of *manche*, sleeve, means small sleeve, and both have their origin in the Latin for hand, *manus*. The following is an extract from a book about cuffs in men's and women's clothing, written in 1801:

'Cuffs are narrow, goffered strips of nettle-cloth, cambric, gauze, net, muslin, *entoilage*, batiste, lace and fine stuffs of a like nature, fastened (sewn) to the sleeve-band of the shirt and serving as ornament to the person of a man or woman. They can be single or two-fold, the latter being narrower at the top. . . . *Pleureuses* (weepers) and *frisettes* are distinctive kinds of cuff associated with court mourning.'

In the second half of the 17th century and early 18th century, the laced linen frilled cuff was attached to the undershirt and showed in the wide sleeve opening. Towards the middle of the 18th century the tighter sleeve came into fashion – elbow length and trimmed with *manches en pagode*. A series of graduated frills were stitched at the sleeve opening and formed the cuff. The ruffles or 'engagements' were stitched below this. A graceful movement of the hand tended to bare the forearm, so long gloves were added, for in fashion one thing leads to another. Thus the lace cuff repeatedly comes to the fore: on pagoda sleeves during the crinoline period, when the wide opening of the sleeves disappeared under a 'cloud of tulle, batiste and lace'.

During the 17th and 18th centuries cuffs, particularly those of lace that fell elegantly over the hand, were a favoured ornament of men's clothing. An authority writes: 'Sleeves must never be so long that they fail to reveal the fore part of the shirt sleeves and lace cuffs in their entirety.' Over and over again, from the time of their introduction, there is striking evidence of the close relationship between collar and cuff. The cuff kept pace with the transformations of the collar; at one time it resembled the ruff and later the lace collar. When the pleated cuff of the late 18th century became narrower, the jabot worn on the shirt dwindled proportionately.

During the Early Victorian period the modern type of cuff made its first appearance and has persisted ever since in men's fashions. Towards the end of the 19th century there was a transitory attempt to economize on wear and tear at vulnerable points of the shirt by the introduction of stiffly starched loose cuffs. The loose cuff was an entirely separate article, being pushed over the wrist and into the opening of the coat-sleeve and it was fastened with a cuff-link. It had its corollary in the dicky. These loose cuffs, though undoubtedly economical, were liable to be propelled from the wrist by an unguarded movement, and they had become an object of social ridicule long before the turn of the century. Before the First World War there was a reaction against the starched cuff, its place being taken by the double cuff.

Starched cuffs are now confined to evening dress, and nowadays shirts for sport and for everyday wear have a variety of cuff forms.

435

731

732

731 Lucas van Leyden. Chess Players.
Berlin Art Gallery. Various kinds of
Renaissance cuff: sleeves are slashed at the
wrist.

732 El Greco. Knight with his hand on his
breast (detail). Prado, Madrid. The only
ornaments worn by the Spanish knight are a

white lace collar, and starched white lace at
the cuff.

733 Sophonisba Anguisciola. The artist's
three sisters at chess. Narodowe Museum,
Posen. The narrow sleeves of the young
noblewomen are ornamented with nothing
but a band of embroidery or lace at the cuff.

733

734

735

736

737

738

734 Wenzel Hollar. Englishwoman taking a stroll in town. Engraving.

735 Wenzel Hollar. Gentleman in ceremonial robes. Engraving.

736 'Costumes Parisiens', 1814. Lace-trimmed dress.

737 Wenzel Hollar. Parisian citizen's wife.

Engraving. The Parisian woman wears a plain bodice ornamented with white cloth cuffs and a wide white collar at the neckline.

738 A costume picture from the time of Louis XVI. A lady of Marie-Thérèse's court, Louise de Savoyan-Carignan, Princesse de Lamballe. Engraving after a painting in the gallery at Versailles.

739 Lucas Cranach. The Amorous Old Man.
Národni Galerie, Prague.

Belts and Sashes

Bandoleer and **Baldrick.** Wide military belt on which powder-flask, match, tinder and lead were carried during the 15th and 16th centuries. In the 17th century it was one of the fashionable accessories of the cavalier who wore a tuck (rapier). It exerted little serious influence on civilian fashion.

Belt. An important item of men's and women's fashion, worn round the waist and frequently separating one item of clothing from another. Apart from being an embellishment – next to the brooch, probably the oldest found in fashion – it was known to have been in existence since the Bronze Age. It relieves the shoulders of part of the weight of the garment. In Crete, and in Greek and Roman antiquity they were a familiar and important element of fashion; only dancers and hetaerae wore their tunics ungirdled. During the Middle Ages when clothing became waisted, belts were often a sign of respectability and position, so women of doubtful repute were, in many cities, forbidden to wear them. During the late Middle Ages a purse was hung from the belt; known as the *aumoniere*, it was the forerunner of the pouch, later to be put to a great variety of uses. The slimness of Gothic and Burgundian fashion enhanced the importance of belts. At this time they were sometimes long and elaborate and worn with bells and later, in the 16th and 17th centuries, women used them to carry mirrors and cosmetics.

During the 17th and 18th centuries, belts were less frequently used. The contemporary line of those fashions had no need of them. Not until the Directoire and Empire periods did they make a general reappearance as a fashion accessory emphasizing the small waist. According to a fashion report of the time, they were either fairly long ribbons simply knotted at the front or side, or shorter strips of velvet, Ottoman silk or crochet-work, fashioned with a steel buckle. The use of the belt in present day male and female fashion began before the First World War. Since then it has been employed over a wide range of women's clothing. In men's fashion it is particularly characteristic of modern sports clothing.

Sash. Band of expensive material, usually silk, worn either from the right shoulder across the chest and over the left hip, or round the waist. The sash was in fact the predecessor of military dress; as late as the Thirty Years' War, soldiers' clothing was not uniform, individual regiments being identified by means of sashes and arm bands. These sashes, also called 'field bands', were at first worn loosely, from the shoulder down to the opposite hip and knotted either at the side or back, with hanging ends. There followed the practice of wearing the sash around the waist and knotting it at the hip. At the Battle of Lutzen in 1632 red sashes identified the Imperial troops and green those of the Swedes. The Brandenburgers, at the Battle of Warsaw in 1651, wore a primitive distinguishing mark in the form of a sprig of oak-leaves attached to their hats while their allies, the Swedes, used wisps of straw. Sashes can also be indicative of rank according to their colour, and are sometimes used for attaching orders and decorations. In the reign of Louis XIV it was fashionable to wear a sash over the *justaucorps* diagonally from the shoulder. During the 17th century nightgowns were sometimes worn loosely tied with a sash. At the end of the 18th century women began to wear round their waists wide bands with hanging ends which were described as sashes. Modern cummerbands are a relic of the sash.

Swordbelt (German, *Dupsing, Dupfing, Teusink*). A low-set belt of the 13th century buckled about the hauberk, a long-sleeved tunic of mail with gauntlets attached. During the second half of the 14th century this wide belt, often of rich goldsmith's work, encircled the gown (similar to the contemporary civilian surcoat) which closely fitted the body and upper parts of the thighs, at hip-level. Much equipment could be attached to this belt: weapons, knives, pouches and even bells. Later it ceased to be a separate article of dress being attached directly to the coat-armour.

740 Portrait of Napoleon III. Lithograph. The last of the French emperors is depicted here with a baldrick over the shoulder and a sash at the waist.

741 Johann Kupecky. The Artist and his Son (detail). Herzog Anton-Ulrich Museum, Brunswick. Especially in the early 18th century, the sash was both a male and a female accessory. The artist portrays himself in informal dress with a striped sash around his waist.

742 John Hoppner. Horatio Viscount Nelson. The sash was also a badge of naval rank. It was worn diagonally across the shoulder and knotted at the hip.

740 741

743

744

743 Pietro Lorenzetti. The Birth of the Virgin Mary (detail). The long scarf was already an accessory of female clothing in the Renaissance period, sometimes having stripes woven into it and also fringes.

744 Karl Skreta. Maria Maximiliana von Šternberk. Národni Galerie, Prague. The walking-stick is not confined to the history of men's fashions, but it is also found in women's. Here it is being used as part of the dress of a young noblewoman who is dressed as a shepherdess in accordance with the pastoral fashion of the time. In the 18th century a fashionable woman's stick was called a *badine*.

745 Francisco de Goya. Dona Maria del Pilar Teresa Cayetana de Silva y Alvarez de Toledo, Duchesss of Alba. Academia de Bellas Artes, San Fernando, Madrid. The sash was in fashion at the end of the 18th century. It emphasizes the high waistline and is tied in a large bow with hanging ends.

746

746 *Costumes Parisiens* 1812. Widow's weeds in the days of the Empire included, as a sign of mourning, a black shawl and a poke bonnet of transparent black material trimmed with feathers.

747 *Wiener Moden* 1829. In the 1820s an indispensable accessory for street wear was the richly embroidered shawl with fringes. The fringes of the shawl are echoed by those worn in the hair, on the sleeves and on the skirt.

747

748 From an English fashion journal, 1841. In the 1840s the shawl was still in fashion; here its colour is plain, as a complement to the popular checked crinoline.

448

Underwear, Housewear and Swimwear

Underclothing is the collective term for all masculine and feminine articles of clothing which are worn next to the skin and under the outer garments. They are made of washable material – of linen, cotton, silk and synthetic fibres, which are produced by knitting or weaving. The history of underclothing is relatively recent; the shirt type of traditional dress worn in ancient times was indeed worn next to the skin, but it served at the same time as the outer garment. Underclothing, as we understand it, was not known until the Middle Ages, when the tendency to wear fine underclothing under the outer garment was first evident, particularly in the higher strata of society. We can still read in the chronicles of the 16th and 17th centuries that an undershirt or shift was a luxury, which only the well-to-do could afford. This garment, basic for both men and women was straight cut, usually knee length, and had the elbow length sleeves set straight into the shoulders.

The women wore their shifts under their corsets, and in the second half of the 17th and 18th centuries the frills at the low cut neckline and at the elbow were intended to show in the openings of the dress. Most was of white linen, easily washable. There was little change in cut or material until the last quarter of the 19th century, when more elaborate trimmings for the majority and not only for the few became possible and permissible. New, more fitted, lower cut shapes were devised for the fashionable, close fitting dresses and it was not until the end of the 19th century that women began to wear decorative, ready-to-wear under-linen, for the most part made of cambric, rarely of silk. It was after 1925 that women's underwear got its present day appearance; natural and artificial silk prevailed for material, pastel shades for colour and the cut was also more elegant (narrow shoulder straps, tailored slips). Men's wear changed even more markedly in this century – the collar was sewn to the shirt, underpants and stockings were shorter. Shortly after the First World War Americans were already wearing very short and tight, close-fitting underpants, similar to bathing trunks.

Bathing Dress. This first came into being at the end of the 18th century, as people began to bathe more in the open air and to take up sport (earlier people had bathed naked). The bathing dress for women at the turn of the 19th century was made of coloured calico, decorated with frills, and black bathing stockings completed the outfit. The bathing suit for men was of cotton jersey material, usually blue and white or red and white striped; but tight close-fitting triangular bathing trunks were also making their appearance. Ladies' bathing costumes were first modernized in the 20th century; they began to be made of woollen jersey material, the Regulation Suit, as it fitted so much better and was warmer. Ladies' modern swimwear is today made of the most varied material; two-piece ones are as popular as all-in-one bathing dresses.

Bliaut (Bliaud). The French medieval term for a shirt type outer garment for men and women, which was evolved from the tunic.

Bust Bodice, Brassière (Bra). Garment to support and shape the breasts introduced early in the 20th century during the 'corsetless' mode. It is usually of elastic material and provided with shoulder straps. In the 1960s the body stocking of elastic mesh was introduced. Worn by young people it affords only very little support.

Caracalla. Narrow tunic, open front and back, originally worn by the Gauls. This led to the hooded Capuchin cloak, the favourite garment of the Roman soldier-emperor Marcus Aurelius Antonius, who on this account was nicknamed 'Caracalla' by his people.

Chemise (French = shirt). Since the Rococo period this has been the term for an under garment with short sleeves; somewhat later (1785–1800) the shirt type garment, the chemise, was the fashion. The name was transferred to a day dress of similar cut.

Chiton. House and every day dress of the ancient Greeks of all classes.

Combinations. Combinations of drawers and chemise introduced for men in 1862 and for women in 1877 provided greater warmth and a smoother line. In the 1920s camiknickers were similar but made of lighter material with shoulder strap tops and looser, shorter legs.

Contouche. Comfortable morning gown in the 18th century.

Corselet. Term for a comfortable, smaller corset, stiffened only with light whalebones or not at all.

Corset, Stays, Bodies. This word contains the French word *corps* = body. Indications of a corset, also of the lacing that made and fashioned the body slimmer, appeared already with the ancient peoples; under the chiton and the tunic leather bands were worn, which shaped the bosom and the hips. A self-supporting garment, similar to the corset, which accentuated waist and bust, came in the 14th and 15th centuries with the Burgundian fashion (men may have then worn a corset).

The shape of corsets changed continuously with the aesthetic conception of the female figure then in fashion and with the type of dress. At one time it was larger than the modern woman's swimsuit, then again as small as a fairly wide belt; sometimes it accentuated or raised the bust, then minimized and flattened it again; often it stressed the waist, narrowed the hips or it emphasized them.

The first great period of the corset in the history of dress came with the spreading Spanish fashion between the middle of the 16th and middle of the 17th centuries. Unlike the Burgundian, the Spanish fashion almost fully suppressed the bust; the corset, stiffened with stays of wood, metal or whalebone, developed into armour plating, which deformed the female figure. The hips were enlarged and supported with the farthingale. Only since the middle of the 17th century were bust and décolleté once more stressed under the influence of French fashion. The tightly boned corsets fastening with lacing at back and front were cut and shaped to lift the bust. Made of canvas they were often covered with rich materials. Short waisted in the 17th century, they became longer waisted and more pointed and cone shaped in the 18th century.

Together with the side-hoop it provided the fashionable outline of the 18th century.

Tight lacing, particularly in France, went into recession with the short waisted styles coincident with the French Revolution and Directoire. It returned about 1810 and continued with different degrees of severity throughout the century. Corsets, hard and stiff to sew, were always made by special craftsmen and women or by tailors. By the middle of the 19th century they were being mass-produced in factories. Even by the middle of the 18th century doctors, philosophers and reformers had begun to campaign against tight lacing, but the first real step towards its abolition was the reform of the Paris fashion-king Poiret, who submitted to the public a proposal to create a chemise type of woman's dress without a corset. After the First World War, the corset disappeared finally and completely out of women's fashions; it was replaced by an elastic and light stockinette belt or girdle and complemented by the bust bodice. Only from time to time are there indications of the return of the corset in modern dress; it always conforms, however, to the natural shape of the body.

Cotillion. Originally the term for an underskirt; in the middle of the 18th century it was transferred to a country dance, probably because the underskirt was to be seen during its performance.

Drawers (feminine), Pants, Knickers (from Knickerbocker). May have been worn in Germany and Holland from the 16th century, but only came into occasional use in England at the beginning of the 19th century, and into general use in the middle of the century with the revealing crinoline styles. Made of washable material they were shaped more or less like men's knee-length trousers. Completely separate legs attached to a band were worn in the second quarter of the 19th century (pantalettes) and were later joined. Calf-length in mid-century, by the end they had become knee-length and more fully cut. Knickers were knee-length, tighter-fitting than drawers and introduced in the late 19th century for wear with sports and tailor made clothes. They are now shorter and smaller.

Drawers (masculine), Underpants,

Trunks etc. Men have worn washable garments under their hose since ancient times. Usually short or knee-length, they were suspended by a tie at the waist. In the 18th century they were shaped like the outer breeches and as long trousers became fashionable in the 19th century, they became tightly fitting and longer reaching almost to the ankles. The fashionable upper classes wore knitted silk, others flannel or flannelette, and in the late 19th and early 20th century wool. Knee-length underpants were reintroduced in late 19th century appealing mainly to the younger man, and very short crutch-length ones (trunks) were introduced after 1945.

Dressing Gown, Undress Gown, Nightgown, Negligé. Term for a comfortable house garment. In the 17th and 18th centuries it was known as a nightgown and worn by both sexes as an informal house-dress. It was originally based on the Far Eastern kimono or banyan. Men's dressing gowns preserved their classical style; they were made of silk or flannel and reached to the calves. They were worn for morning *toilette*, including breakfast. Women's dressing gowns were mostly long, so that they covered the length of the nightdress; in recent times they have also become short or of three-quarter length.

Guépière. Bodice, similar to a corset, used for the tight lacing of the waist; prevailed mainly in the fashion of the New Look after 1947.

Jumps. English late 17th and 18th century. Under-bodice or jacket, an alternative to the stay, providing less restrictive support.

Kalasiris. Shirt type garment of the ancient Egyptians, worn by both sexes. Egyptian sources show it generally as hugging the figure so tightly that it must obviously have been made of a stretch material.

Liberty Bodice. Child's bodice introduced about 1900 to provide warmth and support without harmful restraint. It was reinforced with tape stiffening and often had buttons for the attachment of suspenders.

750 Bible of Wendel IV, circa 1400. National Library, Vienna. The Prague bath-house girls were dressed for work in a white linen chemise with shoulder straps; it reached to the ankles.

Matinée. French term for a loose day garment, especially in use in the 19th century.

Nightshirt. It was first found in the late Middle Ages under the term bedshirt; until then people had either slept naked or had kept on their day clothes. The first nightshirts were very capacious, otherwise they were by and large similar to a day shirt. In general the nightshirt prevailed first in the 19th century, in many countries later. Women often wore at night a night jacket over the day chemise.

Pyjamas. It was brought by travellers from India to Europe in the 19th century. Still in 1882 it was the term used by Edmond de Goncourt for the dress of the matchmaker. Only from the beginning of the 20th century did pyjamas come increasingly into fashion, especially with men, with whom it has to-day fully replaced the nightshirt.

Tunica. The garment for men and women in ancient Rome, which corresponded to the Greek chiton.

Undershirt, Shift, Vest. Loosely cut garment for both sexes, usually of cotton, wool, linen, silk and, in most recent times, of synthetic fibres. The shirt did not exist in the classical age; the shirt-type traditional dress of the Egyptians, Greeks and Romans (kalasiris, chiton, tunic) served at the same time as an outer garment. In cold weather two such garments were worn, without the under one serving as under linen.

Fine linen began to be used for the under-tunic in Byzantium, but this custom did not become general. In the 16th century the shirt was still regarded as a luxury, which belonged only to the well-to-do. Shirts were at that time voluminous, straight cut and had long,

751 The Jena Codex. Bath-house girls and monks. Národni Museum, Prague. The height of the waist also differed.

752 Bible of Wendel IV, circa 1400. National Library, Vienna. The chemises of the Prague bath-house girls varied little in the 15th century from those of the previous period. They had shoulder straps and coloured braid at the neck. The bath-house girls wore a kind of turban on the head.

753 French peasants. 16th century engraving. The woman's chemise is gathered at the neck and covered with a bodice.

754 Pieter Brueghel. The Haymakers (detail). Nárdoni Galerie, Prague. Dutch peasants in their working dress. The shirts of white linen with a round neck are worn over a lace-up bodice. A white or coloured apron is tied over the skirt, which reaches to the knee. A straw hat protects the head; a white cap is also worn.

753

755 Michelangelo da Caravaggio. Mary Magdalene. Gallerie Doria Pamphili, Rome. The deep décolleté of the chemise is ornamented with embroidered braid. The sleeves are wide, but tight at the wrists. A shoulder-strap dress of patterned damask is worn over the chemise.

756 Camille Corot. Agostina. National Gallery of Art, Washington. In the second half of the 19th century the chemise has still the traditional cut, is sleeveless or given short sleeves, has a round neck and is worn with a bodice.

757 Edgar Degas. Women combing their hair. Collection Duncan Philipps, Washington. Long, wide chemises of white linen, with deep round necks and short sleeves were worn at the end of the 19th century.

756

757

758 Wounded Amazon. Roman copy after the Greek original from the 5th century. State Museums, Berlin. The underclothing of the Greek illustrates the exomis, a shirt with only one shoulder band; it is gathered in to a belt at the waist and reaches not quite to the knee.

759 Sarcophagus from Charenton-sur-Cher. Detail of a relief from the 7th century. Musée du Berry, Bourges. The chiton of the ancient Greeks has a belt and is slightly gathered.

760 Isaiah's prayer. Miniature from the Paris Psalter. Bibliothèque Nationale, Paris. The tunic of the ancient times is an under garment. Two tunics were often worn one over the other, a longer and a shorter; the top tunic is sleeveless, the under one has sleeves.

758 759

ΝΥΞ   ΗϹΑΙΑϹ

ὄρθρ

459

761 Ezekiel as a sick man and his miraculous healing. Miniature from a 10th century Psalter. Bibliothéque Nationale, Paris. The tunic was also worn in the late classical period (*centre* and *left*). It was, however, no longer plain, but was ornamented with embroidery.

460

762 Jean Fouquet. The Virgin Mary. Musée Royal des Beaux-Arts, Antwerp. The Madonna is depicted in a chemise under a Gothic dress with lace-up bodice and with an ermine-trimmed cloak. On her head she wears a crown of gold with precious stones.

sleeves. Women's chemises were already made of finer and more varied material and had low necks; at the neck and sleeves they were ornamented with embroidery. Among the people women's chemises were not yet in general use in the 18th century. Women wore only a corset and drawers under the Rococo garment. Elegant men wore fine lace-trimmed shirts with jabot and cuffs. During the Directoire women wore close-fitting knitted

763 Henri de Toulouse-Lautrec. 'Street Conquest'. Musée Paul Dupuy, Toulouse. In the 19th century the feminine fashion was to stress the tiny waist. The corset lacing up at the back achieved this deformation.

764 José Gutierrez Solana. Chorus Women. Museum of Modern Art, Barcelona. The chorus girls are dressing in white chemises with broad shoulder straps, white linen drawers to the knee and corsets.

765 *Nos Loisirs*, 1929. The underlinen of the thirties, for which stockinette was already used, had by and large the present day cut.

763

764

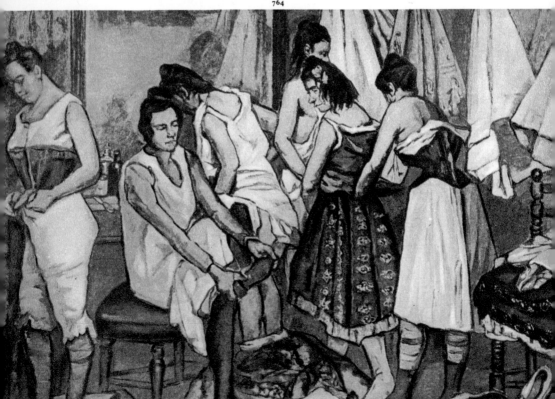

EXPOSITION DE ROSE
Lingerie et Déshabillé

Chemise nuit toile de soie rose thé. Plissés, plastron, col et manches ornés de point de Rhodes.

Déshabillé crêpe satin rose. Un côté en dentelle ocre monté par un feston pointu. Nœud de côté.

Jupon-culotte voile triple. Applications de dentelle vieux ton. Plis «religieuse» dégradés vers le haut.

Combinaison en crêpe mat géranium. Haut et bas garnis d'un crêpe brillant. Broderie au plumetis.

(En haut à gauche)
Chemise crêpe rose incrusté de feuilles bleues. Biais bleu. Combinaison garnie de jours, bordée de dentelle.

(En haut à droite)
Tehina crêpe corail garni d'incrustations brillantes. Chemise et pantalon très plat ornés de jours.

766 Gymnastics. Mosaic from the Piazza Armerina, Sicily. 4th-5th century.

767 'Master with the Bandrolle'. Bathing Women. Woodcut. Gothic women used in general to bathe naked.

768 Hermann Hendrich. Bathing apparel circa 1860. Lithograph. Bathing apparel of the 19th century.

769 *Simplicissimus* (detail). Munich 1919. 'For all that, Kitty is perverse. She is actually in love with a man!' The bathing dress of the twenties was already of clinging material.

770 Contemporary photograph. Bathing dresses from the beginning of this century.

771 *Vogue*, 1928. Jean Patou design. In the twenties bathing dresses had the addition of trouser legs, covered by a short skirt.

772 *Simplicissimus*. Thomas Theodore Heine: 'Madam, you are wife of the chief censor, and now I understand your husband's basic dislike of all nudity!'

766

767   768

769   770

771   772

garments, which were part of the so-called 'naked fashion' of those times. In the early 19th century women wore the chemise voluminous with the square flap neck and short sleeves. Not until the second half of the century did it become appreciably lighter, lower cut and decorated with embroidery. Men's vests of that time were often of wool with short sleeves and button-fastened. Up to the First World War women's chemises were chiefly of batiste, adorned with embroidery and lace; after 1925 they were made of new pastel-shaded material (silk or rayon) and more nearly approached present day design.

Underskirt. A woman's skirt worn under the outer garment. The Spanish farthingale worn in the mid 16th century was actually a linen underskirt, which was stiffened with horsehair or canvas and with a hoop of cane or rope. Women's fashion only paid greater attention to underclothing in the 18th century. Its erotic aspect was soon discovered; the petticoat, which at that time was regarded as the symbol of femininity, developed into an object of feminine coquetry. The top petticoat, which was mostly visible, was made of silk and adorned with lace: the 'under-dress'. In the first half of the 19th century one petticoat was of horsehair, to give support to the bell-shaped overskirt. The number of underskirts was at that time exactly laid down – half a dozen petticoats would belong to an elegant garment; they were of course white; coloured under linen was deemed inelegant and even immoral.

773

774

773 Frans van Mieris. The Morning of a Young Lady. Hermitage, Leningrad. A variation of the *matinée* – the name for an elegant morning jacket – of black velvet with white fur.

774 Gerard Terboch. The Glass of Lemonade. Hermitage, Leningrad. A characteristic component of the Dutch fashion for women was the *matinée*, a short jacket.

775 Johann Peter Molitor. Count Jindřich Pavel Mansfeld. Dobris Castle (near Prague). The Baroque jerkin and waistcoat are richly embroidered with gold. To these belong white stockings and buckle shoes.

775

Accessories are the innumerable unimportant and seemingly trivial features of fashion, which yet, taken together, indicate a style of clothing as much as the actual silhouette or colour. It is in this very toying with trifles that fashion expresses her insatiable desire for novelty. All through history we come across many a commodity which, though taken for granted today, once ranked among the most highly prized and highly priced adjuncts of fashion – the things 'one simply must have, my dear!' A history of accessories can therefore never hope to be exhaustive – the field is too wide. Every epoch created its own particular toys. From the 12th to the 17th century, for example, hand and pocket-mirrors were a favourite female adornment; they were worn on a gold chain round the neck, hung at the girdle, used as the centre of fans, framed in tortoiseshell, ivory or silver-gilt, or combined with miniatures or etchings. The inexhaustible fund of ideas which we admire in the modern fashion industry was limited in those days to the medium of the craftsman's workshop. It was not until plate-glass was invented and large wall-mirrors appeared that little mirrors were outmoded. An exhaustive history of accessories would have to include the vinaigrette, the pomander, the innumerable little caskets and phials, the toothpicks and the watches which all played their part in the image of a period.

Artificial Flowers. Made by the Egyptians in 3000 B.C. and the art was imitated by the women of Greece. Roman ladies wore perfumed flowers made of papyrus or brightly coloured silk. Particularly beautiful artificial flowers were made in ancient China from plants, rare feathers and silk. In medieval Europe they were made principally in Italian and Spanish convents for church decorations. The craft was secularized in France where great centres of the handicraft became established (Lyons, Paris). At the end of the 18th century it began to be industrialized. Nowadays as well as the naturalistic imitation of real flowers, the creation of stylized flowers is a growing industry. They are used for costume

jewellery especially as brooches and ear-clips.

Aumônière. A leather bag for coins (French, *aumône* = alms) which was worn by both sexes tied to the belt in the 14th and 15th centuries and was a part of Burgundian court dress on which no expense was spared. Charlotte of Savoy (d. 1483) left 23 elegant purses of white and red leather, velvet and satin.

Boa. A long, narrow scarf made of fur or ostrich feathers. Especially popular at the height of the 19th century Romantic period and again at the turn of the 19th century, it took its name from the boa constrictor, a huge snake that winds itself around its victim. Its hey-days were the early and late Victorian period when huge sleeves made coats impractical or deep décolletés exposed ladies to the risk of a chill.

Bourse. The French name for a purse or for a pochette for carrying cosmetics. The name was also applied (circa 1730) to the bag in which the hair was worn.

Brandenburgs (French, *Brandebourg*). Twin buttons linked by cords or laces. Originally the name of a loose-fitting man's coat at the end of the 17th and 18th century. Later the name passed to its characteristic trimming which became popular in the 1770s. In the 1820s, 1830s, this trimming was worn by men and women on jackets which buttoned tightly down the front. Today it still appears on men's dressing gowns and pyjama jackets.

Buttons. They serve not only as a fastening but also as a decoration. Basic fashion changes determine the shape, size, material and placing of buttons. Their origin is unknown, but they were in use by the 11th century. The tight-fitting portions of medieval clothing could not be put on or taken off without buttons. The precursor of the button was the lace, brooch or pin and in the 15th century hooks were used. The button used entirely as a decoration first appeared on men's clothes in the Rococo period. It was fashionable circa 1860, especially on men's outer clothing, to conceal the buttons inside, in a 'fly' fastening.

En tous cas. The nickname of a parasol

777

(circa 1870) which could also be used as an umbrella. The name had originally been applied to garments which could be adapted for different needs.

Eye-glasses, Spectacles. First appeared in Europe in the late 13th century. Apart from their real practical use they soon began to acquire value as a fashion adjunct and underwent significant changes both in the shape of the glasses themselves and in the material, shape and colour of the frames. Indeed, in the past glasses were sometimes merely a fashion accessory. From the late 18th century onwards the lorgnette was fashionable in aristocratic circles. Diplomats and army officers began to sport monocles. The pince-nez appeared in the 1840s only to disappear almost completely after the First World War. The sun-worship which began in the 1920s brought sun-glasses into fashion; they have recently become an independent item of summer chic, and act as a latter-day mask, concealing the expression.

Flea-fur. Used in the 16th century and may be seen in portraits of the period. Stuffed sables, martens, polecats and weasels were supposed to attract these troublesome parasites. The fur was carried on a gold chain or even held in the hand. It was richly decorated; the Duchess of Ferrara was presented by her husband with a sable the golden head of which was set with 12 rubies, 3 emeralds and 4 pearls.

Flowers. The earliest of fashion accessories and are still sometimes worn today. They are usually worn in the hair, on the hat, at the bosom or on the hip. On feast days medieval maidens decked their hair with garlands of flowers; a wreath of flowers on the head of an unmarried girl symbolized virginity. In the Rococo and Empire periods elegant gowns and especially ball-dresses were adorned with real flowers and ribbons. In the late 18th century men began to sport a flower in the buttonhole as they still do today (a carnation for a morning coat, a gardenia with evening dress).

Gloves. They were worn in ancient times both as a protection and as an embellishment. Gloves of the 21st Dynasty were found in the Pyramids. Although the earliest gloves were merely sack-shaped coverings without fingers (mittens with thumbs but no fingers appeared later), the ancients did wear complete gloves. The ladies of ancient Egypt and Rome protected their hands not only while they worked, but also for meals. In the Middle Ages people wore a kind of mitten rather like those of today. Soldiers and huntsmen wore iron or leather gloves with a stuff or leather lining.

The gloves of kings and church dignitaries were richly ornamented with gold, silver and precious stones. Gloves often played a symbolic role in medieval times; they were part of the investiture of a knight and of a bishop, and were presented to the holders of civic offices as a token of various privileges. A gauntlet was flung down in front of an adversary as a challenge to battle. Richly decorated gloves made of red material formed part of the insignia of the Holy Roman Empire.

Gloves were not often worn with medieval dress because the sleeve was long and often covered the hand. Silk and leather gloves adorned with embroidery and precious stones became the luxuries of the privileged classes of the time, while the peasantry wore coarse working mittens.

In 16th century Italy and Spain, perfumed

gloves were worn. Although the knitted glove appeared at the same time as the knitted stocking, leather gloves were still preferred by the elegant. In the 17th and 18th centuries, both sexes sported richly embroidered gloves. The Baroque and Rococo styles for men, with their lace ruffles covering the hand almost completely, left little scope for the glove-maker; women's styles compensated for this by making the glove or mitten ending at the knuckles a popular accessory. Leather, plain and embroidered, and silk were both worn. From the second quarter of the 19th century to the end, etiquette prescribed that a lady's hands be covered at all times. Short white or lavender kid gloves were worn for day and evening in the middle of the century, but gloves for evening became longer, reaching to the elbow or upper arm at the end. Net mittens were sometimes worn in the house. Fabric gloves began to be worn after the 1914–18 War and in the 1950s plastic began to replace leather. Nowadays gloves of various materials, colours and lengths are indispensable to elegance. Even gloves designed for drivers are fashionable as well as functional.

Handbags. The lady's handbag is the counter-part of the man's pocket. It has gradually be-come an indispensable part of female dress and is made of the most varied materials. The material, shape and size is dictated by the frequently changing fashion. In the Middle Ages, money and other small objects were carried in purses or small leather bags with draw-strings which were fastened to the belt. The late Gothic style involved the wearing of a whole collection of bags of varying size which jingled at the owner's waist. A leather bag sometimes with a metal mount at the belt also formed part of Renaissance dress. From the Rococo period until right into the 19th cen-tury, ladies had richly decorated, embroidered, knitted or netted draw-string bags. During the French Revolution, a bag on a long cord became fashionable – a 'ridicule' or 'reticule'. In the early 19th century, men also carried purses. Well-to-do Victorian ladies had elab-orate reticules for their sewing and other impedimenta always at hand. The designs of Rococo, Empire and early Victorian hand-bags occasionally influence modern fashions.

Strong, stiff handbags began to appear in the last quarter of the 19th century. A small purse or handbag is called in the United States a 'pocket book'.

Handkerchief (Italian provincial, *fazzoletto*). Adorned with lace it was carried by 16th century Italians and later became fashionable in France and Germany. Not until the habit of snuff-taking transformed it into a vulgar necessity did it lose its ornamental character.

Laces, 'points' (cord, leather thong or ribbon laces). These were used as a method of fasten-

777 *Modealmanach*, 1786–1788. The fashionable German lady wears a gown with a fichu and a wide-brimmed hat trimmed with ribbons and feathers and carries a slender cane.

778 From a 19th century copy of a Louis XVI fashion plate. The period delighted in the most varied costume-dresses. The 'shepherdess' holds a shepherd's crook trimmed with a bow.

778

ing garments before buttons were invented. From the late 14th century they were used to lace doublet and hose together. The metal tips of laces, 'arglets', were a later addition.

Lorgnette. A pair of spectacles held by the handle into which they are folded when not in use. They were a popular upper class accessory from the late 18th century. The art of using a lorgnette became a highly complex social game in the 19th century. Its cult remained largely confined to female aristocratic circles. A lorgnon is similar but has a shorter handle.

Mask. The fashion for half-masks became widespread in the 16th century in France; they were made of velvet or taffeta and were worn mainly for travelling or with outdoor town-clothes. They were supposed to be a protection against the weather but were at the same time an aid to coquetry and amorous intrigue. Courtiers were forbidden to wear masks in the king's presence. Masks attained their widest popularity in Holland and in England. From the 16th century onwards, their use was confined to carnivals of which they remain an essential feature.

779

Miser purse, Stocking purse. A double-ended purse used by men; it was often netted or knitted; it was tubular, and was secured with sliding rings which opened down the side, they were worn twisted through the belt.

Monocle. This single eye-glass was adopted for preference by diplomats and army officers. It sometimes hung from a cord and was either gold-rimmed or rimless. It was always held to be a (much caricatured) status-symbol of the upper class; its final appearance was after the First World War, when it was also worn by ladies. Today it has almost completely disappeared.

Muff. The precursor of the muff was a cone-shaped extension of the narrow sleeve worn by both sexes at the Burgundian court in winter. The cylindrical fur muff, as a separate article of clothing, is first documented in Venice; Vecellio's *Book of Costumes for the Year 1590* contains the portrait of a Venetian matron holding a muff. The fashion spread from Italy to the rest of Europe. In Germany, where furs had long been fashionable, the muff did not appear until the 17th century. In the 17th and 18th centuries, it was a part of male as well as female dress and was a mark of social rank; the ruling class forbade their servants to wear muffs. Muffs were often very large especially in the late 17th century. Ladies wore them not only in the street but indoors and for social gatherings. After the French Revolution, men finally dispensed with muffs; in the realm of female fashion, the muff reappeared from time to time in numerous shapes and sizes.

Parasol. Dates from much earlier than the umbrella. The ancient Greeks and Romans inherited parasols from the Orient, where they had also been a mark of rank, a protection held by servants over their masters. As such they were adopted by the church in the form of baldaquins or canopies. We find the first sunshade used by a private citizen on an ancient Greek vase; it is protecting a rich Greek lady from the sun. The Romans used the same.

Patch (French, *mouche* = fly). A piece of female finery typical of the Rococo period. This tiny decoration was variously-shaped – round, triangular, a flower, an animal or a playing-card symbol – and inevitably appeared where it best set off the wearer's particular charm: upon the alabaster brow, the clear, smooth cheek, the slender, graceful neck or the snow-white bosom. It appeared at the time when gowns attained their maximum width and, as befitted that age of gallantry, was intended to draw the eye of the beholder to the most seductive aspect of his environment.

Petit-point. Tapestry-work in cross-stitch on canvas in characteristic, many-coloured, floral or conventional designs used to decorate Viennese evening handbags, etc.

Pins. These were among the earliest fashion accessories; they were used in Neolithic times to fasten garments together and to secure and decorate the hair and they finally became a pure decoration, an item of jewellery for both sexes. The earliest known pins were made of splinters of bone or horn; sometimes they were just thorns. Their successors, comparatively sophisticated, were of bronze or iron wire. The jewellery of historical times includes pins and brooches of exquisite workmanship.

Pockets. In their modern form they first appeared in the 1670s on the close-fitting coats or *justaucorps* of the Louis XIV period. They appeared on waistcoats in the late 17th century. They have always been inserted in breeches and trousers. Women's pockets in the 18th century consisted of a bag tied round the waist under the hoop. They were always concealed until the early 20th century.

Pompadour (German). A lady's handbag of the 18th century, a draw-string bag of woven stuff (usually velvet) or lace named after the Marquise de Pompadour.

Shawl. A square or oblong piece of material to protect the bare shoulders and neck. Of oriental origin, it was woven in Kashmir from the fine wool of Tibetan goats. Genuine Kashmir shawls were much sought after in Europe in the Directoire period. They were a welcome addition to the flowing neo-Grecian gowns which had short sleeves and low necks. They were gradually replaced by shawls, many beautiful and of fine workmanship made in France (Lyons) and Great Britain (Paisley and Norwich). The fashion for shawls lasted throughout the Victorian period but declined in the last quarter of the century. They were largest in the 1860s.

Walking Stick. They did not long remain merely a support for the walker or a crude weapon, but soon became a personal decoration betokening either chic or the highest military rank. In circa 500 B.C., the Greek historian Herodotus described a Babylonian stick with a decorative handle. Many military leaders of the Middle Ages carried ornamental sticks, the forerunners of the marshal's baton. Ladies began to carry little canes in France at the end of the 17th century as a part of their modish outfits.

779 Fashion plate from the *Theaterzeitung*, a journal of 1834. For some decades the walking stick and the top hat were both indispensable items of male attire, which have scarcely altered, except as to the colour of the waistcoat and trousers, since the 19th century.

780 From a fashion journal. Two-piece outdoor costume. Above the striped skirt a shorter one in a plain colour is looped; the lady carries a lace-trimmed parasol.

780

Umbrella (Latin, *umbra* = shade). Used for protection against sun and rain. The umbrella used by the ancients was cone-shaped and did not fold; the handle was not always attached to the centre. After a long lapse during the Middle Ages, the sunshade reappeared in 16th century Italy, at first as a giant folding umbrella intended for several people at once. Marie de Medici brought the fashion with her to France, where sunshades were made of waxed material and had horn handles. The umbrella for wet weather was not widely used until the 18th century. They were not a fashionable accessory, for the upper classes could use carriages and sedan chairs in bad weather. Early ones were very heavy, made from cane and oiled cloth. But by the late 19th century, early 20th century when they had become an essential for every well-dressed man, improvements in manufacture made it possible to have them light and pencil slim. In 1815 a small sunshade with an adjustable handle was brought out; it gave protection against the oblique rays of the sun. Small folding parasols were popular in the middle of the 19th century, long, heavy ones at the end. Covers were often of fine silk and lace-trimmed. Since the 1920s, the fashion for sport and for the sun-tanned complexion have banished the parasol almost completely from the female wardrobe. As a fashion accessory, it has been replaced by sun-glasses.

781 *Costumes Parisiens*, 1812. The straw hat is trimmed with a gauze ribbon. The lady carries a Chinese sunshade.

782 Auguste Renoir. The Umbrellas. National Gallery, London. At the end of the 19th century the umbrella had become larger and more practical rather than decorative.

783 Giovanni Fattori. Lady in the Shade. Giacomo Jucker Collection, Milan. This sunshade is large and functional. It complements the lady's outdoor dress consisting of a long skirt and cape.

784 Constantin Guys. A Drive in the Bois. Musée du Louvre, Paris. For their afternoon drive in the Bois the ladies carry small, fringed carriage sunshades.

785 *Vogue*, 1928. The parasols of the 1930s were extremely varied both in shape and decorative design. *Top right :* the Chinese influence. They all have straight stems and stout handles.

783

784

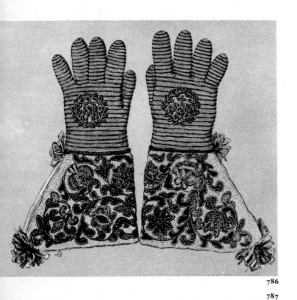

786 Illustration from *Modes et usages au temps de Marie-Antoinette*. Paris, 1885. Silk gloves with gold and silver embroidery as worn by the Knights of the Holy Spirit in the reign of Marie-Antoinette.

787 *Costumes Parisiens*, 1812. Gloves were an essential part of Empire dress. With the short sleeved dresses went long gloves which often covered the elbow.

788 *Costumes Parisiens*, 1809. A straw hat is worn with an elaborately trimmed gown.

786

787

788

789

789 Edgar Degas. Café Singer. Wertheim
Collection, Fogg Art Museum, Cambridge,
Mass. The singer's half-length gloves match
the colour of the dark fur trimming of her
evening dress.

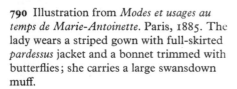

790

791
792

790 Illustration from *Modes et usages au temps de Marie-Antoinette*. Paris, 1885. The lady wears a striped gown with full-skirted *pardessus* jacket and a bonnet trimmed with butterflies; she carries a large swansdown muff.

791 *Gallery of Fashion*, London, 1796. With her delicate sprigged morning gown the lady wears a turban, a scarf and a voluminous muff.

792 Rembrandt van Rijn. Portrait of Jan Six. Six Collection, Amsterdam. Buttons may be ornamental as well as functional, or purely ornamental features of coats and waistcoats. The collar, cuffs and gloves complete this elegant turnout.

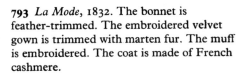

793

794

795

793 *La Mode*, 1832. The bonnet is
feather-trimmed. The embroidered velvet
gown is trimmed with marten fur. The muff
is embroidered. The coat is made of French
cashmere.

794 *Charivari*, Paris, 1833. Winter Style.
The huge muff and the shawl enveloping
half the lady's face contribute to the comic
silhouette of this contemporary caricature.

795 *Wiener Moden*, 1821. The little Empire
handbag is lozenge-shaped, made of woven
material and has a fairly long handle. It
complements the high-waisted gown. The
high hat was known as a Pamela bonnet.

796

797

799

796 *Costumes Parisiens*, 1814. Pamela bonnet. The dress is made of percale.

797 *Deutsche Moden*, 1810-1811. The draw-string bag made of woven material was called a reticule.

798 *Wiener Moden*, 1819. The lady in a redingote and a large frilled bonnet carries a small oblong handbag.

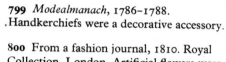

799 *Modealmanach*, 1786–1788.
Handkerchiefs were a decorative accessory.

800 From a fashion journal, 1810. Royal Collection, London. Artificial flowers were particularly popular in the 18th and 19th centuries. They were used to adorn the hat, the coiffure or the gown. Here the sleeves and hem are trimmed with roses.

801 William Hogarth. 'The Harlot's Progress'. Engraving. The girl with the wide-brimmed hat is simply dressed in cap, gown and apron. The elderly woman in the hood has stuck ornamental patches on her face.

798

800

801

802

803

804

802 Wenzel Hollar. The Winter Dress of an English Lady. Engraving. The lady in outdoor dress wears a mask to protect her face from dust, and carries a large muff.

803 Illustration from *Modes et usages au temps de Marie-Antoinette*. Paris, 1885. Lady in a balldress.

804 *Punch*, London, 1880. 'Today – the era of the fan!' The large fans were often a cause of inconvenience, particularly at the theatre.

805 Jan Cornelisz Verspronck. Little Girl in Blue. Rijksmuseum, Amsterdam. She carries a feather fan.

806 *Costumes anglais et français*. The evening gown (*left*) is made of two materials; the skirt hem and neckline are trimmed with a wide frill. The lady wears flowers in her hair and carries a fan.

807 Dress of circa 1905. Prague Museum of Arts and Crafts. Worn with a feather fan and shown at a fashion parade in 1962.

805

806

807

808

809

808 *Costumes Parisiens*, 1811. A cashmere shawl worn with an evening dress.

809 *Wiener Moden*, 1819. Fashionable Viennese outdoor dress included a flower-trimmed hat. The dress is high-necked with a little lace collar and a high waist. The narrow wrist-bands are trimmed with ruffles half-covering the hands.

810 *La Mode*, 1833. A velvet bonnet with a bird of paradise feather. The dress is of satin threaded with gold.

811 Urs Graf. Portrait of a girl in profile. Kupferstichkabinett, Basle.

Jewellery

It seems fairly evident that man's and woman's urge towards self-adornment came prior to their desire for clothing. They have always decorated their bodies and garments with artifacts of precious metals. Jewellery figures among the earliest human relics. Neolithic sculptures depict women wearing long necklaces covering their necks and breasts; they are otherwise naked. The oriental civilizations have been particularly inspired both in their use and their invention of jewellery. Like dress, jewellery is subject to the rule of fashion, which determines not only its form but also the choice of its materials. Opulent display itself depends upon the dictate of current fashion. In the Renaissance and the Baroque period, both men and women vied, each with their own sex, in the splendour of their jewels. This abundance of jewellery was partly due to the fact that the dowry of a wealthy bride was frequently paid in the form of treasure and precious stones.

Agraffe. A kind of hook fastening to a ring and usually used to fasten clothing together. The name was later applied to other ornamental hooks worn as jewellery.

Amber. The fossilized resin of conifers is usually found in various shades of yellows; sometimes it is greenish, brown, blue white or even colourless. It is found chiefly on the Baltic and North Sea coasts. It has been used from earliest antiquity for making jewellery and miniature ornaments; since the 19th century, it has also been a material for smokers' accessories.

Bracelet. Worn at the wrist or above the elbow it has always been a favourite ornament with men and women. It symbolized courage for the Germanic warriors who wore it to protect their wrists in battle. Since the dawn of the Middle Ages it has been worn almost exclusively by women. For modern man, its only surviving form is the gold wrist-band of his watch. Very recently chain bracelets have returned to fashion among young men.

Brooch. A decoration for ladies' dresses and blouses usually worn at the bosom. Brooches were particularly popular in the 19th century; the early Victorians used semi-precious stones

for brooches, while under Napoleon III (1852–1870) gold-enamel became fashionable.

Cameo. A precious or semi-precious stone carved in relief in variously coloured layers, the darkest layers usually forming the background and the lighter lending colour to the relief design.

Chain. A favourite male ornament in the 16th century. Men often wore their medals on massive chains.

Châtelaine. An ornamental metal clasp hooked onto the waist or belt and worn by women from about 1840 to the end of the 19th century. From it hung useful and decorative items; scissors, thimbles, watches, etc. The word derived from the French, *châtelaine* = lady of the castle.

Coral. The marine polypus *corralium rubrum* is found in large colonies in warm oceans; it produces a calcareous deposit which may be red, pink or orange. This is the coral. The bunches of coral are picked, sorted and polished. Both the Romans and the Gauls used corals as ornaments. In ancient times coral necklaces were also worn as a protection against infectious diseases. In the Middle Ages they were used mainly for rosaries. In the 20th century the finest coral jewellery comes from Italy and Japan.

Costume Jewellery. Jewellery made from inexpensive materials such as glass, metal, semi-precious stones, ceramics, leather or synthetic materials. It is not intended as an imitation of real jewellery but goes its own independent way, deriving its own effects from its specific materials and the novelty of its design. In certain moods, fashion despises costume jewellery (for instance during the difficult times of the 1920s and 1930s) but since then it has become a veritable gold-mine.

Cross. An ornament of symbolic significance, is worn on a ribbon or chain hung round the neck. It is usually made of gold and is sometimes set with jewels.

Diadem. A band of material or metal encircling the head or brow. Beloved in ancient oriental civilizations, the diadem has become an established female adornment. It was worn in the East as a symbol of power and achieved luxuriant forms in the splendour-loving Byzantine Empire. Under Justianian it took on its definitive form – that of a crown: a circlet surmounted by an arched head-piece with central cross.

Ear-clip. Fastening to the lobe of the ear by a spring began to replace ear-rings circa 1920 as fashionable women became increasingly reluctant to have their ears pierced.

Ear-ring. Ear ornaments usually made of precious metal but, especially in primitive communities, can be made of bone or wood. They are inserted through a hole pierced through a lobe of the ear. They were introduced from Spain in the 16th century and were worn first by men and then by women. By the 18th century their use was confined to women except for the occasional seaman.

Fibulae. They are amongst the oldest forms of jewellery and were particularly fashionable in ancient Greece and Rome. In form they are basically pins twisted round themselves for security in fastening.

Fob. Watch-chain usually suspended at the waist and worn in the second half of the 18th and 19th centuries by both men and women.

Their use has declined rapidly in the 20th century except among elderly gentlemen. Sometimes trinkets (French, *breloques*; German, *Berlocken*) such as pencils and seals are fixed to them.

Garnet. A vitreous mineral found in slate and volcanic rock, and considered a precious stone. The pyrope (Greek = fiery-eyed) or deep red Bohemian garnet is highly prized. Garnets are set in bracelets, rings, ear-rings, necklaces and brooches.

Gemstone. A precious or semi-precious stone bearing a raised or engraved design either in relief or in intaglio.

Locket. A small oval or heart-shaped ornament usually of precious metal worn around the neck on a ribbon or chain. Lockets enclosed some souvenir of a loved one, such as a miniature or a lock of hair, and were particularly fashionable in the Romantic period.

Necklace. Proved by archaic remains to have been the earliest and most popular ornament. Necklaces were made from the most varied materials; metal, shells, beads, teeth, etc. The most costly necklaces are of precious metals set with precious stones. Fashion determines

812

812 Golden Circlet from Grave III from Mycenae. The people of Mycenae were fond of jewellery. A favourite ornament was a wide circlet with spiral design.

813 Lucas Cranach the Younger. Portrait of a Woman (detail). Museum of Fine Arts, Boston. The lady wears a hair-net and golden chains looped round her neck.

the choice of stones: the women of ancient Egypt wore golden amulets bearing carved miniature reliefs; the primitive Gauls made necklaces of shells and stones. The late 14th and 15th century brought the fashion for livery or heraldic necklaces or collars. In the Renaissance pearls were the favourite jewels.

Pearl. White vitreous concretion formed within the shell of the pearl-oyster and other bivalve molluscs. Their lustre may be blue, pink or yellow, sometimes almost black. In Europe the white pearl is preferred, in the Orient, the yellowish variety. The price of pearls varies considerably. It depends on their shape, size, colour and lustre. They fetched enormous prices in ancient Rome, where they were used to embroider clothes, shoes, etc., as well as for jewellery. It was from antiquity that Renaissance fashion derived its love of pearls. In the East, magic powers were ascribed to them.

Pectoral. A rich ornament worn on the breast. In the Middle Ages, a pectoral was a decorative part of a horse's harness, and, from the 13th century onwards, the name was also applied to a gold or silver cross containing a relic of a saint, which a dignitary of the Catholic Church wore on his breast.

Precious Stones. Minerals distinguished for their durability, colour, brilliance, transparency and rarity. It is above all their rarity which distinguishes them from semi-precious stones. Nowadays many stones can be imitated synthetically. Fashion plays a part in deciding the current value of a stone. In the Middle Ages and the Renaissance, rubies, sapphires, emeralds and chrysolite were the most highly prized stones but, since the reign of Louis XIV (1638–1715), the diamond, the most valuable stone of all, has been supreme. It is found in all colours: the red is the most valuable. For a long time stones were worn in their natural state or table cut. Rose and brilliant cutting were not introduced until the second half of the 17th century.

Watch. Was first made in Nuremburg by Peter Henlein, who had invented the mainspring which made this small portable version of the clock possible. A contemporary (1511) writes: 'He makes little iron clocks with many wheels, which can be wound up at pleasure, have no pendulums, will strike and go for 40 hours together and may be carried in the breast or the purse.' In the 16th century, when a watch was usually worn hung round the neck on a gold chain, some very costly watches were made. The watch became a fashion accessory, and fashion demanded that it should become as small as possible. Watches became quite flat, but not until the 18th century, when they ceased to be worn outside and were kept in the fob-pocket. Today the wrist-watch has become universal but a watch on a chain occasionally reappears as an ornament.

814 Golden Ring with Sapphire. French, first half of the 17th century. Museum of Arts and Crafts, Prague.

815 Gold Pendant, engraved and set with stones, 1923. Museum of Arts and Crafts, Prague.

814

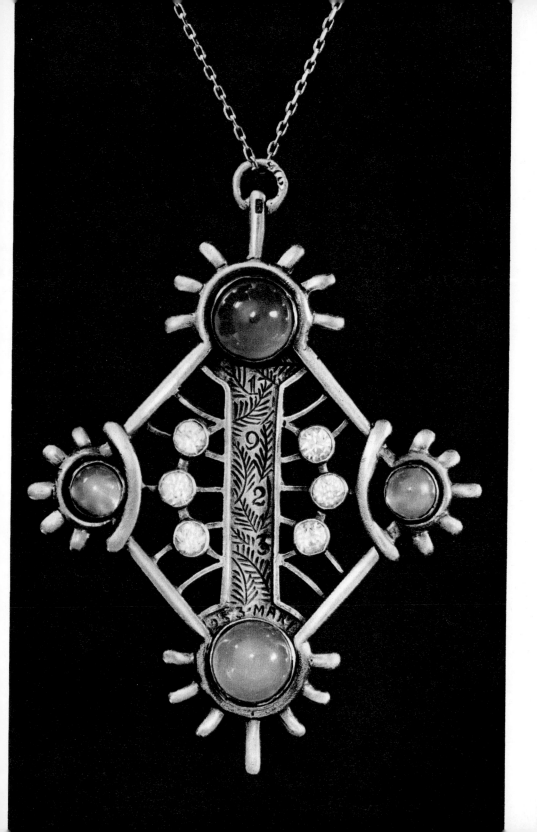

816 Rembrandt van Rijn. Young Lady with a Fan. Buckingham Palace, London. The jewellery of this lady of the Baroque period consists of a pearl necklace round her throat, a pearl bracelet and a few pendants attached to her elaborately laced bodice. She is holding a lace fan.

817 Bartholomäus Spranger. Bianca Capello. Museum of Art, Vienna. Pearls, the favourite jewels of the Baroque period, are used to adorn the lady's hair and rows of pearls are sewn round the collar and bosom of her brocade gown.

817

819

818 Pendant of hollow gold on a finely wrought chain. Circa 1870, Museum of Arts and Crafts, Prague. The pendant is set with white and light blue enamel and red and green stones.

819 Quirin Jahn (?). Portrait of a Lady. Národni Galerie, Prague. The lady wears a dark dress; a white tucker fills the oval neckline. From a ribbon round her neck hangs a miniature.

820 Edward Burne-Jones. Mona Vanna.
The dress of this tragic heroine is
represented with artistic exaggeration.
Her ornaments are three strings of coral,
rings, bracelets and twin jewels in the
form of coiled snakes in her long, flowing
hair.

821 *Gazette du Bon Ton*, 1924–1925. The
designers of the 1920s sought new,
simpler forms in keeping with the new
fashion in dress. The influence of
Egyptian art is apparent here.

822 The liturgical gown of the Patriarch
Nikos (detail). Kremlin,
Moscow. Liturgical vestments were often
embroidered with pearls and precious
stones. Here the pearl embroidery forms a
spiral design.

823 From a fashion journal of the end of
the last century; designs for various
pieces of jewellery and hair-ornaments.

820

821 822

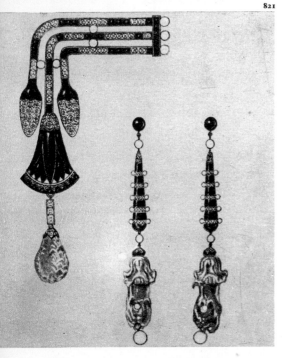

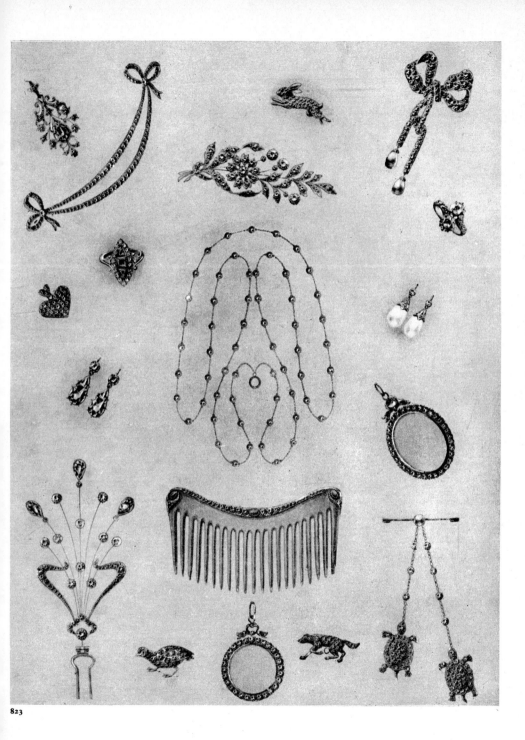

Men's Dress

In the course of its history the fashion in male dress has also developed its special terminology. The technical terms run into hundreds and are steadily increasing, so we must leave them to the experts. We can cite only a few which are illustrated here.

Cutaway. A kind of tail-coat with fronts curving slightly away. It was usually of black cloth; worn with dark striped trousers and light (grey or beige) waistcoat and top hat, it constituted a gentleman's formal day dress for weddings and important occasions. At the end of the 19th century, this English fashion spread to the civilized world, blended with the morning coat and superseded the frock coat. In Germany, it was known as the 'cut'.

Dinner Jacket. A single or double-breasted formal evening jacket, usually black. Occasionally it may be dark blue or purple; in summer or in hot countries it may be white. It has silk revers and is worn with silk-striped trousers. The Germans and French call the whole outfit a 'smoking'; in America the jacket is a 'Tuxedo', the whole a 'monkey suit' in the vernacular. It was introduced in 1888 and the first German reference to the fashion occurs in February 1889 in the Dresden paper *Europäische Modezeitung* in a letter from London. The dinner jacket is referred to as a 'dress lounge' which was very like the modern dinner jacket but was worn unbuttoned.

Frock coat. Originated in the 18th century for country and informal wear. It was distinguished by its collar, and came into more general use in the 1770s; it was worn with knee-breeches. Long trousers were not worn with it until the beginning of the 19th century. In the early Victorian period, the conventional day dress was a light (brown, blue or green) frock coat. In the 1820s a waist seam was introduced. Black became more or less the standard colour, and the length of the tails varied with the fashion. The revers were of black silk. Differences of detail distinguished the dress from the undress frock coat.

Livery. Nowadays the term is used for a servant's uniform, which usually consists of a frock coat, knee-breeches, stockings and shoes. In the Middle Ages courtiers wore the heraldic colours of their lord who supplied their uniform. Soldiers also wore livery before modern national uniform was introduced. The liveries were in the colours of the commander of the unit, usually a regiment.

Tailordress Coat. A coat with the front tails stitched to the back panel. It was mainly, but not exclusively worn for formal day and evening occasions from the late 18th century to around 1860 after which, as today, it was reserved exclusively for formal evening wear.

Uniforms. Not only the working dress of many trades and professions, of doctors, nurses, cooks and waiters, but even sportsmen's dress has the character of a uniform. It is a set of clothes characteristic of the occupation of the wearer and easily identifiable. The dinner jacket and the dress suit are also species of uniform. Uniform in the modern meaning of the term did not come into existence until the 17th century. The Industrial Revolution was to bring the technical advance necessary for its production. The traditional livery of the knight disappeared and those vestiges of it still worn by commanding officers were of purely symbolic significance. In the 16th century the dragoon was no more than a mounted infantryman. In the Thirty Years War, the dress of all the fighting armies was disparate and the only distinguishing marks of most individual bodies of troops and regiments were their sashes. Louis XIV had commanded in 1670 that his troops should be uniformly dressed for parades, but the Swedish king Gustavus Adolphus had already introduced the first true uniform. Its colour, material and cut, its distinctive features and decorations were all exactly prescribed. Many European states lagged a full century behind the leading powers in the matter of military uniforms. At first only the ranks were obliged to wear

uniform; for some decades officers might dress as they pleased. In the 18th century new types of uniform appeared; the variously equipped troops and kinds of regiment became distinct in outward appearance as their separate organization was elaborated. Since the Russo-Japanese War and the Boer War, which finally demonstrated the importance of camouflage in land warfare and led to the minimization of colour in uniforms, khaki and field grey have been universally adopted.

825 From a fashion journal of 1792. With the frock coat the 18th century gallant wore a low-crowned top hat with a gay curled brim. The coat was double-breasted and the tail reached halfway down the thigh at the back. The breeches are decorated with cord appliqué.

825 826

826 From *Modes d'hommes*, 1809. At the beginning of the 19th century the frock coat had undergone little change. The breeches were sometimes trimmed with appliqué stripes and buttons, precursors of the silk stripe of circa 1820; slippers were worn with them. The indispensable cane completes the silhouette.

827 From *Costumes Parisiens*, 1813. A cloth coat worn with nankeen pantaloons.

828 From the *Theaterzeitung*, 1834. In the 1830s the tail of the frock coat reached to the back of the knee. The gentleman wears a flowered waistcoat and a very wide cravat. The trousers are wide at the bottom.

827   828

829 From the *Allgemeine Modenzeitung*, 1842. The man has a dress suit, top hat and cane.

830 From the *Theaterzeitung*, 1834. The riding coat, the popular style for gentlemen, was a forerunner of the walking frock coat. It was buttoned only to the waist or above it to produce the characteristic slim-waisted effect.

831 From *Modes de Paris*, 1840. This fashionable frock coat of the 1840s has a dashing cut-away waist-line, a flowered waistcoat and light trousers.

832 From an English fashion magazine, 1875. The man wears an undress frock coat with long, light trousers, with the dress coat (*left*) a starched shirt and a black waistcoat.

833 From the *Theaterzeitung*, 1834. These model riding coats of the 1830s with shawl or pelerine collars have become fuller and longer.

834 Illustration from *Peacock Pie* by Walter De la Mare, 1924. A caricature by Lovat Fraser of a frock coat and check trousers.

829

830

831

832

833   834

835 Praying figure. Relief.
5th century, Egyptian
Museum, Cairo.

Liturgical Vestments

The liturgical vesture of the Roman Catholic rite consists of: the *alb*, the *amice*, the *chasuble*, the *cincture*, the *cope*, the *dalmatic*, the *fanon*, the *maniple*, the *mitre*, the *pallium*, the *pontifical gloves*, *stockings* and *sandals*, the *stole*, the *subcincture*, the *surplice*, the *tunicle*. Of course no single member of the hierarchy is entitled to wear all these garments. There are also a few garments which, while possessing no liturgical significance, have become associated with the rite in so far as they are worn by the clergy: they are the *rochet* (a surplice), the *cappa magna*, the *amess*, the *mozetta* and the *biretta*. The sacramental vesture, which was originally the dress of the simple layman of the day, has undergone no significant change since the 9th century, when its essential development was completed. It was in 9th century Rome that its chief components were elaborated and defined.

The various colours of the vestments are prescribed according to the liturgical calendar and the requirements of the divine service; they are white, red, green, purple or black. Yellow and blue are non-canonical colours.

Alb. A linen garment reaching to the feet with narrow sleeves; it is tied at the hip with a girdle called the cincture. It is worn by the ordained cleric for the celebration of Mass and other divine service. It was originally the long tunic worn during the Roman Empire.

Amice. Rectangular shoulder-piece of white linen with tapes attached to two corners. It fits round the neck covering the shoulders and is the initial vestment worn beneath the alb.

Biretta. Head-covering of the priesthood. Today it is circular with a hard rectangular base surmounted by three, sometimes four, curved ridges. A cardinal's biretta is red, a bishop's purple, while that of all other clergy without peculiar privilege is black.

Cassock. The uniform of the cleric. It reaches to the ankles, buttons down the front and, in contrast with the talar or academic gown, is close-fitting at the top. It is often tied round the waist with a cincture. Ordinary clerics wear a black cassock, bishops a purple one, cardinals a red one; only the Pope wears a white one. In some countries priests wear a similar garment reaching only to the knees known as a clerical frock-coat. The gown is similar to the cassock but looser at the top with a stand-up collar. It is also worn by certain academic dignitaries and judges.

Chasuble (Latin, *casula*). Vestment in the liturgical colour of the day worn by the priest over the alb at Mass. Its prototype was a secular upper garment worn by the ancient Greeks and Romans, which was originally wide and bell-shaped with an opening for the head (still current especially in the Eastern Church). In the Roman Church its volume was progressively curtailed to free the arms until the Gothic chasuble came into fashion. This was still relatively wide, falling in voluminous folds from the shoulders onto the arms. The chasuble of the Baroque period was straight, flat and rather short.

Cincture. The liturgical girdle pertaining to the alb; it is usually made of flax or hemp, sometimes of silk or wool.

Cope or **Pluvial.** A richly embroidered ceremonial cloak – the so-called 'shield' reminiscent of the earlier hood. The cope originated as a hooded cloak worn by monks from the 9th century onwards at processions or in the choir. Nowadays it is a wide heel-length cloak of the appropriate liturgical colour. It is a processional vestment. A cappa magna is worn by high prelates on ceremonial occasions.

Dalmatic. Liturgical robe of deacons assisting at pontifical High Mass, in solemn procession and at Benediction. It is always of the same colour as the priest's vestments. The name comes from its prototype, a secular garment worn in Dalmatia, which was adopted by the Romans in the 2nd century and worn over the tunica.

Maniple. A part of liturgical dress which is handed to the deacon at the consecration. During Mass the priest wears it on his left forearm. It is a band of material about three feet long of the same colour as the chasuble. Its prototype was a mappa (or small perspiration cloth) carried as part of genteel dress by Roman patricians. Hence the maniple was originally the prerogative of the higher clerics.

Mitre (Latin, *infulae*). Liturgical headdress of Popes, cardinals and bishops. It is a stiffened hat rising to a peak with ribbons hanging from the back onto the wearer's shoulders, is usually silken and often richly embroidered with pearls and gold thread.

Mozetta. The knee-length purple mantle worn by bishops and higher prelates, sometimes by canons. It is worn over the rochet.

Pilos/Pileolus. A little round cap, which is white for the Pope, red for a cardinal, purple for a bishop and black for an abbot. As it must be removed during certain parts of the Mass, it is also known as a 'Soli-Deo' ('before God only') to indicate that it is taken off only to God.

Stole. A long narrow vestment in the liturgical colour worn round the priest's neck. It is similar to the maniple in shape, material, colour and ornamentation but is more than twice as long.

Surplice. A white clerical knee-length robe of linen or lawn with wide sleeves, worn at many liturgical rites. The corresponding, distinctive robe of bishops and prelates is the rochet which differs from the surplice only in its narrow sleeves.

Tiara. A triple crown worn by the Pope on non-liturgical public occasions. Nowadays it consists of three, tiered coronets; the second was added in the 13th century under Boniface VIII, the third at the beginning of the 14th century.

Tunicle. The upper vestment of a subdeacon, corresponding to the dalmatic of a deacon.

836 Priest in attitude of prayer. From a relief in the Church at Mirebeau. Poitiers Museum. The chasuble is wide at the shoulders and falls outwards in a triangle. It is ornamented with patterned strips. The chasuble is the vestment worn by the Roman Catholic priest at Mass. Its form has changed several times in its history.

509

837

838

837 Greek and Roman Fathers of the Church. Mosaic. After 1148. Cefalie Cathedral. The Holy Fathers wear the chasuble and the pall, a vestment which was put on over the tunica.

838 Embroidered Chasuble. San Antonio Abate, Vedeseta. The chasuble bears a raised embroidered cross and designs of figures.

839 Embroidered Chasuble. Upsala Cathedral. Stockholm work of the 15th century. Richly decorated Gothic chasuble with motifs from the Life of the Virgin in star-shaped frames surrounding the central motif, the Madonna and Child.

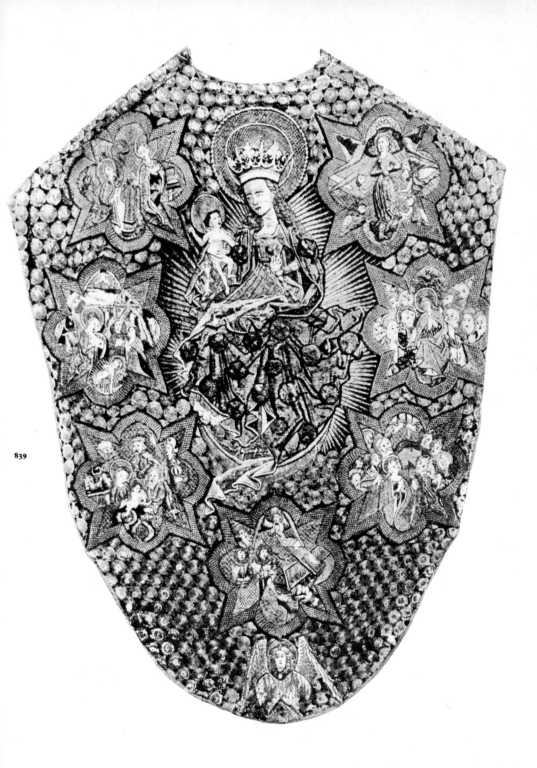

839

511

840 Albrecht Dürer. Adoration of the Holy Trinity (detail). On the right is a bishop in a brocade pluvial and mitre with ribbons, on the left a monk in a cowl, in the centre a cardinal with his hat.

841 Francisco de Zurbaran. The Vision of Peter, the Apostle. Prado, Madrid. St Peter wears a white gathered pluvial; his head is tonsured.

842 Jan van Eyck. Inner wing of the Ghent Altar-piece. St Bavo, Ghent. The singing angels wear brocade copes fastened with metal clasps and embroidered with a pattern.

840

841

XXVa Jasper de Crayer. Four Witnesses (detail). Národni Galerie, Prague.

XXVb Baroque Chasuble from the Břevnov Monastry in Prague.

XXVIa Unknown Master. Count Schönborn. Castle Kozel (Bohemia).

XXVIb Unknown Master. Jan Kazimir Polský of the Family Wasa. Castle Gallery, Rychnov n.Kn. (Bohemia).

842

843 Dalmatic. Gandino Basilica. This Gothic dalmatic is made of velvet damask with the characteristic pomegranate motif; it is decorated with panels of embroidered design.

844 Dalmatic. From the Treasury of St Peter's. Vatican Museum, Rome. The dalmatic is decorated with a richly embroidered representation of Christ enthroned beneath the Cross and surrounded by angels and saints.

845 Sakkos of the Patriarch Nikos. Kremlin, Moscow. It is similar to the dalmatic. The sakkos is of brocade with a design of figures. The sleeves and neck are embroidered with pearls and metal leaves.

843

844

845

846 Masolino. John the Baptist and Saint Jerome. Part of a retable. National Gallery, London. St Jerome wears a hat and cappa magna, St John the Baptist a short cape without ornament.

847 Pesellino. St Zeno and St Jerome (detail). National Gallery, London. The figure in the jewelled bishop's mitre wears a cope of dark monochrome material with a gold border. It is fastened at the breast with a clasp.

847

846

848

848 Jaume Ferrer II. Detail from the
Altarpiece of St Gregory. Mid 15th century.
Museum of Catalan Art, Barcelona.

518

849 Max Liebermann.
Portrait of Dr Linda.
Národni Galerie, Prague.

Jackets, Coats and Waistcoats

In Danish Bronze Age coffins sleeved jackets have been discovered among the female clothing – a proof of the great antiquity of this most versatile of garments. Leaving aside variations in length and width, it has played a leading role both among male and female clothing throughout the ages. It comes in many guises and its variants stretch from a light, often sleeveless tunic, which derived from leather armour, to the coat, and it is difficult to establish clearly the transition in fashion to the overcoat. In modern dress too, the casual jacket, worn independently of costume or suit, has become an indispensable garment for leisure and above all sport. The lumber-jacket, a blouse-like garment usually with knitted cuffs and waistband and named after the Canadian lumberjack, the windcheater and the anorak all belong to this category.

Blouse. This garment developed from the short form of the medieval *bliaut* – a smock-like upper garment worn by both sexes. For many centuries it has been a popular garment with workers and country people. It forms part of soldiers' and sailors' dress and in various colours it has played its role in revolutionary movements, e.g. the Garibaldi red shirt, the Fascist black shirt, etc.

In the 19th century the upper part of women's dress became independent. The division into skirt and blouse – in contrast to the hitherto customary one-piece garment, was already in evidence in the mid-forties of the last century, but this form of dress, so popular today, became widespread only at the end of the century. The blouse first resembled a bodice fastened high at the neck. It began to be called a blouse in the middle of the 19th century. As the tailored coat and skirt increased in popularity, the blouse or 'shirt waist' (US) grew in popularity. The blouse, generally in unobtrusive colours, has remained an important and interesting item in the female wardrobe.

Bolero. Originally a gaily embroidered, open waistcoat of the Spanish *torero*, it was intro-duced into fashionable ladies' dress about 1850 reappearing at intervals.

Canezou. After 1820 a short spencer, which covered the wide neckline of ladies' dresses. In the course of the following decades it changed into a lace-trimmed collar, broad enough to cover the shoulders.

Casaquin. A loose, short ladies' gown. It was also a lightly waisted overgarment worn with the crinoline. The **caraco** is a mid 18th century fitted, knee-length gown often worn by the unfashionable.

Cassock (French, *casaque*). The typical feature of this garment, and the only one, which all its many variants in the history of costume have in common, is its length. We meet it as *casaque* or as *casaquin*. The *casaque*, which was already in use in the 16th century, was the characteristic garment of the French companies of musketeers. It kept its place as an overgarment generally with loosely hanging sleeves till the 19th century. By the end of the 18th century, provided with long tails and with chevrons and buttons, it formed part of the elegant man's wardrobe as a travelling or hunting coat.

Doublet (German, *Wams*). This name was originally given to the padded coat worn beneath the breastplate. From the 15th to the 17th centuries it was the chief garment worn on the upper part of the body and immediately underneath the outer coat or cloak; it was always made with sleeves. In its style it followed the vagaries of fashion: sometimes it fitted tightly, sometimes it was slashed and puffed and sometimes it assumed the curious form of the peasecod or goose belly. In the 17th century it became increasingly shorter; the coat with tails gradually turned into a jacket which barely reached the waist. Its function was then taken over by the waistcoat.

Gipon or **Jupon.** Close-fitting, slightly waisted, medieval garment falling without folds or gathers to just above the knee. Its body was padded, usually throughout.

Jacket (German, **Sakko**). This is a short single or double breasted coat or (lounge) jacket for men. It became popular in England in the 19th century. We meet its predecessors in the jerkin and the loose coat worn by country folk in the 17th century and later by sportsmen.

In the second half of the 17th century the three basic elements of the male costume of today emerged: jacket or coat, waistcoat and trousers. In the France of Louis XIV it was called the *justaucorps*, because the coat clung rather loosely to the body – *juste au corps*. It was knee-length and made of heavy, richly embroidered materials with wide sleeves, large pockets and many buttons. In the middle of the 18th century the lower part of the *justaucorps* was stiffened with whalebone or waxed cloth giving a similar outline to the side-hoop, supported skirts of contemporary ladies.

Kamisol (German) or **Jerkin.** A close-fitting jacket or short coat often made of leather. In the 16th and 17th centuries it was an undergarment with sleeves (the word derives from the Latin for shirt = *camisia*).

Lendner (German). This close-fitting garment, a sort of jerkin, which came to the upper part of the thighs and was generally sleeveless and made of leather, was worn in the second half of the 14th century.

Pourpoint. This was the characteristic upper portion of male dress during the second half of the 14th century. Tight fitting, it was fastened with buttons or laced. A strongly accentuated waist characterized this garment, which lent itself to the exaggeration of fashion features. The sleeves were puffed near the shoulders and often adorned with dags. Of the doublet worn beneath it only the narrow sleeves could be seen, since the shape of this garment was adapted entirely to that of the tight-fitting pourpoint.

Waistcoat (French, **gilet**). In the Baroque and Rococo the waistcoat sometimes had sleeves and was made of costly materials, richly decorated. During its development, which extends over three hundred years, it frequently changed its shape; it shortened from knee to waist length, and in the course of the last century it also lost its sleeves. The backs are usually of less expensive material than the front. To this day it has preserved its colourful appearance and very striking specimens may be seen. Usually, however, it is made of the same material as the suit, although there is an increasing tendency to omit it altogether.

850 Edgar Degas. Portrait of Manet. Drawing. Bibliothèque Doucet, Paris. In the seventies of the last century the short jacket as we know it today, took the place of the tail-coat. The trousers were often made of a lighter material than the jacket.

851 *Modealmanach*, 1786–1788. From the *justaucorps* depicted here, lavishly trimmed with brandenburgs and facings on pockets and cuffs, the *frac* developed towards the end of the 18th century, into a more comfortable garment made of a lighter material.

852 *Modes d'hommes*, 1828. The coat of the twenties of the past century has a tight waist and flares at the hips. The sleeves too are gathered at the shoulders.

850

851

852

853 *Allgemeine Modenzeitung*, 1836. The festive frockcoat for evening wear is worn with a flowered waist-coat; the trousers are provided with straps at the ankle. A bicorne completes the outfit.

854 *Allgemeine Modenzeitung*, 1836. The coat tails are lined with moiré silk. The waistcoat is of the same material. Side-whiskers and moustache are much in evidence.

853

854

855

855 Eugène Delacroix. 'Freedom leads the people to the barricades' (detail). Musée du Louvre, Paris. The young revolutionary in cap and shirt is wearing an open waistcoat with large metal buttons.

856 Hans Memling. Warrior from 'The death of St. Ursula' in the shrine of St. Ursula at Musée de l'Hôpital Saint-Jean, Bruges. The warrior is wearing a jerkin with tied on sleeves over a mail shirt.

857 The Money Changer. Nuremberg engraving, 1539. The German citizen is wearing a cap and a belted doublet.

858 Giambattista Moroni. 'The Tailor'. National Gallery, London. The short doublet is fastened with small buttons.

859 Florentine School. Portrait of the poet Garcia della Vega. The Italian poet's doublet is embroidered. The sleeves are in a contrasting material.

856

857

858

859

860 *Modealmanach*, 1786–1788. The overloaded hat dominates the fashion picture. The street dress, the *caraco*, has a very tight waist, the skirt is full. The lady is carrying a stick.

861 Raphael. Soldiers of the Swiss Guard. Detail from the Mass of Bolsena. Fresco in the Stanza di Eliodoro. The bare-headed, kneeling soldiers are wearing *Schecken* with wide sleeves, and skirts.

862 Francisco de Goya. Self Portrait. Prado, Madrid. The embroidered bolero is part of Spanish national costume.

860

861

863 After a playing card from the late 15th century. A Renaissance dandy: the clothes are very tight fitting, only the shoulder and sleeve portions are artificially widened, (*Mahôitres*). The points of the shoes in this bizarre fashion were often longer than the shoe itself.

Trousers are probably of oriental origin. In Europe they were first worn by the Gauls and certain Germanic tribes. The Romans were introduced to them by the Teutons, but they generally employed puttees, as did the Carlovingian Franks, who nevertheless on occasions wore trousers and sometimes also the long tunic of antiquity. Not until the 12th century did hose come into general use in men's clothing. Basically they were long stockings. In the 15th and 16th centuries trousers acquired numerous names (trunk hose, round hose, Venetians, etc.), for which many yards of silk material were necessary. But each country developed its own style. The Landsknechts introduced fantastic slashed and pouched styles – *Pluderhose*. The most extravagant trouser fashions were further enriched by the intervention of the lansquenets, who slit them. The Rhinegrave breeches of the 17th century were wide and hung loose to below the knee so that they produced the same frilly effect as a woman's petticoat. The kneebreeches, which were introduced in the reign of Louis XIV only went out of fashion with the French Revolution, which popularized the long trouser or pantaloons, hitherto worn only by the lower orders and sailors. The trousers remained fashionable until the end of the 19th century, and they became narrower or wider as fashion demanded. Kneebreeches remained the correct formal wear until 1820, but were worn into the 20th century with court dress. In our time kneelength trousers are part of sports dress, worn above all by alpinists. Women first wore trousers as underwear in the 16th century, but the fashion was not general in Europe, and it was only at the beginning of the 20th century that the majority of women began to wear them generally. As outer wear for women trousers have only really been accepted in recent years, but today they may be said to have 'arrived'.

Braies (Bruche). In the course of the 12th century the leg covering was divided into a trouser-like garment called braies, which covered the hips and upper thighs. To it were attached the long, narrow hose by means of strings or laces. Cross-gartering was often

used. (From the 14th century onwards hose were no longer attached to the braies but to the doublet.)

Canions. In the 16th and early 17th century, the tubular extension covering the thighs between the trunk hose. The stockings were pulled over them.

Galligaskins (German, **Pumphose**). They were worn in the 16th century and first half of the 17th century and were distinguished by the fact that they were knee length. They could be padded or smooth at the hips.

Heerpauke (German), **Round Hose.** These heavily padded, short and rotund-looking breeches, a product of Spanish fashion during the second half of the 16th century, were mostly worn in western Europe.

Keilhose (Trousers with gusset). This type of trousers became fashionable for skiing at the end of the thirties and since then – thanks to the modern elastic fabrics – they have become increasingly tighter. Nowadays these slim-fitting and elegant trousers are the accepted wear both for skiing and 'après-ski'.

Knickerbockers, Plus Fours. The length and width of these sports trousers, which are reminiscent of the 16th and 17th century slops or galligaskins have undergone frequent changes. Today knickerbockers are regarded as having the correct cut if they extend a good handsbreath below the knees.

Pantaloons. These long, tight trousers became widespread after the French Revolution and paved the way for modern male fashion.

Rhinegrave breeches. They are sometimes, incorrectly, said to have been called after the Rhinegrave brother of the Princess Palatine. They antedated his arrival in 1670, and were already worn in the 1650s, remaining fashionable until the 1670s. They were generously cut, of even width and lavishly trimmed with ribbons. With them skirt-like puffed over-trousers were worn which came to about the middle of the thighs. They consisted of strips of different materials, which were laid length-wise over a contrasting and thickly padded lining and the whole was sewn on to the actual breeches. Generally the strips consisted of velvet or silk with gold embroidery or small

slashes. As the overtrousers increased in volume they were referred to as *tonneaux*. The development of breeches which only cover the upper part of the thighs would have been unthinkable without the invention of stockings, which were designed to display the beauty of the legs.

Riding Breeches. In order to make them fit comfortably, extra width is allowed over the thighs; it is this which gives them their characteristic shape. When seated no crease must show on the inner side of the rider's leg.

Slops. In contrast to the trunkhose, they were worn straight and loose and were also worn during the late 16th century and early 17th century.

864 Pieter Aertsen. Market scene. Museum of Fine Arts, Budapest. The working dress of the Dutch trader consists of a soft hat, a shirt, a sleeveless waistcoat, long trousers and clogs.

865 Terence, Heautontinoroumenos 9. Syrus, Klitipho, Bacchus, Chremes. In the 16th century ordinary dress always consisted of cap, belted doublet with wide sleeves, narrow-legged trousers and boots with turned-down tops.

866 Jost Amman. Flagbearer. The adventurously coloured clothes of the flagbearer are richly decorated. The cap is trimmed with feathers and the bodice and sleeves of the waistcoat as well as the wide trousers are slashed.

867 Wenzel Hollar. From the cycle 'Dress for State occasions'.

868 Jacob Seisenegger. The Emperor Charles V. Gemäldegalerie des Kunsthistorischen Museums, Vienna. The width of the shoulders in the Imperial costume is achieved by the padded sleeves. Broad slits in the gown permit free movement of the arms. The codpiece, called *braguette*, which was considered decorative, is conspicuous in this outfit.

864

XXVII Jodokus Verbeeck. Norbert Leopold, Count Libenstein of Kolovrat. Castle Gallery, Rychnov n.Kn. (Bohemia).

XXVIII Wenzel von Brožik. Young girl. Národní Galerie, Prague.

XXIX Luděk Marold. Lady in the snow. Národni Galerie, Prague.

XXX Auguste Renoir. The actress
Jeanne Samary. Hermitage, Leningrad.

865

866

867

868

870

Trunk hose. In the second half of the 16th century breeches were slashed, puffed and underlaid with padded lining. In spite of their amazing appearance – they are among the most eccentric manifestations in the history of costume – the cut was extremely simple; only their size distinguished them from the earlier breeches.

869 Jacob Geyn. Guitar player. The masked musician is wearing a waistcoat with pleated collar and cuffs; the fantastically slashed trunkhose are tied with bows at the knees.

870 Dirck Barendz. Venetian Ball. Rijksmuseum, Amsterdam. Ladies' Renaissance court dress is of heavy satin. The bodice tapers to a triangle, the deep décolleté is adorned with pearls and a circlet crowns the hair. The gentleman is wearing cap, doublet and short padded breeches. He has thrown a cape-like wrap over his right shoulder.

869

871 *Costumes Parisiens*, 1810. Evening dress worn by the fashionable lady of the Empire has a high waist and mamelouk sleeves. The gentleman is wearing a gold-embroidered *frac* with flowered waistcoat and a lace jabot. White stockings complement the knee breeches.

872 Francisco de Goya. Don José Miguel de Carvajal y Vargas, Duke of San Carlos. Prado, Madrid. Spanish court dress of the late 18th century is lavishly decorated with gold embroidery and worn with stand-up collar, sash, feather-trimmed bicorne and walking stick.

871

872

873

874

875

876

877

878

879

873 From a contemporary fashion magazine of the 1840s. The tails and cuffs of the evening *frac* are ornamented by piping, and worn with breeches.

874 *Journal des Dames et des Modes*, 1812. The spencer-jacket, Canezou, was fashionable.

875 *Modes d'hommes*, 1839. The street outfit consisted of frockcoat, waistcoat, long trousers, top hat and walking stick.

876 Eugène Delacroix. Baron Scheiter. National Gallery, London.

877 Fashion plates for the *Theaterzeitung*, 1845–1848. The tight waistcoat and short front of the tailcoat accentuate the waist.

878 Lithograph. Lams after Joh. Wenzel Zinke. A caricature of the mid 19th century fashion for check trousers.

879 *H. Buschmanns neue Frauentracht*, circa 1900. Ladies' sports dress.

880 Francisco de Goya. Doña Isabel Cobos de Porcel. National Gallery, London. She wears a mantilla.

Fashion is open to every kind of influence and grateful for any stimulus. For this reason alone and in view of the international character of fashion, any attempts to create an exclusive 'national costume' and to keep away all foreign impulses and tendencies were doomed to failure. Extra-European cultures, too, have contributed to fashion and there is a constant influx of ideas from such fringe areas as Norway, Sweden, Russia, Spain and Greece into the centres of European fashion. Canada as well as America contribute their share. One big fashion sensation of the late 18th century and early 19th century, the long shawl came from India. No one today can imagine the furore produced by the Indian shawl among the European society ladies; no one today will think it possible that thousands of francs were paid for certain costly specimens and that society ladies stooped so low as to rob one another.

But one need not go so far back into the past in order to be aware of the manifold influences which affect fashion. The blazer, a brightly coloured sports jacket, formerly the preserve of the English gentleman whereby he proclaimed membership of his sports club, and which was later taken up by schools and colleges, suddenly, at the beginning of the sixties, became a great fashion hit with men and women of all ages. This shows that not only working dress but also uniforms or parts of uniforms are avidly welcomed among the civilian population by fashion creators, who are constantly on the look-out for new ideas. In 1965/66 a regular 'military look' was fashionable in Europe – not surprising for those who have experienced the spontaneous acceptance by both sexes of the trench coat in the twenties and of the duffle coat in the fifties.

In recent years certain features of 'national' dress have crept into fashion designs.

Amazon or **Riding Habit.** The Amazons were a legendary, warlike race of women according to a Greek myth, which were already known to Homer. Later on all female riders were referred to as Amazons. Their habit, which in the 16th century was not noticeably different from the ordinary dress of the time, later acquired a more and more masculine flavour. It is said that Catherine de Medici was probably the first women to wear trousers and, lavishly adorned, allowed them to be seen. In the 17th century these 'Amazons' took over the men's *justaucorps*, worn with a skirt. In the 19th century, women riders wore masculine trousers under a very long skirt, as well as boots and tight jackets. At that time it was fashionable to wear a top hat with veil attached. Riding astride was not introduced for women until the early 20th century. Women first rode astride in a divided skirt over breeches, and did not wear breeches alone until after the First World War. Jodhpurs – riding trousers full at the hips and narrow at the ankle – were introduced for informal riding dress well after the First World War. They are copied from the Indian trouser, and are now worn by both men and women. The modern horsewoman has entirely assumed male riding costume.

Dirndl. The national dress of the Bavarian and Austrian Alps. Between the wars the fashion spread over Europe, and found its way to America and even to Australia. The whole outfit includes the wide skirt with coloured or white apron and tight-fitting bodice.

Kimono. This forms the basis of the costume of Japanese men and women. Basically the kimono – the word means 'thing for putting on' – is a long coat-like robe with wide sleeves, held together by a sash called obi. This brocade belt, which is about half a yard in width and several yards long, is wound several times around the body and tied at the back in a large bow. In the 20th century Paul Poiret introduced the comfortable kimono into European female fashion. The sleeves, which are cut in one with the rest of the garment, and which to this day have kept their place in fashion, are known as kimono sleeves.

Mantilla and **Mantelet.** The black, or sometimes white, lace veil is part of the festive garb of Spanish women; it is draped over head, shoulders and neck. In the fashionable costume of the 17th and 18th centuries a light shoulder wrap was known as Mantelet. In the

19th century the name also referred to short ladies' coats.

Sari. The long wrapping garment of Indian women, which covers head and body, was used at the end of the forties by Paris fashion designers as a model for some of their creations.

Gown, Robe, Frock, Dress. 'Gown' is the general term current for a woman's dress from medieval times onwards. In the 18th century the term 'robe' or *manteau* began to be used interchangeably, implying a front fastening overgown. 'Frock' began to be used at the end of the 18th century and at the beginning of the 19th century for a one-piece gown usually fastening at the back. 'Dress' began to be used for a woman's main garment in the 20th century.

881 *Magazin des Demoiselles*. In the 19th century the mantle and mantelet were no longer merely decorations but part of street clothing, kinds of wraps, which were worn over the dress and came to the knee.

882 *Allgemeine Modenzeitung*, 1844. Children's fashion also copied the mantelet of the adults.

883 *L'Iris*, 1854. Another type of mantelet is shorter and trimmed with strips of fur and fabric.

884 J. D. de Saint Jean. Lady in church. The elegant Frenchwoman's wrap is similar to the Spanish mantilla. It is regarded as decorative and worn above all to church, where the head must be covered. The mantle is lightly tied under the chin and falls in soft folds to the hips.

885 Wilhelm Leibl. Three women in church. Hamburger Kunsthalle. Bavarian traditional costume for women is the dirndl dress: skirt with bodice and white blouse or a scarf, which is tucked into the bodice. This costume too, has more than once been an inspiration for world fashion.

881

882 883

884 885

886-888 The Japanese kimono has also been accepted into world fashion; here, however, it serves as house rather than outdoor dress.

886 Women on the Terrace. Engraving. Kionoka. Musée Guimet, Paris.

887 Kabayashi Kokkei. The hank of black hair. Ilosokawa Collection, Tokyo.

888 Embroidered kimono. 16th century. National Museum, Tokyo. The style of the sleeves in particular contributes to the comfort of the kimono.

887

888

889 From an English fashion magazine, 1831. In the Biedermeier period the riding habit includes a top hat with veil; the dress has balloon sleeves.

890 *La Mode de Paris,* 1834. The ladies in black Amazon costume are fashionably clad in dresses with puffed sleeves and top hats with veils of black lace.

891 *Journal des Dames,* 1799. Lady riding in a dress of lawn and a jockey cap.

889

890

891

541

892 After Moreau le Jeune. Lady in waiting to the Queen. Circa 1777. The huge hooped skirt from the era of Marie Antoinette is adorned with flounces and flower garlands.

The lower portion of a woman's dress, which extends from the waist downwards over the hips, is known as the skirt. The original skirt of the Middle Ages was a draped garment, which reached from the neck to the knees in one piece and was generally girded. It was worn by men and women until about the 13th century. The female Gothic suckeny is known to have had a bodice and skirt; this is the beginning of the skirt as we understand the word today. Changes in length, width and shape of the skirt have had a decisive effect on the formation of the fashion line.

Apron. The oldest item of clothing which has remained virtually unchanged from the time of the ancient Egyptians to the present day. Its purpose, which has changed as little as its shape, was to protect clothing during work. In the course of the last 500 years, however, it has, on occasions, formed part of fashion. On such occasions it is made of fine materials and decorated with embroidery and lace (fancy apron, cocktail apron).

Bell-shaped or **circular skirt** (*Glockenrock*). Wide skirt consisting of a single piece or several sections cut to form a circle, which gives the skirt a bell-like appearance.

Bustle, Tournure, Dress-improver, Crinolette, Cul de Paris. A skirt which is widened at the back and stands away from the body in the region of the buttocks. This effect is achieved by means of a padded cushion, or a whalebone or wire contraption. The overskirt is richly decorated with flounces and bows. Variations were fashionable in the 1780s and around 1870–86.

Crinoline. Originally a material of horsehair and therefore stiff, used first of all for soldiers' collars and only later for skirts. The wide skirt, which stood away from the body, was made either from stiff material or was made to stand out by means of another stiff skirt worn underneath, by padding, wood or wire contraptions, whalebone, hoops of bamboo or cane, air-filled rubber rings or petticoats of stiffened linen. It has entered the history of fashion on several occasions, the last of these was in the years 1850–1870. Skirt supports such as farthingales were used in the 16th century, side-hoops and paniers in the 18th century.

Divided skirt. Sports skirt for women, which came into fashion around 1930. Its trouser form is well concealed by the deep pleats. This form of skirt is again high fashion today, when it is described as a culotte-skirt.

Hobble skirt. Long skirt which was so narrow round the ankles that women could not walk properly and had to hobble instead. It was fashionable between 1910 and 1914 and is an interesting example of how fashion can prevail over all considerations of sound sense. It is said that this skirt, a creation of the House of Paquin, did not, at first, arouse much enthusiasm and that the actress Sarah Bernhardt declined to wear it. Mme Sorel, reputed to have excellent taste, needed an original dress for an original role, in which she had to remain leaning against a pillar for a considerable length of time. It was necessary that her figure should form an aesthetic contrast with the pillar and at the same time should present a harmonious whole with it, and the hobble skirt appeared to fulfil these conditions, the more so that she need not take large steps which would destroy its line. Unfortunately this fashion found favour with the *demi-monde*, who, for a time, formed a kind of fashion-link between the other social classes, and for this reason the skirt became generally accepted. The writer of this anecdote reflects that this skirt, 'suitable only for statuesque poses, was used for walking, nay, even dancing, and this nonsense fashion carried off the victory, without effort, without a fight, as it were in spite of itself'.

Pleated skirt. A skirt laid into pleats which are then pressed. The cut and width of the pleats vary according to fashion. Pleated skirts were worn by men during the Renaissance.

Train. The hem of the dress is lengthened at the back and dragged along the ground. The train helps above all to increase and lengthen the figure and lends its wearer a superior and dignified appearance. The train was therefore largely reserved for court circles. It could be either fastened to the shoulders as a separate part of the costume or was merely an elongated part of the dress as we know it already from medieval miniatures of the 12th century. At the Burgundian court the length of the train was prescribed exactly: the longer the train the greater the importance of the wearer. At that time men too wore a gown with train called houppelande. The largest known garment is the coronation gown of the Russian Czarina Catherine the Great: the train was over 70 metres long and 7 metres wide. It was carried by fifty pages.

The train did not fit in with the costume of the Baroque, it only returned when skirts gathered up high at the back came into fashion – the *bouffantes* around 1680, the *cul de Paris* in the second half of the 18th century, and the bustle a hundred years later. The train was fashionable for the last time around 1900 when it was worn with street dresses; today it is disappearing even from ball and wedding gowns.

893 From a fashion journal. A hooped skirt with lace and fur trimmings. A close-fitting bodice and a tightly laced waist are part of court dress. The tall coiffure is decorated with feathers and bows.

894 *Gallery of Fashion*, 1796. Side-hoops continued to be used for court dress long after they had ceased to be fashionable for everyday wear. According to English fashion garlands of flowers and ribbons with tassels decorate the hooped skirt. A turban with ostrich feathers belongs to this ensemble.

895 Satirical copperplate engraving of the *Bouffantes*. Circa 1785. The caricature mocks at skirt, side-hoops and corset.

896 *Allgemeine Modenzeitung*, 1836. In the 1830s the skirt is full, supported on starched or horsehair reinforced petticoats. Instead of the high wigs bonnet-like hats are worn.

893

894

XXXI Unknown Master. Cecilie Renata, daughter of the Emperor Ferdinand II. Castle Gallery Rychnov n.Kn. (Bohemia).

XXXII Unknown Master. Sabine Victoria von Kolovrat, née Countess of Wolkenstein. Castle Gallery, Rychnov n.Kn. (Bohemia).

895

896

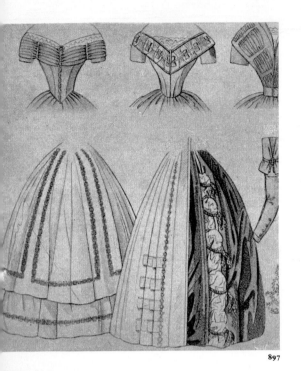

897/898 *Die Wiener Elegante*, 1843 and 1845. These fashion plates clearly show the cut of various bodices and skirts, as well as a number of fabric combinations and types of pleats. Skirt and bodice are often trimmed with various kinds of braid.

899 *Petit Courrier des Dames*, 1864. The crinoline of the sixties still makes use of combinations of materials and flounce trimmings. It is worn with shawl or mantilla and a bonnet, the *fanchon*.

900 *Allgemeine Modenzeitung*. The street dress, too, must have a crinoline, a small bonnet and a parasol.

901 *Le Charivari*, 1865. 'We shall spend the rest of the summer in the country and live here underneath the crinoline.'

897

898

899

900

901

902 From a fashion journal. The crinoline becomes the bell-shaped skirt, which does not broaden the hips and is flared not gathered.

903 From a fashion journal of 1860. Correct evening wear of the sixties is the crinoline with many flounces, ribbons and braids. The fashion creators again pay great attention to the sleeves.

904 *Vogue*, 1924–1925. Model by Jean Patou. The finely pleated skirt of the twenties falls loosely and naturally. It reaches to mid-calf.

905 From an English fashion magazine, 1898. The street costumes of the turn of the century have floor length, flared skirts and are worn with hats trimmed with veils and feathers and with a stick.

906 *Le Charivari*, 1885. Caricature of a lady with bustle: 'If only these baskets could be used for doing the shopping!'

902
903

904   905

906

907   908

909

907/908 From fashion magazines of 1875 and 1884. In the last third of the 19th century the crinoline was replaced by the bustle which, together with the tightly laced corset, produced an S-shaped figure. The bustle was embellished with flounces, lace and bows.

909 *Fliegende Blätter*. The fashion outline of the bustle is caricatured in this silhouette.

910 Caricature by Heinrich Lossow. German Can Can.

910

911   912

913

914 915

916

917

911 Hans Holbein the Younger. Citizen of Basle. Kupferstichkabinett, Basle. The dragging, richly draped outer garment allows the petticoat to be seen.

912 Hans Holbein the Younger. Study of a woman of Basle. Kupferstichkabinett, Basle.

913 Matthäus Zasinger. Ball at the court of Munich in the year 1500. Engraving.

914 Egyptian Relief from a tomb in Benihasan, Middle Kingdom. In Egypt the apron was a basic part of clothing.

915 Wenzel Hollar. Lady from Zurich going to town. Engraving. The lady's apron, which extends to the hem, is edged with lace.

916 *Modes de Femmes*, 1827. The French lady's apron with embroidered hem and pockets serves to adorn the day dress.

917 Edgar Degas. The Family Ballelli (detail). Musée du Louvre, Paris. The little girl wears a sleeveless overall.

Coats and Mantles

By the word mantle in its widest sense we understand every outer garment worn over the rest of the clothing as a protection against the weather, that is to say, from the Greek himation and the Roman palla onwards to ladies' and gentlemen's overcoats and rain-coats of today. In the Middle Ages mantles were sleeveless – they were rectangular, circular, semi-circular or segments of a circle and were either fastened in front or at the shoulders, or else they had a hole for the head. Later the word coat came to mean an overgarment with sleeves and button fastening.

Adrienne (French). A wide, comfortable overgarment with a loosely pleated back, dating from the time of the Rococo. It received its name from the comedy *Adriana* by Terence, in which, in the year 1703, the actress Doncourt, playing a pregnant woman, appeared for the first time wearing this garment. Soon it came to be worn also as a house and travel gown. Other names for it were: *Sacque, Contouche, Innocente, Trollopee, Slammerkin*, etc.

Burnous. The characteristic garment of the Bedouins. Originally it was not sewn but draped round the body rather like the Roman toga. Later it was sewn, had sleeves of varying length and a hood. In the Beidermeier period it served as a model for fashionable ladies' and gentlemen's cloaks.

Chesterfield. Single or double breasted man's overcoat without a waist seam, named after the sixth Earl of Chesterfield.

Chlamys. Smaller version of the himation; oblong woollen mantle of the ancient Greeks, measuring about 5 ft or 6 ft by 3 ft. It was worn above all by youths, riders, soldiers and travellers. In Imperial Rome it was also worn by women. In ancient iconography the god Hermes, or Mercury, is depicted wearing the chlamys.

Diploidion (Diplois, Diplax). Large piece of cloth folded double, serving the Greeks as a mantle. It was distinguished from the chlamys and himation only by its double thickness. The pallas of the Romans, too, was often doubled.

Domino. Originally the large hood worn by monks, protecting head, neck and part of the shoulders against the vagaries of the weather. Later it became a wide cloak with attached hood and since the second half of the 17th century it has been traditional carnival dress with a small mask.

Garde-Corps. Chief outer garment for men from the end of the 14th to the middle of the 15th century. Fashion points to note especially are the voluminous sleeves, the lower part of which had a pouch-like extension which reached to the knees; moreover, the sleeves were sometimes richly dagged. The garment frequently had a hood, which either stood open or was fastened by means of laces or buttons. The tabard was similar, but sleeveless.

Garrick (or Carrick). Winter and bad weather coat, probably named either after the actor Garrick or the Irish town of Carrick. The coat was long – it came to within a few inches of the ground – had a large ornamental collar which fell to the shoulders and was often made of fur. The fashion spread around 1800 from England to the rest of Europe. A lady's version of this coat came into being in the 1870s.

Glocke (German = bell). In the Middle Ages a circular cloak with a central hole for the head – the simplest form of male overcoat. A similar version of it is worn today, especially in the mountainous regions, in the form of a cloak made from the rough woollen cloth known as loden.

Heuke (Arabic, *Haik*). Bell-shaped, sleeveless cloak, much worn in France, Italy and Flanders at the beginning of the 14th century, first by men only and later also by women. The men wore it over the shoulders, the women also over the head. Sometimes the upper part of the women's version was stiffened with wire and so formed a kind of cage over the head, sometimes it was fixed to the head with the aid of a round cap. Another variant (*Tipheuke*) consisted of a rounded piece of wood in the form of a small cap, decorated with a projecting point and wool tassels; it kept the mantle in position. In some traditional costumes this garment was preserved until the 18th century.

Himation. Mantle of the ancient Greeks, generally made of wool and worn over the chiton. Its rectangular shape was the same for men and women. To assist with the draping it was weighted at the four corners. It was usually thrown over the left shoulder and held together in front, the right shoulder remaining bare. The woman's himation sometimes covered the whole body including the head. It was about 5 ft wide and 10 ft long. Great care was taken by the wearer with the draping of this garment, because the way it was draped showed the degree of her personal taste and culture.

Houppelande. Long, wide gown with long full sleeves and high collar, worn from the end of the 14th century by French-Burgundian fashion. First masculine, but later also feminine ceremonial dress. For court occasions it was lined with fur and lengthened into a train. It often had dagged edges. Later heralds wore a short version of it with the insignia of their lord.

Inverness Cloak. Mid 19th century long coat for men, sleeveless, with removable pelerine.

Caftan. Long, loose robe of oriental origin, open in front, sometimes girded and generally with wide sleeves. Until recently it was part of the costume of orthodox Jews. In the mid 1960s it became fashionable for female evening wear.

Lacerna. Roman mantle (analogous to the Greek chlamys) with hood. In rainy weather it was worn over the toga.

Paenula. Bad weather cloak of the ancient Romans. It was sleeveless, circular and later elliptical and was made of rough sheeps' wool or pelts. It had an opening for the head and was always provided with a hood.

Paletot. (The word derives from the Dutch *paltrok*, a combination of *pals* = palace and *rok* = garment, in other words palace cloak.) In the 19th century the word always described an overcoat for town wear – in contrast to the sports coat – and is still used in that sense in German.

Paludamentum. Military cloak, purple in colour, worn by Roman generals, identical in

cut with the lacerna. Later, and especially in the Middle Ages, also the purple cloak of the Emperor.

Pelerine. From the French for 'pilgrim' (*pelerin*) or from the Latin *peregrinus*, meaning a stranger. Originally a sleeveless cloak or cape worn by pilgrims. The pelerine appears at various periods, generally in the form of a shoulder-cape of varying length.

Peplos. Long woollen shawl which was draped round the body and fastened at the shoulder with a pin. It was the long, gracefully falling over-garment of Doric women. An exactly similar garment for men was called the chlaina.

Raglan. An overcoat in which sleeves and shoulders are cut in one piece, named after the English Field Marshal Lord Raglan (1788–1855). It has remained in fashion to this day, because of its comfortable style.

Redingote. (Corruption of English 'riding-coat'.) This coat originated in England in the middle of the 18th century, evolving from the *justaucorps*. It had cutaway tails and was used for riding. It soon became popular also in France. By the last quarter of the 18th century women, too, began to wear it, though no longer for riding, but rather as an all-purpose coat. The redingote had a shaped waist, a large collar and revers and was single or double-breasted. Whereas in due course it disappeared from male fashion, variants of it have survived in women's fashion to this day.

Schaube (German = gown). From the last two decades of the 15th, and the first half of the 16th century, it was the generally worn male overcoat. It was open in front with a broad, often fur-trimmed, collar and voluminous sleeves. This garment was characteristic of the 16th century.

Spencer. Short, tight, tailless jacket of light-coloured material. (The story goes that Lord Spencer burned the tails off his coat while warming himself by the fire and thus started a new fashion!) It was worn by both sexes. It was fashionable with women from the 1790s to the 1820s, because thin fabrics and insufficient underwear created a demand for a warmer outer garment which would serve as dress and coat at one and the same time. Anyone merely wanting to cover the bodice found it adequate for the purpose. It was a continuation of the *caraco*, worn at the time of Marie-Antoinette. Its long sleeves followed the contemporary fashionable line. It was an early 19th century masculine fashion sometimes worn over a coat for extra warmth. Nowadays it has become a sort of woollen, usually knitted undergarment worn unfashionably for extra warmth.

Surcoat or **surcot**. Elegant over-garment of ladies of rank, worn during the late Middle Ages, the 13th and 14th centuries, and identical with the suckeny. It was made of precious fabrics, often of fur or with a fur lining, sleeveless, with deep arm openings extending to the hips, through which the tunic worn beneath could be seen.

Surtout (French = over all). 18th and 19th century male overcoat, usually with a collar, wider and more comfortable than the redingote.

Toga. Outer garment worn by the free male citizens of ancient Rome, a privilege denied to slaves, exiles and strangers. To begin with the toga was small but later it began to emulate the Greek himation and eventually greatly exceeded it in size. In its classical form the toga may frequently be seen on statues of Roman generals, statesmen and Emperors. It was semi-circular, elliptical or semi-elliptical in shape, about 12 ft wide and 18 ft long. It proved to be too elaborate for everyday wear and became reserved for ceremonial occasions. The wealthy had special servants (vestiplici) who at night carefully draped the toga round a dummy figure and fixed the folds into their exact positions by means of clasps and small weights. The toga had many variants. Its most common form was the *toga virilis* which was worn by all freemen; the *toga candida* was pure white and worn by candidates for public office; the *toga praetexta* had a purple border, distinguishing the higher official; the *toga purpurae* was the purple toga of the senators; the *toga palmata* was decorated with patterns of palms and worn by consuls, etc.

Ulster. A double-breasted heavy male overcoat of a rough woollen material with high buttoned collar and a half belt. It is called after the Northern Irish province, where in the towns of Belfast and Londonderry heavy woollen cloth for overcoats is manufactured.

Zimarra. Garment of the Italian Renaissance, worn both by men and women, and as *simarre* continues to be worn by French magistrates and university professors.

919 The Virgin Mary praying. Relief from Santa Maria in Porto, Ravenna. Over the tunica the women of ancient Rome wore the paenula, a medium length cloak with hood.

920 Evangelistary of Cutbercht. English, circa 770. State Library, Munich. Although the medieval mantle derived from the toga of antiquity, it was less richly draped.

921 The Three Kings. Mosaic. Early 6th century. St. Apollinare Nuovo, Ravenna. The Kings are depicted wearing patterned trousers, unknown in antiquity, and wraps (lacernae), which were fastened at the shoulders with ornamental clasps.

922 Maso Finiguerra. Illustration from the Florentine Picture Chronicles. British Museum, London. For a long time the mantle retained the form of a toga – an unsewn piece of fabric, draped in rich folds. Here it has an ornamental border. The old man is wearing a headdress of Eastern form.

920

921

922

923

924

925

923 The Adoration of the Magi. Church of
St. Croix de la Charité-sur-Loire. Middle of
12th century. The paludamentum of the
Romanesque period remains as a cloak, which
is loosely draped round the body.

924 Angel. Cathedral of Lleida. Second
half of 13th century. The angel is wrapped
in a Romanesque cloak laid in folds.

925 Porphyry Group of the Tetrarchs.
Southern façade of St. Mark's, Venice. The
Emperors are wearing short tunics and
paludamenta, fastened on the right shoulder
with a clasp.

560

926 St. Michael. Ivory carving. 9th century. Stadtbibliothek, Leipzig. Over the tunica with ornamental border, St. Michael is wearing a paludamentum.

927 Master of the Legend of St. Catherine. King with retinue (detail from the Martyrium of the Ten Thousand). Museum Narodowe, Warsaw. The late Gothic houppelande in the foreground has wide sleeves and a train. It is worn girded and the neck-opening is trimmed with fur. To the right a wide cloak with hood. Far right a sleeveless cloak.

926   927

928

929

930

928 Fra Filippo Lippi. Three Women
(detail from the Miracle of St. Ambrose).
State Museums, Berlin. The women's
cloaks cover the head so as to form hoods.

929 Master of the Life of the Virgin. The
conversion of St. Hubert (detail). National
Gallery, London. The saint is wearing a
short gown, the so-called *giornea*, with fur
trimming and slashed sleeves.

930 Jaime Huguet. The Saints Abdon and
Senen. Retable of the Saints. Centre Panel.
Tarrasa, San Pedro. The kneelength
garde-corps of the two saints are of a
patterned fabric.

931

932

933

931 French School. Louis XII and his Court in front of the Fortuna. Atelier de Rouen. The King is wearing a *garde-corps* with hanging sleeves.

932 Francesco del Cossa. St. Lucy. Cress Collection, National Gallery of Art, Washington. The saint is depicted wearing a Renaissance cloak after the manner of the *garde-corps*. The slits and the hem are trimmed with braid. The sleeves of the dress beneath are open and laced over the undergarment.

933 Hans Holbein the Younger. Sir John Godslave. Royal Art Collection, Windsor Castle. 16th century gentleman with cap, wearing a gown with fur collar.

934   935

939

934 German cloth merchant. 1620. The gown in a patterned fabric is lined with fur. Collar and cap are of the same fur.

935 Nuremberg Merchant, 1610. Another type of gown is trimmed with fur strips and fur collar.

936 German merchant. 15th century. The young merchant's gown is simple in style without embellishments and without collar. With it he is wearing a cap.

936   937   938

940

937 Wenzel Hollar. Woman from Antwerp.
The woman is wearing a *heuke* which
envelops her entirely from head to foot.

938 Wenzel Hollar. Woman of Antwerp
dressed for town. A special version of the
Heuke, the *Tipheuke*, is attached to the
forehead by a round disc which is sometimes
decorated with feathers.

939 Nuremberg Merchant, 1577. The
Spanish cape – known as such in the history
of costume – is a short, flaring cloak with
stand-up collar. It is worn with trunk hose
and a cylindrical cap.

940 Anton Möller the Elder. Virgins in
church. The girls wear pleated pelerines
with millwheel ruffs.

941

942

943

945

941 *Deutsche Modenzeitung*, 1823. In the 1820s pelerines came in various materials, often lined with fur and trimmed with embroidery. They were part of evening dress and worn with turbans.

942 *Modes d'hommes*. During the Biedermeier period the cloak was an elegant accessory of the *frac*.

943 *Deutsche Modenzeitung*, 1923. The numerous versions of the pelerine demonstrate the wealth of fashion ideas: here it has a circular upstanding collar and imaginative shoulder decorations.

944 Fashion plates for the *Theaterzeitung*. Short pelerines are part of day dress. They are edged with fur and worn with feather-trimmed hats.

945 Louise Abbema. Place de la Concorde. In the late 19th century the pelerine had a broad collar and reached to the waist. Here it is worn with a small veil-trimmed hat.

946 Illustrations from *Modes et usages au temps de Marie-Antoinette*. Paris, 1885. A lady of the late 18th century in a redingote with wide collars. She is wearing a fashionable hat and a *bandeau d'amour* with initials.

947 *Costumes Parisiens*, 1813. Redingote with silk lining and trousers ending in gaiters.

948 *La Mode*, 1831. English costume. Winter redingote.

944

946

947

948

949

950

951

955

949 Duhamel. Engraving. The double-breasted coat, called Garrick, with several shoulder-capes, reached to mid-calf. It is worn with hat, cravat, buckled shoes and a long stick.

950 *Modes d'hommes*, 1811. The elegant gentleman in *frac*, caped cloak, top hat and walking stick.

951 Leonetto Capiello Worth. The Raglan coat is a basic garment of modern fashion and only varies in length and type of lapels.

952 *Wiener Moden*, 1823. In the 19th century the caped cloak was popular. Here it is depicted trimmed with fur.

952   953   954

956

953 From a fashion magazine, 1827. The gentlemen's caped cloak – it is usually a man's coat – has the same cut as the women's, but it is wider. Here it is depicted lined with white satin and with a fur collar.

954 Illustration from *Modes et usages au temps de Marie-Antoinette*, Paris 1885. Lady wearing a domino of yellow taffeta and carrying a mask.

955 Fashion plates for the *Theaterzeitung*, 1834. The gentleman's caped cloak is of plain coloured material, the lady's has a pattern.

956 *Le Rire*, Paris 1925. 'Oh, pardon me, miss, I thought you were a pansy.' A caricature making fun of the similarity of male and female attire.

957 From a French fashion journal. The robe *à la française* forms a cloak in a light material with hood, which hides the wig.

958 *Modes de Paris,* 1837. The lady is wearing a hooded cloak with long sleeves turned up at the cuffs; the gentleman a top coat with checkered edging.

959 *Costumes Parisiens,* 1812. Hair style *à la chonoise.* She wears a *pelisse.*

960 *Vogue,* 1928. The evening coats have fur collars and are narrow, but not waisted. They are worn with small, close-fitting hats.

958

959   960

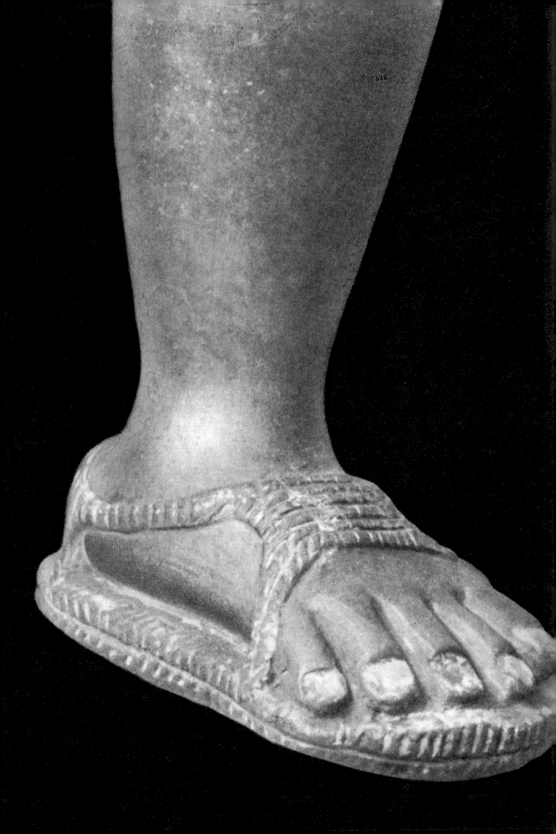

961 Foot with sandal; unknown place of discovery in Peru.

Stockings and Footwear

The first knitted children's socks were found in Coptic graves dating from the 5th century B.C.; for a long time after the art of knitting was lost, indeed for many centuries. Until then stockings were sewn, first of linen and then of fine leather. In medieval times the stocking was unknown as a separate item of clothing; during the period of Burgundian and Spanish fashion, that is to say, until the 17th century, coloured, and often multi-coloured hose were worn. In the Middle Ages the legs, from the soles of the feet to the knees, were sometimes bound with strips of material in the manner of puttees. It was not until the 16th century that the use of hand-knitted stockings became widespread in Spain. King Henry VIII received a pair of stockings from Spain as a precious gift. The Spanish stockings were decorated with colourfully embroidered clocks.

In 1589 William Lee, an English clergyman, built the first stocking frame; in the following years frame-knitted stockings gradually replaced hand-knitted stockings. Sewn stockings were sometimes used as 'boot-hose', and were used until the end of the 18th century to protect breeches from leather boot tops. The fashionables of the Baroque and Rococo wore knitted silk stockings with their tight-fitting breeches – sometimes several pairs for warmth. Under Louis XIV kneelength hose in light blue or red was worn. Elegant ladies liked embroidered clocks at the ankle, taking their cue from the Marquise de Pompadour. In the 19th century, with the advent of long tubular trousers, stockings for men became superfluous and they gradually shortened into socks, which are part of men's costume to this day.

Women began wearing stockings in the middle of the 19th century; the shorter the skirt the greater was the attention paid to stockings and shoes; in the 20th century the legs have achieved a prominence as never before. In the years 1900–1914 openwork stockings became fashionable, they were mostly made of lace in a great variety of floral patterns; some of these patterns had a symbolic significance (anchors and spiders' webs). The materials employed were chiefly silk and fine cotton (crêpe). Finely woven stockings with hand or machine embroidered motifs of flowers or birds with insets of Brussels lace were considered particularly elegant. In addition to these 'best' stockings, textured or striped stockings were worn generally, even with elegant outfits. With the development of the knitting industry after 1920 silk stockings carried the day, especially in flesh-coloured tones. In recent years silk and artificial silk (rayon) have given way completely to synthetic fibres such as nylon in the manufacture of stockings. From time to time coloured wool or cotton stockings came back into fashion, but usually woollen stockings and socks, whether hand or machine knitted, are reserved for sportswear. Tights, a revival of the medieval all-in-one hose came into use in the late 1950s.

Under footwear we mean any kind of covering for the feet; in its original form it was a covering for the sole, extending over its entire length and protecting the foot from injury. The laced sandals of antiquity were also in general use in the Middle Ages. To this day in the Balkans sandal-like shoes are worn, which are attached to the foot by means of straps; they are called *Opanky*. In the Middle Ages socks made of leather or felt were worn, which came to the knees and over which, especially in bad weather, wooden sandals were put on. Heels did not appear until the 17th century, when shoes of ankle height were worn, decorated with tongue, ribbons and rosettes. Red-coloured heels, and sole-edges at that time were the privilege of ladies and gentlemen of the Court. Besides, in the 17th century, enormous boots were worn with flaring funnel-shaped tops, later even to be trimmed with lace. In the 18th century ladies' shoes with high waisted heels came into fashion and in the 19th century these were replaced by high or medium-high boots. Today distinctions are made in footwear according to the raw material from which it is made, such as leather, wood, rubber, cloth, raffia and recently also synthetic fabrics.

Brognes, These consisted of a piece of leather which was strapped round the ankles with thongs. This shoe was known to have been worn by the old Germanic tribes; among country people it continued in use until the 16th and 17th centuries. It is still worn in the wilder parts of Ireland and the Scottish Highlands.

Calceus. The ankle-length leather shoe of the ancient Romans, taken over by certain of the Germanic tribes.

Cothurnus (Greek). A shoe with thick soles, worn frequently by members of the upper classes in ancient Greece. Since Aeschylus they were also worn by Greek tragic actors in order to appear taller on the stage. The cothurnus was made of coloured leather and lavishly decorated.

Duckbill-toed shoe. After 1450 the points of the shoes became shorter and rounder, receiving the name of duckbill, etc. These flat, low-cut shoes with rounded toe-cap, were especially characteristic of the Reformation period. They were made for the most part of yellow or blackened leather; the nobility wore coloured shoes of a fine leather, of velvet or of silk.

Elastic-sided or laced boots (*Stiefcletten*). This type of low boot was worn generally in the first two-thirds of the 19th century.

Gaiters. A covering of cloth, linen or leather for the ankle and lower leg. Laced stockings, similar to gaiters were worn already by the Franks and Lombards as a protection against the vagaries of the weather. Gaiters as worn today, without soles, made their first appearance in the 17th century in France, whence they spread to other countries. Side-buttoning is the typical form of fastening for gaiters. In the 18th century they were mainly worn with soldiers' uniform. In the 19th century, with the advent of goloshes, gaiters lost their importance in ladies' fashion; for men, short gaiters or spats have come back into fashion from time to time.

Ledersen (German). For the sake of convenience round 1500 peasants, knights and travellers wore this combination of leather breeches and shoes.

Leggings. In the course of the 12th century the leg-covering was divided into breeches or braies and long hose, which were fastened to the breeches. In addition ankle-high slippers were worn. Sometimes long hose, the foot reinforced with leather soles, were found sufficient without shoes. In the 15th century breeches and hose merged into trousers.

Pantofle (French, *Pantoufle*). It developed from the cothurnus and the name formerly applied also to the thick cork-soled wooden *chopines* which were worn in the street as a protection against the mud. The pantofle played an important role in Byzantium, then came to Italy where it was called pantofla (i.e. corkshoe) and reached France at the end of the 15th century. It became the fashionable footwear of men, expensively made of silk or fine leather. In the 16th century pantofles were worn exclusively by women. These were overshoes in the form of mules. At the end of the 18th century they degenerated into ordinary slippers.

Patten or **Clog** (*Trippen*). A kind of wooden sole or platform mounted on two 'heels' (one

962

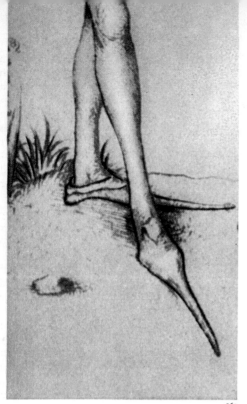

963   964

962 Sandals. Shoe Museum,
Gottwaldov (Moravia). The basic
type of shoe, which was made of any
kind of material accessible to
primitive peoples, is similar almost
everywhere in the world.

963 Master of the Housebook.
Death and the Maiden (detail).
The peaked shoes – here in their
extreme form – belong to the oddest
manifestations in the history of
fashion.

964 Pointed shoes from the 15th
century. Shoe Museum, Gottwaldov
(Moravia). In Gothic shoes the
point was turned upwards; in others
it lay flat.

each end) and strapped to the foot underneath the shoe. Pattens were worn in the 15th and 16th centuries as a protection for the ordinary shoes, which at that time generally were the pointed type. In the 18th century in England, the patten iron replaced the wooden sole support.

Peaked shoes. They were brought to Europe from the Orient during the Crusades. In France they were known as *poulaines* or *crakowes*; they gained ground among those who adopted Burgundian fashion. The shoes were colourful, as were all the clothes of that period. The points might be as long as two feet. They were worn in the late 12th century but their main period of fashion was in the second half of the 15th century.

Pumps (French, *Escarpin*). This shoe which at first was heelless, made its appearance in the late 17th century and continued to be worn especially for dancing. Ribbon trimmed they were worn in the 19th century as part of gentlemen's ball dress.

Sandal (Greek). A protective covering for the sole of wood, cork, leather or matting,

965

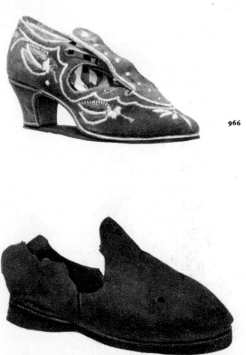

966

968

967

965 Jost Amman. The Shoemaker. Wood carving. In this shoemaker's workshop of the late Gothic period, pantofles and clogs are made. Of interest also are the working clothes with rolled up shirt sleeves and aprons.

966 Shoes from the 17th century. (a) Pantofle of a titled lady; (b) English shoe; (c) Shoe from the Königsberg tomb of Baron Grisbek; (d) Cothurnus. Shoe Museum, Gottwaldov, Moravia.

967 Pietro Longhi. The Dancing lesson (detail). Casa Rezzonico, Venice. The man's dancing shoes are ankle high and fasten with buckles. They are worn with white stockings.

968 Shoes from the 17th–18th century. Shoe Museum, Gottwaldov, Moravia.

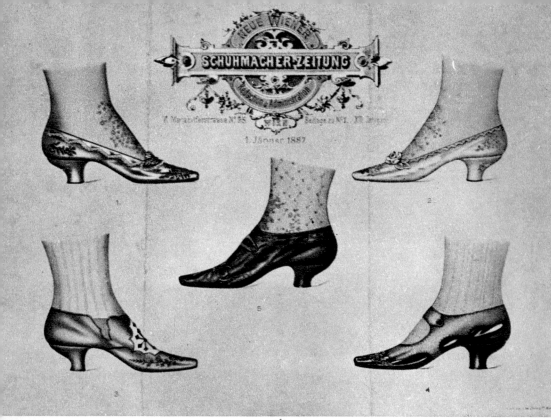

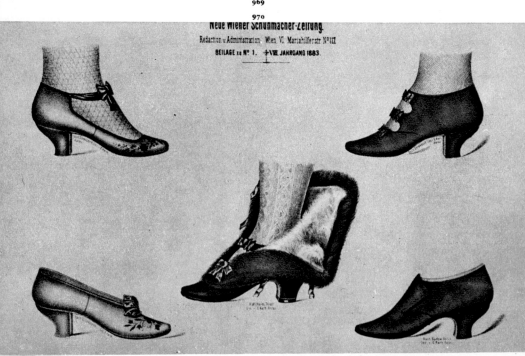

971   972

973

969 From a shoemaker's magazine, 1887.
The fashion magazine of the late 19th
century shows the line of ladies' shoes. They
have a lower, broader heel. Often two kinds
of material are combined or else the shoes
are decorated.

970 *Neue Wiener Schuhmacher-Zeitung*, 1883.
At the same period shoes for winter are
higher and more closed in, but the general
line is the same.

971 Copy of the shoes belonging to the
Czech author Božena Němcová. Shoe
Museum, Gottwaldov (Moravia).

972 Dancing shoes from the 18th century.
Shoe Museum, Gottwaldov (Moravia).

973 *Gazette du Bon Ton*, 1924. In the
twenties the slim sandal cut returned, and
shoes were cut high or fastened with an
ankle strap.

fastened to the foot with thongs – it is the oldest type of footwear in existence. The ancient Egyptians made it of straw, raffia or papyrus. Its classical form is known to us from Greek sculptures. The Romans called the sandal solea. Finds from Coptic tombs reveal, in addition to sandals, also a kind of laced shoe made of leather pieces, the edges of which have been slashed to form thongs. Sandals were also worn in the Middle Ages, then they went out of fashion for a long time and did not reappear until the 18th century in France under the Directoire, when the 'antique' fashion was in vogue. Today any kind of light shoe is indiscriminately referred to as sandal.

Children's Costume

Children's dress as such only came into existence in the second half of the 18th century in England, doubtless in consequence of Rousseau's revolutionary ideas on education. Until then children's costume had merely been a smaller version of adults', with a few utilitarian additions like pinafores and 'reins' or leading strings attached to the shoulders. This applied particularly to the children of well-to-do parents. As long as clothing continued in the tradition, begun in antiquity, of adapting itself to the natural requirements of the human body, special clothes for children were unnecessary. But as fashion grew in complexity – one need only consider Burgundian, Spanish or Rococo fashion – the slavish copying of adults' clothes must have meant a great amount of discomfort for lively and active children. Liberation, begun in the 18th century, and insisted on by all the reformers of the 19th, was not fully achieved until the 20th century.

Writing of her youth, Johanna Schopenhauer describes the torture of being cooped up in this armour called clothing: 'An enormous tower of hair, supported by a contraption of wire and horsehair and crowned with masses of feathers, flowers and ribbons, added at least an *ell* to my height; the little white stilts, hardly more than an inch thick, which I wore underneath my ball shoes decorated with gold-embroidered ribbons, sought to redress the balance at the other end of my little person; but although they came nowhere near the height of the headdress, they were nevertheless high enough only to allow me to touch the floor with the tips of my toes. A tightly constructed harness of whalebone-sticks, sufficiently firm and stiff to withstand a bullet, violently pushed back arms and shoulders, pushed the chest forward and constricted the waist above the hips to wasplike proportions. And as for the hooped skirt . . . !' (the description continues). This is

how the children of the 'better' families were dressed in the last third of the 18th century.

But it was already a great step forward, the beginning of the emancipation of the child, as it were, when one could read at the end of the 19th century that it was 'horribly tasteless and inelegant for the clothing of small and growing children to be modelled on the lines and in the style of adults' costume'. The book, entitled *The Elegant Housewife* instructs the bourgeois reader that upper class families, in particular, lay great stress on allowing their children to remain young as long as possible, both in spirit and especially in dress. While it becomes clear, on reading further, that there was still a long way to go before clothes would be designed especially for children, credit must be given to the author for recognizing that the exuberant spirit of small children is not exactly uplifted by the wearing of silk and velvet and high boots with high heels.

But with a typical 19th century attitude the author urges one luxury upon the reader, namely the lavish use of lace for small children. 'Nothing', she says, 'so enhances the delicate tender bloom of a child's complexion as a soft frame of lace', and she advises the utmost simplicity of style so as to counteract 'any possible pretentiousness' inherent in the lace. 'But', she warns further, 'on no account must the elegant effect be spoiled by the use of a coloured sash.' (Sashes for children at that time were considered high fashion.)

The 20th century has at last solved the problem of light, practical and hygienic clothes for children. A special market with its own manufacturers and its own distributors has come into existence, with a steadily rising turnover; existence as a consumer now starts in infancy. Naturally children's clothing remains in touch with current trends and has many fashion points in common with the dress of the 'grown-ups'.

975

976

977

975 Diego Velasquez. Infant Balthasar Carlos. Prado, Madrid.

976 Gerard Terborch. Portrait of Helene von der Schecke. Rijksmuseum, Amsterdam.

977 Jean-Baptiste Siméon Chardin. Little girl with racket. Private Collection, Paris. The little girl in play-clothes is wearing a bonnet, a low-cut dress with apron and a ribbon round the neck.

978 *Costumes Parisiens*, 1808. Under the influence of the Revolution and pedagogic ideas children's clothes became more comfortable.

979 Camille Corot. Portrait of Louise Robert. Musée du Louvre, Paris. The small girl is wearing a bonnet and a princess style dress.

980 *H. Buschmanns neue Frauentracht*. The girls are wearing wide, kneelength dresses with short sleeves – the head, however, is crowned with the indispensable large hat with ribbons.

978

979

980

Techniques, Colours and Materials

Fashion changes do not manifest themselves only in the more or less rapid transformations of the silhouette or in the see-saw movements of the hem-line, although these are the changes that immediately leap to the eye. Fashion's restless nature is not content with the search for new styles; it seeks to express itself also in the colours and the textures of fabrics and other substances – leather, for instance, for a long time, was featured as high fashion material.

In the beginning there is the yarn. It can be of wool or polyester, of cotton, of cotton and silk, of flax or hemp. The yarn, which is to be processed into fabrics so varied that each variant can inspire a new fashion, must be dyed. Until late in the 19th century this was done with vegetable or animal dyes, later chemical dyes were added. To the costume historian certain periods in history seem to stand out as colour-motivated. Tendencies towards light or dark, dazzling or delicate, dull or glowing shades are discernible. In the 15th century, a period which used colours garishly, the secretary of Duke Henry of Saxony describes the wedding gown of Princess Katharina of Mecklenburg: 'It was very strange and composed of several hundred pieces; the principal colours were red and yellow and there were lines half an *ell* in length and a quarter in width set close together, and other lines, two fingers in breadth, going crossways; parts of it looked like a chessboard and in other parts four colours had been sewn together in the form of dice, namely rose red, yellow, ash colour and white. Such a dress must have caused much labour and was all patchwork.'

In the Middle Ages the colour of the costume denoted differences in social standing (e.g. black for the burgher) or else it indicated association with a certain social or philosophical group or circle (the 'white court' of the Empress Eugénie, for instance). Many colours or shades have certain conventional connotations, such as black for mourning or formal occasions, white for brides, 'royal' purple etc. Moreover the optical qualities of the range of cold and warm colour shades and of degrees of brightness and richness play an important role in the composition of the ensemble.

Fashion always goes hand in hand with technical advances in textile production. The transition from draped garments to tailored ones was a turning point in the history of costume. To spin and to weave plant fibres and animal hair is an achievement of the human intelligence which dates back thousands of years. The development of silk in China is an early example of human ingenuity, as is the weaving of velvet in Italy.

But it is only since the beginning of the industrial era that truly revolutionary developments have taken place in the textile industry – and then only after a lengthy period of rather slow technical progress. The 18th century saw the invention of the most important machines: in 1764 James Hargreaves invented the spinning-jenny; in about 1767 Richard Arkwright set up his spinning-frame; in 1785 Edmund Cartwright patented a power-loom; in 1792 Eli Whitney devised the cotton gin; lastly, in 1805 Joseph Marie Jacquard invented the silk-weaving loom called after him. Apart from the production of textiles, endeavours were made to develop a machine, which would take over the laborious work of sewing. In the early 19th century Thimonier and Baltasar Krembs had some success, but it was not until 1845 that Elias Howe built his lock-stitch machine using a double thread, the immediate predecessor of the sewing machine of today. It is owing to these machines that the large-scale production of cheap ready-made clothes became possible. In the 20th century animal and vegetable fibres have been joined by chemical fibres, of which the first was rayon. It has been shown that in some respects chemistry has been able to correct nature and even to improve on it, for the chemical fibre is capable of being produced in any strength desired and in infinite lengths. Owing to its versatility, numerous types of materials and textile mixtures can be produced, which are a determining factor in fashion creation.

982

983

984

982 Franz Hals. Nurse with child. State Museums, Berlin. The girl's dress is of patterned silk. Bonnet, collar and cuffs are adorned with starched lace.

983 Petrus Christus. St. Elijah in his shop. Robert Lehmann Collection, New York. The woman is wearing a brocade dress with pomegranate motif and a bonnet, the so-called *sella*. The man is dressed in a velvet cloak with fur trimming.

984 Henri de Toulouse-Lautrec. Marcelle Lender dancing the ballet *Chilpéric*. Mrs. John Hay Collection, New York.

985 Contemporary photograph. In the 19th century cashmir shawls with woven pine patterns were much worn with outdoor dress.

986 *Die Wiener Elegante*, 1842. The 19th century had a predeliction for braid and tassels, which adorned neckline and hem.

987 Drinker and Hetaera. Picture of the inside of the calix of Brygos. Circa 490–480 B.C. Museum of the University of Würzburg.

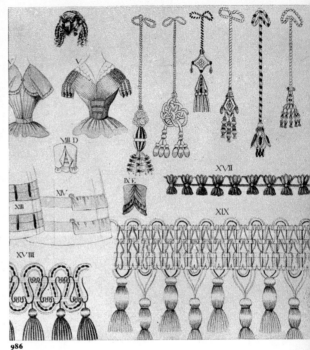

985

986

987

988

989

990

991

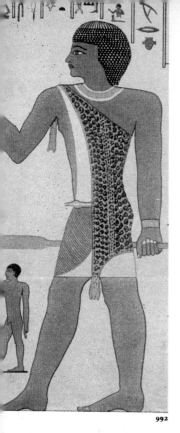

992   993   994

995

988 John S. Copley. Ann Tyng. Museum of Fine Arts, Boston. She wears satin.

989 Quirin Jahn. Portrait of the artist's wife. Národni Galerie, Prague.

990 Renoir. The Swing. Musée du Louvre, Paris.

991 *Victoria*, Berlin, 1872. Ribbons and bows were indispensable to the bustle.

992 Painting from an Egyptian tomb of the period of the IVth Dynasty (detail). Animal skins were among the oldest materials used by man as clothing.

993 Horace Vernet. *Merveilleuse* wearing fur-trimmed *pelisse*.

994 *Costumes Parisiens*, 1814. Velour fichu and redingote.

995 *Allgemeine Modenzeitung*, 1837. Ermine, in the past reserved for court dress, in the 19th century became used in ladies' fashion.

Acknowledgements

Black and white photographs by Jan Splichal, Drahomir Paseka, Camera Press, Keystone Press, Basil Partridge, Mary Quant Ginger Group, Syndication International and from the collections of the authors.
Colour photographs by Ladislav Neubert and Karel Neubert.
Fashion plates from the Museum of Arts and Crafts in Prague, and from private collections.

Thanks are due to the following institutions for the reproduction of individual works:
Academia, Florence; Academia de Bella Artes, San Fernando, Madrid; Academy of Fine Arts, Bruges; Acropolis Museum, Athens; Alte Pinakothek, Munich; Archbishop's Palace, Prague; Austrian Gallery, Vienna; Bavarian State Library, Munich; Bayerische Staatsgemäldesammlungen, Munich; Béhague Collection, Paris; Berlin Art Gallery; Biblioteca Apostolica Vaticana; Bibliothèque Doucet, Paris; Borghese Gallery, Rome; Brancacci Chapel of Santa Maria del Carmine, Florence; British Museum, London; Buckingham Palace, London; Castle Gallery, Prague; Castle Gallery, Rychnov n. Kn. (Bohemia); Castle Kozel (Bohemia); Castle Museum, (Reichenau); Castle Slavkov, Moravia; Chiaranda Collection, Naples; Choir of San Francesco, Arezzo; Choir of San Vitale, Ravenna; Choir of Santa Maria Novella, Florence; Chrysolakkos Museum; City Art Collection, Dusseldorf; City Art Gallery, Manchester; Civic Museum, Cortone; Collection Duke of Infantado, Madrid; Collection Duke of Liechtenstein, Vaduz; Collection Duncan Philipps, Washington; Collection Earl of Pembroke & Montgomery, Salisbury; Collection Grant-Cateret; Collection Henry P. McIlhenny, Philadelphia; Collection of the Library of Art and Archaeology of the University of Paris; Collection Pierre Laudry, London; Collection Prince Wagram, Paris; Collection Vicomtesse de Noailles, Paris; Coptic Museum, Cairo; Corneto Museum; Courtauld Institute Galleries, London; Czatoryski Collection, Paris; Damascus Museum; Dobřiš Castle, near Prague; Den Hirschsprungske Samling, Copenhagen; Duc de Mouchy Collection; Egyptian Museum, Cairo; Etruscan Museum, Chiusi; Gallerie Doria Pamphili, Rome; Galerie Strohmayer, Zagreb; Giacomo Jucker Collection, Milan; Hamburger Kunsthalle; Henry E. Huntington Library & Art Gallery, San Marino, California; Hermitage, Leningrad; Herzog Anton-Ulrich Museum, Brunswick; Historical Museum of Crete, Heraklion; Howard Young Gallery, New York; Ilosokowa Collection, Tokyo; Institut Royal du Patrimoine Artistique, Brussels; Kaiserliche Galerie, Vienna; Kremlin, Moscow; Kunsthalle, Basle; Kunsthistorisches Museum, Vienna; Kunstmuseum, Dusseldorf; Kupferstichkabinett, Basle; Lateran Museum, Vatican City; Library of the Cathedral Chapter, Prague; Lord Ellesmere's Collection, Edinburgh; Magyar Nemzeti Galéria, Budapest; Metropolitan Museum of Art, New York; Monza Cathedral; Mrs. Huntington's Collection, New York; Mrs. John Hay Collection, New York; Musée des Augustines, Toulouse; Musée des Beaux-Arts, Nantes; Musée des Beaux-Arts, Pau; Musée du Berry, Bourges; Musée de Cluny, Paris; Musée Condé, Chantilly; Musée Fabre, Montpellier; Musée Guimet, Paris; Musée du Jeu de Paume, Paris; Musée du Louvre, Paris; Musée du Luxembourg, Paris; Musée Nationale de Versailles; Musée Paul Dupuy, Toulouse; Musée de Peinture et de Sculpture, Grenoble; Musée du Petit Palais, Paris; Musée H. Rigaud, Perpignan; Musée Royal des Beaux-Arts, Antwerp; Musées Royaux, Brussels; Musée Saint-Remi, Rheims; Musée Toulouse-Lautrec, Albi; Museo Arcivescovile, Ravenna; Museo Archeologico, Florence; Museo Archeologico Nazionale, Naples; Museo Archeologico, Milan; Museo de Bellas Artes, Toledo; Museo Capitolino, Rome; Museo Correr, Venice; Museo Nazionale Romano, Rome; Museo e Gallerie Nazionale di Capodimonte, Naples; Museo de Palazzo Venezia, Rome; Museo Poldi Pezzoli, Milan; Museum of Art, Bucharest; Museum of Art, Vienna; Museum of Arts and Crafts, Prague; Museum Boymans van Beuningen, Rotterdam; Museum of Catalan Art, Barcelona; Museum of Fine Arts, Boston; Museum of Fine Arts, Budapest; Museum of Modern Art, Barcelona; Museum Narodowe, Krakow; Museum Narodowe, Warsaw; Museum of the University of Würzburg; Národni Galerie, Prague; Národni Museum, Prague; Narodowe Museum, Poznan; National Art Collection, Kassel; National Gallery, London; National Gallery, Urbino; National Gallery of Art, Washington; National Library, Paris; National Library, Vienna; National Museum, Athens; National Museum, Damascus; National Museum, Tokyo; National Portrait Gallery, London; National Trust Regional Representative, Shrewsbury; Nelahozeves Castle (Bohemia); Ny Carlsberg Glyptotek, Copenhagen; Palace at Poitiers; Palazzo Conservatori, Rome; Palazzo Pitti, Florence; Pergamonmuseum, Berlin; Pierce Collection of Antiquities; Poitiers Museum, Poitiers; Prado, Madrid; Pushkin Museum, Moscow; Rijksmuseum, Amsterdam; Robert Lehman Collection, New York; Royal Art Collec-

tion, Windsor Castle; Royal Collection, London; Rožmberk Castle (Bohemia); Shoe Museum, Gottwaldov (Moravia); Sistine Chapel, Vatican; Six Collection, Amsterdam; Smolny, Leningrad; Soprintendenza alle Gallerie per le Provincie di Firenze, Arezzo e Pistoia, Florence; S.P.A.D.E.M., Paris; Städt. Groeningemuseum, Bruges; State Art Collection in Wawel, Krakow; Staatliche Kunstsammlungen, Gemmäldegalerie, Kassel; Staatliche Museen, Gemäldegalerie, Berlin; Städelsches Kunstinstitut, Frankfurt on Main; State Library, Leipzig; State Library, Munich; State Museum, Department of Antiquities, Berlin; Szepmuveszeti Museum, Budapest; The Duke of Devonshire's Collection; Thermal Museum, Rome; Treasury of Saint Peter, Vatican; Uffizi Gallery, Florence; University Library, Cambridge; University Library, Prague; Vatican Museum, Italy; Vichy Museum; Victoria & Albert Museum, London; Villa Giulia, Rome; Wallraf-Richartz-Museum, Cologne; Wallace Collection, London; Wertheim Collection, Fogg Art Museum, Cambridge (Mass.); Wittelsbacher Ausgleichsfond, Munich.